Other books by Nina Simonds

Classic Chinese Cuisine
China's Food
Chinese Seasons

Nina Simonds

William Morrow and Company, Inc.
New York

Library of Congress Cataloging-in-Publication Data

Simonds, Nina.
    China express / Nina Simonds.
        p.   cm.
    Includes index.
    ISBN 0–688–11478–4
    1. Cookery, Chinese.   I. Title.
TX724.5.C5S593   1993
641.5951—dc20   92–46413
                                                                  CIP

Printed in the United States of America

First Edition

1 2 3 4 5 6 7 8 9 10

BOOK DESIGN BY RICHARD ORIOLO

For M.C.
Like many working mothers,
she loved to nurture,
but had little time
to cook

Acknowledgments

China Express benefited from the inspiration and input of many people. It's impossible to list each person by name but I would like to express my special thanks to:

Mat Schaffer for his inspiration and encouragement.

Debby Richards and Susan Mason for their unflagging assistance in testing recipes.

Zanne Zakroff and Kemp Minifie at *Gourmet* magazine for their continued friendship and encouragement.

The crew at *Eating Well*, past and present, particularly Patsy Jamieson, Rux Martin and Barry Estabrook.

The Warren Street tasting team and all of my Salem friends for enthusiastically sampling my recipes and still coming back for more.

My professional colleagues in Boston and beyond whose enthusiasm and warmth has been constant through the years.

Ann Bramson, my editor, Sarah Guralnik, her assistant, Judith Sutton, my copy editor, and Ann Cahn, who were all a pleasure and a joy to work with.

Richard Oriolo, my designer, and Ann Field, the illustrator, for their talent, creativity, and sensitivity in pleasing my aesthetic as well as their own.

Rose Schwartz and Joy Marcus for their prudent legal advice.

Maureen and Eric Lasher, my ever-dedicated agents, for their inspiration, hard work, and encouragement.

My family and close friends who have been incredibly supportive to me.

Last and certainly not least, I want to thank Don and Jesse for the constant love and joy they both bring to my life.

CONTENTS

INTRODUCTION

I used to cook Chinese food for dinner almost every night. After several years of living in the Orient, studying with Chinese chefs in the seventies, and subsequent annual visits to the Far East throughout the eighties, I was intent on re-creating many of the specialties I had come to adore in my travels.

That was before my son was born. With the arrival of a newborn, I didn't have the time to travel to Chinatown to buy ingredients (I was lucky to make it to the local supermarket). And I didn't have the patience to spend a good chunk of the afternoon chopping, slicing, and mincing.

Yet I longed for the vibrant flavorings as well as the healthy approach to eating that the Asian regimen offered. I needed, I decided, to develop a whole new set of recipes that streamlined the classic techniques and used ingredients available in any market. The dishes that emerged from this line of thinking became the first recipes created for this book.

At about the same time, a close friend called one day on his way home from work. He had just purchased a chicken breast and wanted some suggestions for a fast Chinese chicken dish. He was adamant about eating within the hour, but he couldn't think of a single recipe that didn't require extensive preparation time. That provided further inspiration to develop material for this book.

I realized that there was a shortage of Chinese cookbooks that took into account the harried schedule of the contemporary cook. In fact, there seemed to be no book that remained true to the basic tenets of classic Chinese cuisine yet was user-friendly for a non-Chinese audience. Here is my answer to the problem.

The dishes in this book use readily available ingredients that can be found in most supermarkets. The recipes are so accessible that even cooks who have been intimidated by the idea of cooking Chinese food in the past may be persuaded to try it now.

This book is a direct reflection of the simplified way I cook today. I love to steam fresh vegetables and dress them lightly in a piquant sauce. I delight in stir-frying seafood or chicken and serving the dish simply with steamed rice or noodles. And I take great pleasure in blending Western cooking methods, like grilling and roasting, with Chinese ingredients and techniques. The results have often proved to be even better than I had hoped.

I have tried to streamline traditional cooking methods while retaining the essence of the classic Chinese style. Most of the recipes reflect my informal and open approach toward cooking: Be creative and use ingredients that are fresh, readily available, and of the best quality. The ultimate aim of *China Express* is to allow you to enjoy real Chinese cooking without spending hours preparing it.

THE NEW CHINESE BASICS

INGREDIENTS

This book is designed to demonstrate that you can prepare Chinese food with provisions that are readily available. Most of the ingredients for these recipes can be found in any well-stocked supermarket. Fortunately, stores now carry an extensive selection of ethnic condiments and a lush supply of fresh fruits and vegetables, both familiar and exotic.

The basic ingredients, with suggestions for substitutions, are listed here. Feel free to improvise if necessary. Most of the bottled ingredients and spices keep indefinitely stored in a cool, dry place. Once opened, pastes, sauces, and other perishable items should be transferred to tightly sealed containers and stored in the refrigerator.

Chili Paste Chili paste (or sauce, depending on the manufacturer) is a piquant seasoning made of crushed chile peppers, vinegar, and assorted other seasonings, including garlic. I prefer the Vietnamese brands in jars since the canned Chinese varieties tend to be salty. Chili paste will keep indefinitely in the refrigerator but tends to lose its bite over time.

Substitution: Use a slightly smaller amount of crushed dried red chile peppers or chile pepper flakes.

Chinese Cabbage There are dozens of varieties of Chinese cabbage grown in this country alone. The most commonly available types are bok choy, with a stalky body and leafy stems; Napa cabbage, with an oval-shaped, broad-leafed head; celery cabbage, with a long, thin, leafy head; and Chinese broccoli, a slender-stalked, slightly bitter version of its American cousin. Bok choy, Napa, celery cabbage, and Chinese broccoli are all good in stir-fried dishes, but Napa and celery cabbage are preferable for soups and pickles.

Substitution: None.

Chinese Ham Chinese ham is salty and slightly smoky. It is cured using a method similar to that for Smithfield ham. Tightly wrapped, it will keep for at least a month in the refrigerator.

Substitution: Use equal amounts of prosciutto or Smithfield ham.

Chinese Rice Vinegar Rice vinegars tend to be lighter and sweeter than wine and fruit vinegars. Chinese cooks generally use two types of rice vinegar: clear and black. Clear rice vinegar is used for pickling vegetables and to flavor sauces and dressings. Chinese black vinegar has a more mellow taste and is used primarily in seafood sauces and dressings and as a dipping sauce. If possible, use Japanese clear vinegars, which are generally of better quality than the Chinese clear vinegars available here. The black vinegar I recommend is the Chinkiang brand, imported from China.

Substitution: Cider vinegar has a slightly different flavor but can be used in place of clear vinegar; reduce the quantity by one third. For black vinegar, substitute an equal amount of Worcestershire sauce.

Cilantro Cilantro, Chinese parsley, and coriander are all names for an herb that is similar in appearance to flat-leaf parsley but has a unique musky fragrance and flavor. People tend to love it or hate it. Chinese cooks use it primarily in soups, salads, and cold platters. Store it with its roots in water in the refrigerator.

Substitution: None.

Cornstarch In this country, cornstarch is the most popular thickener for Chinese dishes. It is also used in marinades and to coat foods for deep-frying. Cornstarch has a tendency to break down upon reheating.

Substitution: Potato starch and arrowroot are excellent substitutes for thickening and for coating foods.

Dried Chile Peppers Dried chile peppers are available in a range of sizes in most Asian markets. Usually the smaller the pepper, the more intense the heat. Chile peppers, fresh as well as dried, are used to infuse oils, sauces, and dressings with their powerful flavor. Store tightly wrapped in plastic bags.

Substitution: Use a smaller amount of bottled crushed red chile peppers or chile pepper flakes.

Dried Chinese Black Mushrooms Dried black shiitake mushrooms, admired for their pungent, smoky flavor, are available in a variety of grades, with prices to match. The best and most expensive are those with the thickest caps, and they are generally reserved for banquet dishes where the caps are used whole. Dried mushrooms will keep indefinitely tightly wrapped in plastic bags in the freezer.

Substitution: Dried Italian porcini mushrooms have a very different flavor, but they make an adequate substitute; fresh shiitake mushrooms have a much milder taste than the dried version, and are not really an appropriate alternative.

Dried Tangerine or Orange Peel This pungent aromatic is used in braising sauces and to season spicy stir-fried dishes. Usually the peel is reconstituted in water before using. I generally prefer to use the skin of the fresh fruits; the store-bought variety tends to be bitter and should be blanched before using.

Substitution: Use fresh tangerine or orange zest (without the pith) instead of the dried peel.

Fermented or Salted Black Beans This popular condiment is made from black beans that have been preserved in a salty brine that contains ginger and orange peel. The beans should be rinsed and drained before using.

Substitution: None.

Five-Spice Powder This fragrant spice mixture is made with a blend of spices, which vary depending on the manufacturer. The usual seasonings are star anise, powdered licorice root, cinnamon, Sichuan peppercorns, cloves, and fennel. Five-spice powder is used to flavor marinades and as a dipping salt.

Substitution: You can make your own five-spice powder by combining ¼ teaspoon each ground aniseed, ground coriander, ground cinnamon, and ground ginger, and ⅛ teaspoon freshly ground black pepper.

Ginger Ginger, the knobby root of a flowering plant, is one of the primary Chinese seasonings. The ginger available in most markets is a mature form, with a thick skin. On occasion, spring ginger, which has a papery skin and delicate flavor, is available. Select plump roots with smooth, unwrinkled skin, and peel before using. Store ginger unpeeled in a pot of sand, or peeled in a jar of rice wine or sake in the refrigerator.

Substitution: None. Ground ginger is not an adequate substitute for fresh.

Hoisin Sauce Ground bean sauces such as hoisin are found in various forms all over China. This southern condiment is made with fermented beans, salt, sugar, and garlic. Its primary uses are in marinades for barbecuing and roasting and in dipping sauces. Stored in the refrigerator, it will keep indefinitely.

Substitution: Sweet bean sauce (see page 6).

Oyster Sauce Lustrous and rich, oyster sauce is a concentrated mixture made from fermented oysters, salt, and assorted seasonings. It is an especially appropriate seasoning for seafood and many vegetable dishes. Stored in the refrigerator, it will keep indefinitely.

Substitution: None.

Plum Sauce Plum sauce, or duck sauce, is a condiment made from plums, apricots, vinegar, and sugar. In China, it is served only infrequently, usually with roasted duck and goose. In the West, it has become a staple dipping sauce for deep-fried appetizers.

Substitution: The flavor will not be the same, but if plum sauce is unavailable, use bottled sweet-and-sour sauce.

Rice Wine Rice wine, or yellow wine, made from fermented rice, is the all-purpose Chinese wine, used in cooking or consumed as a beverage. "Cooking" rice wine, which contains salt, is now widely available. For both cooking and drinking, I recommend Shaohsing, which can be purchased at Asian markets.

Substitution: Although many Chinese cooks recommend dry sherry as a substitute for rice wine, I find its flavor strong and cloying. Sake, Scotch, or dry white vermouth are more appropriate.

Sesame Oil Pleasantly nutty and rich, Asian sesame oil is made from roasted sesame seeds. Chinese and Japanese brands are preferable. It is not interchangeable with the pressed sesame oil found in health foods stores. Asian sesame oil is used primarily as a seasoning and only infrequently as a cooking oil, since its flavor can be overpowering.

Substitution: None.

Sesame Paste Made from toasted and ground sesame seeds, sesame paste is used as a base for cold noodle dishes and salad dressings. Chinese sesame paste is richer and stronger than tahini, the Middle Eastern sesame paste, and the two are not interchangeable. Chinese sesame paste is sold at all well-stocked Asian markets. It will keep indefinitely in the refrigerator.

Substitution: Peanut butter has a different flavor, but it is a suitable substitute in most recipes.

Soy Sauce Chinese soy sauce is available in three grades: low-sodium, or light; medium, or all-purpose; and heavy, or dark. Light is generally reserved for cold sauces and dressings; medium is used for all types of cooking; and heavy is reserved for barbecuing or roasting. Japanese soy sauce, found in most supermarkets, is appropriate for all dishes.

Substitution: None.

Sweet Bean Sauce The northern version of hoisin sauce (see page 5), sweet bean sauce is similarly made from fermented ground beans, along with flour, salt, and water. It is used mainly as a dipping sauce for Mandarin pancakes and as a base for stir-fried sauces. There are many different types of brown bean and yellow bean sauces, which vary in taste and texture, but sweet bean has the best and most consistent flavor. Once opened, it should be transferred from the can to a plastic container, and it will keep indefinitely in the refrigerator.

Substitution: Hoisin sauce (see page 5).

Star Anise This eight-pointed star-shaped spice has a pleasant licoricelike flavor. It is used as a seasoning in marinades, braised dishes, and stews. Star anise will keep indefinitely wrapped in plastic and stored in a cool, dark place.

Substitution: Substitute about 1 teaspoon aniseed per 1 star anise.

Water Chestnuts These days, fresh water chestnuts are becoming more widely available. When selecting them, squeeze them to make certain that no parts are rotten. Fresh water chestnuts should be peeled and blanched for about 2 minutes before being used in savory dishes. The sweet flavor of the fresh chestnut makes it preferable to the canned variety. If you do use canned water chestnuts, they should be blanched for about 15 seconds in boiling water and refreshed in cold water.

Substitution: None.

EQUIPMENT

Chinese food can be prepared with the most rudimentary kitchen tools, if the traditional ones are not on hand. The following glossary offers some information on the basic cookware with suggestions for substitutions. Feel free to improvise whenever necessary.

Wok and Dome Lid This all-purpose pan is used for all methods of Chinese cooking from steaming (with a steaming tray or bamboo steamer) to stir-frying, deep-frying, braising, and smoking. The sloping sides offer an extended cooking surface so that ingredients can be tossed about without spilling out of the pan. Ideally, the heavier the pan, the better it conducts heat and the more efficiently it will cook food. Heavy rolled steel or iron is the preferred material, and a 14-inch-diameter wok is a good all-purpose size. A dome lid is recommended for steaming and braising.

Substitution: A deep skillet or frying pan, made of a heavy metal such as cast iron, is ideal.

Steamers The traditional layered steamers used in Chinese cooking are manufactured in bamboo, stainless steel, and aluminum. Individual steaming trays or racks made of aluminum or steel are also available. For the traditional method, a wok or steamer is filled with several inches of water and heated until boiling. The food to be steamed is placed directly on a steamer tray, or arranged on a plate and placed on a tray or in a layered steamer, and then suspended over the boiling water. The wok or pot is tightly covered and the food steamed over the boiling water.

Substitutions: Any type of large pot with a tight-fitting lid is appropriate for steaming. To suspend a plate of food over the boiling water, you can use several chopsticks crisscrossed to form a rack; or place an empty tuna can with both ends cut off, or a trivet or cooling rack, in the pan as a shelf. A standard collapsible steamer will work for steaming some foods, but you can also use aluminum pie plates with holes punched in them.

Shovel A basic spatula with slanted sides designed to conform to the shape of a wok, this is the traditional choice for stir-frying and tossing food. The most useful type is stainless steel with a wooden handle.

Substitutions: Two ordinary spatulas or a large spoon—even a wooden spoon can be used.

Handled Strainer The most commonly available handled strainer in this country is one with a bamboo handle attached to a woven wire mesh basket. In the Orient, you can find a slightly sturdier version made with a round perforated steel body and a hardwood handle. This useful piece of equipment allows you to remove food easily from hot oil or water and then rest the strainer in a pan or bowl to allow the food to drain.

Substitution: A slotted spoon in combination with a standard colander works well. (Use the spoon to remove food from a hot liquid and drain it in a colander set in a pan or bowl by the stove.)

Cleaver Any Chinese cook would feel lost without this all-purpose utensil. Once a cook has become accustomed to using a cleaver, it is indispensable: The sharp edge cuts; the side of the blade flattens; and the blunt edge tenderizes foods. Chinese cleavers are sold in different weights and grades, with the smallest and lightest being used for chores like cutting vegetables; the medium-weight blade used for virtually all tasks; and the heaviest cleaver is reserved for tougher jobs like cutting through bones.

Substitution: Any sharp, good-quality, heavy knife is suitable for Chinese cooking, but a large chef's knife is ideal. Most important, the cook should be comfortable using the knife.

STREAMLINED CLASSIC TECHNIQUES

Over the centuries, Chinese chefs have developed a highly sophisticated battery of cooking techniques and cutting methods, but all are quite basic and require no special skills other than organization and common sense. The following techniques serve as a foundation for any type of Chinese cooking.

Stir-Frying Stir-frying is the quintessential cooking method used universally by Chinese cooks. Since this quick cooking method emphasizes the inherent flavor of the ingredients, only those of the best quality should be used. A strong source of heat is imperative for stir-frying. Gas is the first choice; if you use electric heat, keep the burner at the highest setting. The process of stir-frying can be divided into two parts: preparation and cooking. For optimum results, follow the steps outlined below.

PREPARATION

1. All of the main ingredients, including meat, poultry, seafood, and/or vegetables, should be cut to the size and shape specified in the recipe. The pieces should be uniform to encourage even cooking. In most recipes, the meat, poultry, or seafood is marinated for a brief period to give it more flavor. Cornstarch, potato starch, or arrowroot is added to marinades to coat the food, sealing in the natural juices so the cooked food will be tender and juicy. Usually, the longer the food marinates, the more flavor it will have.

2. Seasonings such as garlic, ginger, and scallions should be cut as directed in the recipe, and the ingredients for the sauce assembled.

3. Vegetables that require precooking or blanching in boiling water, such as broccoli, cauliflower, or carrots, should be precooked, then immersed briefly in cold water to prevent them from overcooking and to keep their colors bright.

COOKING

1. It is important to heat the wok or skillet until very hot, then add the oil and heat it. If cold oil is added to a cold pan and then heated, the food will stick. I usually recommend corn or safflower oil for stir-frying, but peanut or canola oil can be used. For beef, pork, and chicken, the oil should be heated until extremely hot, about 400°F. For fish and seafood, a temperature of 350°F is acceptable. Once the oil is hot, the meat, poultry, or seafood is added to the pan and stir-fried over high heat until done. The food should be stirred constantly for even cooking. In general, no more than a pound or so of food should be cooked at one time or the ingredients will just steam in their own juices. As soon as it is cooked, the food is removed from the pan and drained thoroughly in a handled strainer or a colander.

2. The pan is cleaned out and reheated. Fresh oil, usually only a tiny bit, is added and heated, and the various seasonings are tossed in the hot oil until fragrant. Any precooked vegetables are added, along with the cooked meat, seafood, or poultry, and tossed over high heat until heated through. Then

the sauce ingredients are added. The mixture is cooked just until it thickens and is transferred to a serving platter. For best flavor, most stir-fried dishes should be eaten immediately.

Steaming Like stir-frying, steaming is a cooking process that accentuates the natural flavor of the ingredients. Consequently, only the freshest, top-quality ingredients should be used. Generally, steaming requires only two or three easy steps:

1. The food to be steamed is cut, scored, and/or marinated as directed in the recipe. If a Chinese steamer is used, it should be lined with parchment paper, cheesecloth, or a moistened tea towel. (Otherwise, the food may pick up a bamboo flavor.) Then the food is arranged in the steamer with space to allow for expansion in cooking.

2. Water for steaming is brought to a boil in a wok or a sizable pot. The heat should be as high as possible, and the water should boil vigorously throughout the steaming period. If the steaming period is lengthy, additional boiling water may be added from a saucepan or a kettle. If more than one steamer tray is used, the order of the trays should be reversed midway through the steaming period.

3. The cooked food is removed from the steamer and is usually served immediately.

Braising Braising is a simple process that usually involves three basic steps:

1. The food to be braised is cut, scored, and/or marinated as directed in the recipe. Often the marinade is reserved and added to the braising mixture. The ingredients for the braising mixture are assembled, along with any other seasonings. The most popular style of Chinese braising is called red-cooking; in this process the food is cooked in a soy sauce–based cooking liquid until tender and colored reddish-brown.

2. The food to be braised is first seared on the stove top or in the oven to seal in the juices and give the ingredients an attractive color. For stove top searing, a small amount of oil is heated in a wok or skillet until very hot, the food is added, in batches if necessary, and seared until golden brown on all sides. Alternatively, the food can be arranged on a rack on a baking sheet and seared in a very hot (450°F) oven until golden brown on all sides.

3. Usually, the braising mixture is then heated until boiling in a heavy pot. Occasionally, some of the seasonings are stir-fried until fragrant in a little oil, the braising liquid is added, and then the mixture is brought to a boil and simmered for a short period to marry the flavors. The food is added to the boiling liquid and simmered, covered or uncovered, until tender. The

food may be served hot, at room temperature, or chilled, as directed in the recipe. Red-cooked meats, are often served at room temperature or cold.

Simmering Simmering is a simple cooking process that follows the same blueprint as braising except that the food is not seared to start.

Smoking Although smoking is used as a cooking technique in the West, in the Orient it is merely a flavoring and coloring process. The food is first cooked, then smoked. Like the other cooking methods, Chinese smoking is very straightforward if the proper steps are followed:

1. The poultry, meat, or seafood to be smoked is cut, scored, and/or marinated as directed in the recipe. The smoking mixture, which usually consists of loose black tea, brown sugar, and aniseed or other seasonings, is combined.

2. The food is precooked, usually by poaching or by steaming, and allowed to cool slightly.

3. A wok and its dome lid are converted into a smoker by lining them with heavy-duty aluminum foil. The smoking mixture is distributed evenly on the bottom of the pan and a rack or crisscrossed chopsticks arranged at least two inches above the mixture. The food is placed on the rack or chopsticks, and the pan is covered securely with the lid. To prevent any smoke from escaping, the ends of the aluminum foil should be folded together to create a seal.

4. The pan is placed over high heat and the food is smoked for the prescribed period; timing begins once the fragrance of smoke becomes apparent. Then the pan is removed from the heat and the food is left to cool in the pan before serving. Sesame oil is often brushed over the surface to make the smoked food look more attractive.

A NOTE ABOUT MENU PLANNING Traditionally, Chinese meals fall into two categories: formal and family-style. At family-style meals, all the dishes are served simultaneously. They usually consist of a staple dish of rice, noodles, or steamed bread and a combination of various other dishes, including meat or poultry, seafood, and vegetable dishes, and a soup.

For a streamlined family-style meal, serve a meat, poultry, or seafood dish, a vegetable, and a staple. Many of the entrées in this book contain vegetables, eliminating the need for a separate vegetable side dish.

For a simplified Chinese banquet, serve appetizers or hors d'oeuvres; seafood entrée; meat entrée; vegetable dish; noodle, pancake, or rice dish; soup (optional) and dessert and fruit.

FINGER
FOODS

he Chinese are serious snackers. Although few balk at the idea of sitting down to an elaborately formal meal, most would probably prefer a meal composed of small bites or finger foods along with rice or noodles.

The most notorious "pickers" are the Cantonese who have elevated the practice of sipping tea and nibbling on dumplings, stuffed vegetables, and sweet and savory pastries to a fine art in their dim sum parlors. The Sichuanese run a close second. They too like to prepare a variety of small dishes, such as tea-smoked chicken and skewered tangerine beef.

Traditionally, Americans have not been quite as passionate about "grazing" as the Chinese, but in the last ten years our eating habits have changed considerably, especially where entertaining is concerned. Today, Americans are far more likely to prepare a selection of hors d'oeuvres than a sit-down dinner for a social gathering. Informality and innovation reign. And it is here that Chinese finger foods fill the bill.

The list of possibilities is endless. Crisp, deep-fried Hundred-Corner Crab Balls, Barbecued Chicken Wings, and Spiced Peanuts are a few examples offered in this chapter, where classic recipes are interspersed with newly created dishes.

Like the young, innovative chefs in Hong Kong who have been exposed to new ingredients and techniques and are constantly expanding this versatile food form, I have been similarly inspired. Some of my creations, like steamed Lemon Asparagus and Drunken Mussels, use ingredients more familiar to Americans than exotic Chinese ones. Others, including Saucy Barbecued Spareribs and Chinese Crudités with a Roasted Sesame Dip, are streamlined and simplified versions of classic preparations.

Overall, simplicity is the key and thus these dishes demand the best-quality and freshest ingredients. Most can be prepared in advance and then reheated briefly or served at room temperature. These appetizers need not be served with eating utensils: Fingers and a generous supply of napkins will suffice.

SPICED PEANUTS

Crisp, irresistibly appealing peanuts redolent of five-spice powder, a basic Chinese flavoring, are often served with cocktails or tea prior to a banquet. These freeze well, so make them in large batches and freeze some in plastic bags to have on hand. To serve, just defrost them at room temperature and crisp in a moderate oven. ● Serves 6 (Makes about 2 cups)

1 pound raw peanuts, skins removed
3 cups water
1½ teaspoons salt
¼ cup sugar
2 tablespoons five-spice powder (see page 5)

Pick through the peanuts and discard any blemished or rotten ones. Combine the water and salt in a medium saucepan and heat until boiling. Add the peanuts and boil for 20 minutes. Drain the nuts, and spread them out in a single layer on a baking sheet. Let air-dry for 1 hour, stirring occasionally.

Preheat the oven to 275°F. Grease a cookie sheet with corn or safflower oil.

Combine the sugar and five-spice powder in a paper bag and toss lightly to mix. Add the peanuts and shake until lightly coated. Spread the nuts out in a single layer on the greased cookie sheet and roast, stirring occasionally, for 45 minutes to 1 hour, until pale golden and slightly crisp. Let cool, and transfer to a serving dish. (These will keep for up to 1 week in a tightly covered container, but they may need to be crisped in a moderate oven before serving.)

CRISP PECANS

When nuts such as pecans, cashews, or walnuts are simmered in water with a little honey, their inherent sweet flavor is accentuated. Baked in a low oven until they become dry and crisp, they make ideal snacks or nibbles. ● Serves 6 (Makes about 2 cups)

4 cups water
6 tablespoons honey
1 teaspoon salt
1 pound pecan halves

Place the water, honey, and salt in a large heavy saucepan and heat until boiling. Add the pecans and bring back to a boil, then reduce the heat to medium and simmer for 15 minutes. Drain the pecans, spread them out in a single layer on a baking sheet, and let air-dry for about 1 hour, tossing occasionally.

Preheat the oven to 250°F. Lightly grease a cookie sheet with corn or safflower oil.

Spread the nuts in a single layer on the cookie sheet and roast, stirring occasionally, for 25 to 30 minutes, until crisp and golden brown. Let cool completely, and transfer to a serving bowl. (These will keep for up to a week in a tightly covered container.)

LEMON ASPARAGUS

Although asparagus was introduced only recently to China, it has become an integral ingredient in modern Chinese cooking and is relished in both cold platters and stir-fried dishes. The easiest and best cooking method is steaming, which brings out the vivid green color and fresh flavor of the vegetable while preserving its crisp texture. Here a light lemon dipping sauce complements the succulent asparagus spears. ● Serves 6

2 pounds tender asparagus

Lemon Sauce

2½ tablespoons freshly squeezed lemon juice
½ cup Chinese Chicken Broth (page 367)
1½ tablespoons sugar
½ teaspoon salt
1 teaspoon sesame oil
2 teaspoons cornstarch

Fill a wok or a large pot with water for steaming and heat until boiling. Meanwhile, snap off the tough woody ends of the asparagus and rinse the stalks. Line a steamer tray with a damp cheesecloth, a wet linen dish towel, or parchment paper and arrange the asparagus in the tray, or place in a collapsible steamer basket (see page 7).

Place the steamer tray over the boiling water, cover, and steam for 4 to 5 minutes, or until the asparagus is just tender. While the asparagus is steaming, combine all the Lemon Sauce ingredients in a nonreactive saucepan and heat, stirring to prevent lumps, until thickened.

Transfer the sauce to a bowl and arrange the asparagus on a serving plate. Serve hot or at room temperature.

CHINESE CRUDITÉS WITH TWO DIPS

A colorful basket of raw red and yellow peppers, fresh snow peas, and carrots coupled with a flavorful dipping sauce is a festive hors d'oeuvre for any gathering, be it summer or winter. Here I offer a choice of a spicy peanut butter–based dip and a pungent Sichuanese sesame paste dip, both seasoned with generous amounts of garlic, ginger, and black vinegar. Serve either of these with other vegetables, such as cucumbers, celery, and zucchini, if you like, or add orange, purple, and green bell peppers for even more color.

To prevent the dipping sauces from separating, it's important to have all the ingredients at room temperature. ● Serves 6

1 red bell pepper, rinsed, cored, halved lengthwise, and seeded
1 yellow bell pepper, rinsed, cored, halved lengthwise, and seeded
2 carrots, peeled and trimmed
⅓ pound snow peas, ends trimmed and veiny strings removed
Roasted Sesame Dip or Spicy Peanut Dip (recipes follow)

Cut each pepper half lengthwise into 3 to 4 strips and remove any white membrane. Then cut each strip on the diagonal into pieces about 1½ inches long. Cut the carrots into sticks roughly 3 inches long and ½ inch thick. Arrange the peppers, carrots, and snow peas in separate mounds in a decorative basket, leaving a space in the middle for the dip.

Roasted Sesame Dip

1 tablespoon minced garlic
1 tablespoon minced fresh ginger
3 tablespoons Chinese sesame paste
3 tablespoons sesame oil
3 tablespoons soy sauce
2 tablespoons rice wine or sake
2 tablespoons Chinese black vinegar or Worcestershire sauce
2 tablespoons sugar
1 teaspoon toasted sesame seeds (optional)

Combine the garlic, ginger, and sesame paste in a food processor fitted with a steel blade and blend until smooth. Add the remaining ingredients, except for the sesame seeds, one at a time, processing until smooth after each addition. Transfer to a serving bowl and sprinkle with the sesame seeds (if using). Place in the basket of vegetables, and serve.

Spicy Peanut Dip

1 cup peanut butter, or more if necessary
2 tablespoons soy sauce
2 tablespoons rice wine or sake
2 tablespoons sugar
2 tablespoons Chinese black vinegar or Worcestershire sauce
2 tablespoons sesame oil
1 tablespoon minced garlic
1 tablespoon minced fresh ginger
1½ teaspoons hot chili paste, or to taste
7 tablespoons Chinese Chicken Broth (page 367) or water, or more if necessary

Place the peanut butter in a blender or a food processor fitted with a steel blade. Add the remaining ingredients one at a time, blend until smooth after each addition. If the dip seems too thick, add a little more chicken broth or water; if it seems too thin, add more peanut butter. Transfer to a small bowl, place in the basket of vegetables, and serve.

Note: Both dipping sauces can be prepared up to 3 days in advance, covered, and refrigerated. They may break down slightly upon sitting; if so, beat lightly with a whisk just before serving.

SPICY OMELET WEDGES

In this recipe, an omelet studded with fresh snow peas and red peppers is cut into triangular-shaped wedges and served with a warm and spicy hot-and-sour sauce for a unique finger food. ● Serves 6

Spicy Dipping Sauce

¾ cup Chinese Chicken Broth (page 367)

2½ tablespoons soy sauce

2 tablespoons rice wine or sake

1¼ tablespoons sugar

2 teaspoons Chinese black vinegar or Worcestershire sauce

1 tablespoon cornstarch

1 teaspoon sesame oil

Omelet

2½ tablespoons corn or safflower oil

½ cup red onion cut into thin slices

1 small red bell pepper, rinsed, cored, seeded, and cut into thin julienne strips (about ¾ cup)

½ cup trimmed snow peas cut into julienne strips (about 1½ ounces)

2 teaspoons rice wine or sake

6 large eggs, lightly beaten

1 tablespoon corn or safflower oil

Seasonings

2 tablespoons minced scallions (white part only)

1 tablespoon minced fresh ginger

1½ tablespoons minced garlic

1 teaspoon hot chili paste

Combine the Dipping Sauce ingredients in a small bowl and blend well.

Preheat the oven to 200°F.

To make the Omelet, heat a well-seasoned wok or frying pan, add 1 table-spoon of the oil, and heat until hot. Add the red onion and bell pepper and toss lightly over high heat for about 20 seconds. Add the snow peas and toss lightly for another 15 seconds. Add the rice wine or sake and toss to mix.

Transfer the vegetables to a bowl and let cool slightly, then add the beaten eggs and stir to mix.

Heat a nonstick frying pan or a well-seasoned wok, add the remaining 1½ tablespoons oil, and heat until moderately hot. Add the egg mixture and cook over moderate heat for about 1½ minutes, or until golden brown on the bottom. Reduce the heat to low, cover, and cook until set, about 7 to 9 minutes. Remove to a heatproof platter and keep warm in the oven.

Heat a frying pan or wok, add the corn or safflower oil, and heat until very hot. Add the seasonings and stir-fry for 10 seconds, or until fragrant. Add the sauce mixture and cook, stirring constantly to prevent lumps, until thickened. Transfer the sauce to a serving bowl.

Cut the omelet into 12 wedges, arrange on a serving platter, and serve with the dipping sauce.

STUFFED MUSHROOMS

Stuffed mushrooms, the perfect pop-in-the-mouth finger food, can be prepared with a wide variety of fillings. In this version, the stuffing combines fresh and dried mushrooms, leeks, garlic, and toasted pine nuts. Dry sherry and five-spice powder impart a subtle yet delicious taste.

● Serves 6

24 medium white mushrooms

½ pound small button mushrooms

2 tablespoons corn or safflower oil

½ ounce dried Chinese black mushrooms (about 10), softened in hot water for 20 minutes, stems removed, and caps chopped

2 tablespoons minced garlic

1½ tablespoons minced fresh ginger

2 cups chopped leeks

3 tablespoons dry sherry

3 tablespoons dried bread crumbs

3 tablespoons minced parsley

1 cup lightly chopped toasted pine nuts

1 teaspoon five-spice powder (see page 5), or more to taste

1 teaspoon salt, or more to taste

½ teaspoon freshly ground black pepper, or more to taste

2 tablespoons chopped cilantro (fresh coriander) or parsley

Rinse the fresh mushrooms briefly in cold water and drain thoroughly. Trim the stem ends of the button mushrooms, and remove the stems from the medium mushrooms. Set the caps aside. Chop the stems and the small mushrooms.

Heat a wok or a deep skillet, add the oil, and heat until hot. Add the chopped dried mushrooms, garlic, and ginger and toss over high heat for about 10 seconds. Add the leeks and cook for about 1½ minutes. Add the chopped fresh mushrooms and cook, stirring occasionally, over medium heat until they render their liquid and it evaporates. Remove from the heat, add the dry sherry, bread crumbs, parsley, pine nuts, five-spice powder, salt, and pepper and toss to mix. Taste for seasoning and add more salt, pepper, and/or five-spice powder if necessary.

Preheat the oven to 375°F. Line a cookie sheet with aluminum foil.

Stuff the mushroom caps with the filling mixture. Arrange on the cookie sheet and bake for 30 minutes, or until the caps are tender. Transfer to a serving platter, sprinkle with the chopped coriander or parsley, and serve hot or at room temperature.

OYSTER SAUCE BROCCOLI

The rich briny taste of oyster sauce enhances the flavors of many ingredients, but it has a particular affinity for certain foods, such as broccoli, snow peas, asparagus, and clams. Serve this as an appetizer or an easy vegetable side dish. ● Serves 6

2 bunches broccoli (about 1½ pounds)

Oyster Sauce

¾ cup Chinese Chicken Broth (page 367)

3 tablespoons oyster sauce

1 tablespoon rice wine or sake

2 teaspoons sugar, or to taste

1 teaspoon soy sauce

½ teaspoon sesame oil

1½ teaspoons cornstarch

Minced Seasonings

1 tablespoon minced garlic

2 teaspoons minced fresh ginger

1 teaspoon corn or safflower oil

Fill a wok or a large pot with water for steaming and heat until boiling. Meanwhile, with a sharp knife, cut off the broccoli florets. (Reserve the stalks for another dish.) Arrange in a steamer tray lined with a damp cheesecloth, a wet linen dish towel, or parchment paper, or in a steamer basket (see page 7). Place the steamer tray over the boiling water, cover, and steam for 7 minutes, or until just tender.

While the broccoli is steaming, prepare the Oyster Sauce: Combine all the sauce ingredients and blend well. Heat a wok or a skillet, add the oil, and heat until hot. Add the minced seasonings and stir-fry over high heat for about 10 seconds, or until fragrant. Add the sauce mixture and cook until thickened, stirring to prevent lumps. Pour into a bowl and place in the center of a serving platter.

Arrange the broccoli around the bowl of sauce, and serve warm or at room temperature.

BROILED SCALLOPS
WITH BACON

The popular appetizer of scallops wrapped in bacon is given a new twist with the addition of a mustard-spiked plum sauce. Serve these delicious morsels hot from the oven. If you like, set aside a little of the spicy sauce for dipping. ● Serves 6

1½ pounds sea scallops

Plum Sauce

1 tablespoon mustard powder

2 tablespoons hot water

½ cup plum sauce or duck sauce

½ teaspoon sesame oil

½ teaspoon low-sodium soy sauce

¾ to 1 pound thinly sliced bacon

20 to 22 six-inch bamboo skewers, soaked in water for 1 hour

Lightly rinse the scallops and drain thoroughly. Slice any very thick ones in half horizontally.

Heat a broiler or prepare a medium-hot fire for grilling.

Combine the Plum Sauce ingredients and blend well. Cut the strips of bacon in half. Place the scallops in a bowl, add half the sauce, and toss lightly to coat. Wrap a piece of bacon around each scallop and thread onto the bamboo skewers. If broiling the scallops, cover a cookie sheet with aluminum foil and arrange the skewered scallops on top. Place the scallops about 3 inches from the heat source and broil or grill, basting with the remaining sauce, for about 8 to 9 minutes on each side, or until the bacon is cooked. Serve hot.

Variation: Substitute shelled and deveined medium shrimp for the scallops.

GRILLED SWEET-AND-SOUR SHRIMP

This dish couldn't be simpler, yet the various flavors make it a masterful delicacy. Plump scampi are drenched with a ginger-scallion marinade, charcoal-grilled, and served with a chili paste–spiked sweet-and-sour sauce. They are equally delectable served straight from the fire or at room temperature. ● Serves 6

1½ pounds large shrimp (16/20 count), peeled

Marinade

2 tablespoons rice wine or sake

1 teaspoon sesame oil

6 slices fresh ginger (about the size of a quarter), lightly smashed with the flat side of a cleaver or a knife

6 scallions, trimmed and lightly smashed with the flat side of a cleaver or a knife

Sweet-and-Sour Sauce

¾ cup ketchup

1½ tablespoons sugar

1½ tablespoons clear rice vinegar

1 teaspoon soy sauce

½ teaspoon salt

1 teaspoon hot chili paste

10 six-inch bamboo skewers, soaked in water for 1 hour

With a sharp knife or a cleaver, score each shrimp down the back to butterfly and remove the dark vein. Rinse and drain. Combine all the Marinade ingredients in a bowl and pinch the ginger and scallions to release their flavors. Add the shrimp and toss to coat. Cover with plastic wrap and let marinate for 30 minutes at room temperature, or refrigerate overnight. Prepare a fire for grilling or preheat the broiler.

Combine all the Sauce ingredients and blend well. Transfer to a serving bowl and set aside.

Thread the shrimp on the skewers, opening them up. Reserve the marinade.

Place the skewered shrimp 3 inches from the heat source and grill or broil them, basting occasionally with the reserved marinade, for 7 minutes, or until cooked through. Arrange the shrimp on a serving platter, and serve with the sauce.

Variation: Substitute sea scallops that have been blanched for 30 seconds in boiling water for the shrimp, and grill or broil for about 2 to 3 minutes per side.

CILANTRO SHRIMP

Cilantro is a pungent herb that is used frequently in Chinese soups and cold salads. It is especially good with seafood. Serve these shrimp with plenty of napkins; their juices are brimming with the fresh flavors of the sea.

● Serves 6

1½ pounds medium shrimp in the shell

Marinade

2 tablespoons rice wine or sake

1 teaspoon sesame oil

6 slices fresh ginger (about the size of a quarter), smashed with the flat side of a knife or a cleaver

6 scallions, trimmed and smashed with the flat side of a knife or a cleaver

Cilantro Dipping Sauce

½ cup Chinese Chicken Broth (page 367)

1 teaspoon salt

½ teaspoon freshly ground black pepper

½ teaspoon sugar

1 teaspoon sesame oil

1 teaspoon cornstarch

1 tablespoon minced fresh ginger

2 teaspoons corn or safflower oil

3 tablespoons minced cilantro (fresh coriander)

With a sharp knife or a cleaver, score each shrimp down the back, cutting through the shell, and remove the dark vein. Rinse and drain. Combine all the Marinade ingredients in a bowl. Pinch the ginger and scallions to release their flavors, and add the shrimp. Toss to coat, cover with plastic wrap, and let sit for 30 minutes at room temperature, or refrigerate overnight.

Combine all the Cilantro Sauce ingredients except the ginger and blend well. Set aside.

Heat a large pot of water until boiling. Add the shrimp with the marinade, bring back to the boil, and cook until the shrimp turn pink, about 3 minutes.

Meanwhile, heat a wok or a skillet, add the corn or safflower oil, and heat until hot. Add the minced ginger and stir-fry over high heat until fragrant, about 10 seconds. Add the chicken broth mixture and cook until thickened, stirring to prevent lumps. Remove from the heat and stir in the cilantro. Transfer to a serving bowl.

Drain the shrimp, discarding the liquid and seasonings. Arrange on a serving platter, and serve with the dipping sauce.

Note: Cooking shrimp in the shell, say some chefs, intensifies their sweetness. If the shells are split before cooking, as in this recipe, they will peel away very easily.

HUNDRED-CORNER CRAB BALLS

Shrimp paste is a versatile medium that can be used as a base for a variety of stuffings. Here it is combined with chunks of crabmeat, shaped into balls, and coated with tiny cubes of bread (hence the name "hundred-corner balls"), then deep-fried until golden brown. Serve these unusual tidbits with plum sauce and hot mustard for dipping.

● Serves 6 (Makes about 60 balls)

⅔ pound medium shrimp, peeled, deveined, rinsed, and drained

⅓ pound lump crabmeat, picked through to remove any shells and cartilage

½ cup minced water chestnuts, blanched in boiling water for 10 seconds, refreshed in cold water, drained and thoroughly dried with paper towels

Seasonings

1½ tablespoons minced fresh ginger

1½ tablespoons minced scallions

1 tablespoon rice wine

¾ teaspoon salt

1 large egg white, lightly beaten

1 teaspoon sesame oil

2 tablespoons cornstarch

20 to 22 slices thin-sliced sandwich bread, crusts removed

Corn or safflower oil for deep-frying

Wrap the shrimp in a linen towel or paper towels and squeeze out as much moisture as possible. Place in a food processor fitted with a steel blade and process to a paste. Transfer to a large bowl and add the crabmeat and water chestnuts. Stir in the seasonings in the order listed, and stir vigorously in one direction until the mixture forms a stiff paste. Chill thoroughly for easier handling before shaping into balls.

Using a sharp knife, cut the bread into ¼-inch cubes and spread on a cookie sheet. If time permits, let dry for 2 hours, turning several times.

Moisten your hands with water, take a heaping teaspoonful of the crabmeat mixture, and shape it into a ball. Roll the ball in the bread cubes to coat, pressing lightly to make the cubes of bread adhere. Set aside on another cookie sheet, and repeat with the remaining crabmeat mixture and bread cubes.

Preheat the oven to 200°F.

Heat a wok, add the oil, and heat the oil to 350°F. Add 6 or 7 of the crabmeat balls and deep-fry, turning constantly, until golden brown all over. Remove with a handled strainer or a slotted spoon and drain briefly in a colander, then transfer to absorbent paper to drain. Place on a cookie sheet and keep warm in the oven while you deep-fry the remaining balls, reheating the oil between each batch. Arrange on a platter and serve warm.

DRUNKEN MUSSELS

In eastern China, seafood and chicken are often served in a "drunken" state—that is, after brief cooking, the food is marinated in a rice wine or sake mixture flavored with scallions, ginger, and garlic. I like to adapt the traditional recipe, using mussels, which are not traditional, but clams and shrimp are also excellent. Choose the freshest seafood available to you.

● Serves 6

3 pounds mussels

Marinade

1 tablespoon sesame oil

10 cloves garlic, smashed with the flat side of a knife or a cleaver and peeled

10 scallions, trimmed and smashed with the flat side of a knife or a cleaver

10 slices fresh ginger (about the size of a quarter), smashed with the flat side of a knife or a cleaver

4 small dried hot chile peppers, cut crosswise into ¼-inch-thick slices and seeded

1½ cups good-quality rice wine, such as Shaohsing, or sake

1½ cups shredded leaf lettuce

Discard any mussels that are not tightly closed, and pull off the beards. Scrub the mussels well under cold running water to remove any sand or seaweed. Place in a large bowl, add cold water to cover, and let sit for 1 hour; drain.

Heat a large heavy pot, add the sesame oil, and heat until hot. Add the garlic, scallions, ginger, and chile peppers and stir-fry over high heat for 10 seconds, or until fragrant. Add the rice wine and boil for 1 minute. Add the mussels, cover, and cook, shaking the pan occasionally, for about 6 to 8 minutes, until the mussels open. Using a slotted spoon, transfer the mussels to a bowl, reserving the cooking liquid, and let cool slightly.

Remove the top shells from the mussels and discard. Arrange the mussels in a single layer in a nonreactive pan and pour the warm cooking liquid over them. Cover with plastic wrap and refrigerate for at least 3 hours, or overnight, basting occasionally with the marinade.

Line a serving platter with the shredded lettuce and arrange the mussels on top. Spoon some of the marinade onto each mussel and serve.

BARBECUED CHICKEN WINGS

Chicken wings are a popular hors d'oeuvre in any cuisine, and there are infinite variations. In this simple yet delicious rendition, the wings are marinated in a garlicky hoisin-based sauce and then baked until crisp. The longer the wings marinate, the more flavor they acquire. These are as appropriate on a cocktail-party platter as they are in a picnic basket.

● Serves 6

Barbecue Sauce

½ cup hoisin sauce

3 tablespoons soy sauce

3 tablespoons rice wine or sake

2 tablespoons sugar

2 tablespoons ketchup

2 tablespoons minced garlic

3 pounds chicken wings (about 16)

Combine the Barbecue Sauce ingredients in a bowl. Add the chicken wings and toss lightly to coat. Cover with plastic wrap and let marinate at room temperature for 1 hour, or refrigerate for several hours or overnight, turning occasionally.

Preheat the oven to 375°F. Line a rimmed cookie sheet or a baking pan with aluminum foil. Arrange the chicken wings skin side down on the cookie sheet. Bake for 25 minutes, turn over and bake for 20 minutes longer, or until a deep golden brown. Transfer to a serving platter, and serve hot, at room temperature, or cold.

Variation: Grill the chicken wings over a medium-hot fire, turning several times, for 20 minutes, or until cooked.

TEA-SMOKED CHICKEN DRUMETTES

Tea-smoking is an unusual Chinese technique used to flavor a variety of meats and seafood. The smoking mixture may vary slightly (some cooks prefer cinnamon sticks and orange peel to aniseed), but a strong black tea and brown sugar are always necessary for the desired mahogany color and distinctive smoky flavor. ● Serves 6

Marinade

1 tablespoon rice wine or sake

1 teaspoon salt

6 scallions, trimmed and smashed with the flat side of a knife or a cleaver

6 slices fresh ginger (about the size of a quarter) smashed with the flat side of a knife or a cleaver

24 chicken drumettes

Tea-Smoking Mixture

½ cup black tea leaves

¼ cup light brown sugar

6 tablespoons aniseed

2 tablespoons sesame oil

Cilantro Dipping Sauce

¼ cup soy sauce

1 tablespoon sugar

2 tablespoons sesame oil

3 tablespoons clear rice vinegar

1 tablespoon rice wine or sake

⅓ cup chopped cilantro (fresh coriander)

Combine the Marinade ingredients in a bowl. Add the drumettes and toss to coat thoroughly. Cover tightly with plastic wrap and let marinade for at least 4 hours, or overnight, in the refrigerator.

Fill a wok or a deep pot with water, for steaming, and heat until boiling. Line a steamer tray (or two if necessary) with parchment or wax paper. Or use an aluminum pie plate with holes punched in it (see page 7). Arrange the drumettes on the tray(s), place the tray(s) over the boiling water, and steam for about 20 minutes, or until cooked. (If using two trays, stack the trays and increase the cooking time to 25 minutes, rotating the steamer trays midway through the cooking time.) Remove the drumettes and set aside.

Drain the wok or pot and line it with heavy-duty aluminum foil. Cover the inside of the lid with foil as well. Combine the ingredients of the Tea-Smoking Mixture and spread half in the bottom of the wok. Place a smoking rack over the mixture, or crisscross chopsticks to form a rack, and arrange half the drumettes on top. Cover, place over high heat, and cook for about 10 to 15 minutes from the time a smoky smell is first perceptible. Remove from heat and let stand for 10 minutes.

Transfer the drumettes to a plate, and brush with 1 tablespoon of the sesame oil. Discard the used tea mixture and reline the wok and lid with heavy-duty foil. Place the remaining smoking mixture in the bottom, and smoke the remaining drumettes. Brush with the remaining 1 tablespoon sesame oil. Arrange the drumettes on a platter.

Combine the Dipping Sauce ingredients and blend well. Transfer to a serving bowl. Serve the drumettes at room temperature or cold with the sauce on the side.

Variation: Substitute minced fresh tarragon or scallions for the cilantro in the dipping sauce.

SESAME CHICKEN FINGERS

When it comes to coatings for fried foods, Chinese cooks are extremely innovative. In this recipe, chicken is tossed in a flavorful marinade, then dredged in egg and covered with a mixture of cornstarch and sesame seeds. The cornstarch provides a crisper coating than flour and the buttery seeds highlight the sweet, delicate flavor of the marinated chicken. Try this dish with turkey cutlets, boneless pork loin, shrimp, or scallops, or vary the coating by substituting chopped nuts for the sesame seeds. ● Serves 6

1½ pounds boneless skinless chicken breasts

Marinade

2 tablespoons soy sauce

1½ tablespoons rice wine or sake

1 teaspoon sesame oil

1 tablespoon minced garlic

1½ tablespoons minced fresh ginger

1 teaspoon five-spice powder (see page 5; optional)

½ cup cornstarch

1 cup raw sesame seeds

1 large egg yolk, lightly beaten

14 six-inch bamboo skewers

Corn or safflower oil for deep-frying

Trim the chicken of any fat or sinew and cut into 1½-inch chunks. Place in a bowl, add the Marinade ingredients, and toss lightly to coat. Cover with plastic wrap and refrigerate for at least 3 hours, or overnight.

Combine the cornstarch and sesame seeds on a plate. Add the egg yolk to the chicken and toss. Thread the chicken chunks onto the skewers. Dredge the chicken in the sesame seed mixture, pressing lightly to coat well. Place the skewers on a cookie sheet lightly dusted with cornstarch. Let air-dry for 1 hour, turning once.

Heat a wok or a deep skillet, add the oil, and heat to 375°F. Add 4 or 5 of the chicken skewers and deep-fry, turning constantly, until golden brown all over. Remove with a handled strainer or a slotted spoon and drain briefly in a colander, then transfer to absorbent paper. Fry the remaining chicken, reheating the oil between each batch. Serve immediately.

If you like, serve this dish with a dipping sauce such as Spicy Dipping Sauce on page 22.

Note: Allowing the cornstarch coating to air-dry helps it adhere to the chicken during deep-frying.

SKEWERED CHICKEN WITH MUSHROOMS, PEPPERS, AND ONIONS

Skewered meats, heady with pungent flavorings of scallions and ginger, are a favorite snack in China, where vendors barbecue them on make-shift sidewalk grills. I like to improvise on that popular street food, mixing different meats and vegetables—in this case, chicken and onions, bell peppers, and mushrooms. ● Serves 6

1½ pounds boneless skinless chicken breasts

Marinade

⅓ cup light soy sauce

3 tablespoons rice wine or sake

1 tablespoon minced garlic

1 tablespoon minced fresh ginger

1½ tablespoons sugar

1 teaspoon sesame oil

15 small white boiling onions

15 medium button mushrooms, trimmed and cleaned (about ¾ pound)

2 medium green bell peppers, rinsed, cored, seeded, and cut into 1-inch pieces

15 six-inch bamboo skewers, soaked in water for 1 hour

Trim chicken of any fat or sinew and cut into 1- to 1½-inch cubes. Place in a bowl. Combine Marinade ingredients and pour over chicken. Toss lightly, cover with plastic wrap, and marinate for 8 to 10 hours in the refrigerator.

Parboil the onions for 2 to 3 minutes, until barely tender. Drain and cool under cold running water. Trim the ends and slip off the skins.

Prepare a fire for grilling, or preheat the oven to 450°F. Place the skewers on the grill about 3 inches from the heat source or arrange in a baking pan and place on top oven rack and cook for about 5 to 6 minutes on each side, basting occasionally with reserved marinade. Serve hot or at room temperature.

Thread the chicken, onions, mushrooms, and peppers alternately onto the skewers; reserve the marinade.

CHICKEN LIVERS WITH BLACK MUSHROOMS

Chicken livers are ideal for red-cooking, a braising process that involves a soy sauce–based cooking liquid. They turn a rich, dark color as they cook and they can be cut neatly into slices or left in chunks. Red-cooking also traditionally acts to preserve foods, so the livers may either be served immediately or refrigerated for several days. ● Serves 6

1½ pounds chicken livers

Red-Cooking Liquid

3 cups water

¾ cup soy sauce

⅓ cup rice wine or sake

2 tablespoons sugar

1 star anise, smashed

2 cinnamon sticks

1 teaspoon aniseed

10 dried Chinese black mushrooms, softened in hot water for 20 minutes, stems removed, and caps cut in half

Drain the liquid from the chicken livers, rinse briefly, and drain again. Blanch the livers in a large pot of boiling water for about 30 seconds; drain. With a sharp knife or a cleaver, separate the two halves of each liver, removing the connective tissue.

Combine the Cooking Liquid ingredients in a heavy stock pot or casserole and heat until boiling. Reduce the heat to low and simmer for 20 minutes to combine the flavors. Add the chicken livers and mushrooms and bring to a boil, then reduce the heat and simmer for 15 minutes. Remove the pan from the heat and let cool slightly.

Drain the livers and mushrooms, reserving the cooking liquid, and cut the livers into thin slices if desired. Arrange the livers in a serving dish and scatter the mushroom caps over them. Pour a little cooking liquid on top. Serve warm or at room temperature, or refrigerate and serve cold.

STUFFED PEPPERS

In this recipe, bell pepper sections are filled with ground turkey gener-ously seasoned with a heady combination of garlic, salted black beans, ginger, and scallions. Baked until tender, the peppers are succulent in the nat-ural juices that collect as they cook. They are delectable as an appetizer or, served with rice, as a light entrée. ● Serves 6

6 medium green or red bell peppers, rinsed, cored, halved
    lengthwise, and seeded

Seasonings

1 teaspoon corn or safflower oil

3 tablespoons fermented black beans, rinsed, drained, and minced

2 tablespoons minced garlic

2 teaspoons minced fresh ginger

2 tablespoons minced scallions

1 tablespoon soy sauce

1 tablespoon rice wine or sake

1½ tablespoons cornstarch

1 pound ground turkey

1 tablespoon cornstarch

1 teaspoon corn or safflower oil

2 tablespoons minced, fresh cilantro (optional)

Remove any white membranes from the pepper halves, and cut each half into 2 or 3 sections along the natural membranes.

To prepare the Seasonings, heat a wok or a frying pan, add the oil, and heat until very hot. Add the black beans, garlic, ginger, and scallions, and stir-fry until fragrant, about 15 to 20 seconds. Transfer to a medium bowl and let cool.

Lightly chop the ground meat until fluffy. Add the turkey to the bowl with the stir-fried seasonings, and add the remaining seasoning ingredients. Stir vig-orously in one direction to combine evenly.

Lightly dust the inside of the pepper sections with the cornstarch. Stuff the peppers with the ground turkey mixture, and smooth the surface with the back of a spoon dipped in water.

Preheat the oven to 350°F.

Heat a skillet or a wok, add the oil, and swirl the pan to coat it evenly with the oil. Heat the oil until hot, add half the stuffed peppers, meat side down, and fry over high heat until golden brown. Remove and arrange stuffing side up in a casserole or a lasagne pan. Reheat the pan and fry the remaining peppers until golden brown. Place in the pan with the other peppers and bake for 20 to 25 minutes, until tender. Sprinkle the minced cilantro over the peppers (if desired), and serve.

Variation: Substitute ground pork or chicken for the turkey.

STEAMED PEARL BALLS

Pearl balls take their name from their appearance: Coated with shiny steamed rice, these meatballs are said to resemble pearls. In traditional recipes, ground pork is favored. I prefer ground turkey, which is leaner but no less flavorful. ● Serves 6 (Makes about 30)

1¼ cups glutinous rice (see Note)

1 pound ground turkey

10 dried Chinese black mushrooms, softened in hot water for 20 minutes, stems removed, and caps finely chopped

1 cup water chestnuts, blanched in boiling water for 10 seconds, refreshed in cold water, drained, and coarsely chopped

Seasonings

1½ tablespoons minced fresh ginger

1 tablespoon minced scallions

3 tablespoons soy sauce

1½ tablespoons rice wine or sake

1½ teaspoons sesame oil

2 tablespoons cornstarch

Soy sauce for dipping (optional)

Using your fingers as a rake, rinse the rice under cold running water until the water runs clear. Drain and transfer to a baking pan.

Place the ground turkey in a bowl and add the black mushrooms, water chestnuts, and the Seasonings. Stir vigorously in one direction to combine evenly.

Line one or two steamer trays with parchment or wax paper. Or use an aluminum pie plate with holes punched in it (see page 7). Scrape teaspoonfuls of the turkey mixture into balls and roll each ball in the glutinous rice until it is completely coated, lightly pressing the rice so it adheres. Arrange the balls about 1 inch apart on the steamer tray(s).

Fill a wok or a large pot with water for steaming and heat until boiling. Place the steamer tray(s) of pearl balls over the boiling water, cover, and steam over high heat for 25 minutes, or until cooked through. Serve directly from the steamer, with soy sauce for dipping if desired.

Note: Glutinous rice, or sweet rice, is a type of round sticky rice used primarily in stuffings and sweet dishes. Do not substitute long-grain rice, which would fall off the cooked pearl balls. You may, however, substitute ¾ cup Arborio rice for the glutinous rice in the recipe.

The cooked pearl balls can be reheated by steaming them for 8 to 10 minutes over vigorously boiling water.

SKEWERED
TANGERINE-PEEL BEEF

Flavored oils, such as the tangerine-chile oil in this dish, are an integral element of Chinese cooking. To prepare any of these oils, a combination of sesame oil and safflower or corn oil is heated until near smoking, then seasonings such as dried chile peppers, ginger, and scallions are dropped in the oil and the mixture is left to stand at room temperature until the oil is infused with flavor. The seasoned oil can be used in dressings, dipping sauces, or marinades. ● Serves 6

Tangerine-Chile Oil

2 tablespoons corn or safflower oil

2 tablespoons sesame oil

2 tablespoons dried hot chile peppers, cut into ½-inch pieces
  and seeded

6 2-inch strips tangerine or orange peel

1½ pounds flank steak or London broil

Marinade

¼ cup soy sauce

2 tablespoons rice wine or sake

1 teaspoon Chinese black vinegar or Worcestershire sauce

1 tablespoon minced fresh ginger

1½ teaspoons sugar

¼ teaspoon freshly ground black pepper

14 six-inch bamboo skewers, soaked in water for 1 hour

14 orange sections (optional)

To prepare the Tangerine-Chile Oil, combine the corn or safflower oil and the sesame oil in a saucepan or a wok and heat until almost smoking hot. Add the chile peppers and tangerine peel, remove from the heat, cover, and let cool.

Meanwhile, trim any fat or gristle from the meat. Cut the meat lengthwise, with the grain, into strips about 2 inches wide. Cut the strips across the grain into thin slices and place in a bowl.

Add the cooled tangerine oil to the beef slices, along with all the Marinade ingredients, and toss lightly to coat. Cover with plastic wrap and marinate for at least 3 hours, or preferably overnight, in the refrigerator.

Prepare a hot charcoal fire for grilling or preheat the broiler.

Thread the slices of beef onto the skewers. Grill or broil the beef, turning several times, for about 5 to 15 minutes, on each side. Garnish the end of each skewer with an orange section (if desired). Serve warm or at room temperature.

SPICY LAMB IN LETTUCE PACKAGES

For this unique and delicious stir-fry, ground lamb, crunchy water chestnuts, and buttery pine nuts are tossed in a piquant hot-and-sour sauce that is amply seasoned with scallions, ginger, garlic, and chili paste. The cooked lamb is scooped into fresh lettuce leaves, rolled up, and eaten informally like tortillas. It's equally good hot from the pan or at room temperature; served with rice, it's substantial enough for an entrée. ● Serves 6

1½ pounds ground lamb

Marinade

1½ tablespoons soy sauce

1½ tablespoons rice wine or sake

1 teaspoon sesame oil

1½ cups pine nuts

Sauce

3½ tablespoons soy sauce

3 tablespoons rice wine or sake

1 tablespoon Chinese black vinegar or Worcestershire sauce

2 teaspoons sugar

½ teaspoon salt

¼ teaspoon freshly ground black pepper

1 teaspoon sesame oil

⅓ cup Chinese chicken broth (page 367) or water

2 teaspoons cornstarch

1 large head leaf lettuce or 2 heads Boston lettuce, rinsed, leaves separated, and drained

¼ cup corn or safflower oil

Minced Seasonings

¼ cup minced scallions

2 tablespoons minced garlic

2 tablespoons minced fresh ginger

1½ teaspoons hot chili paste, or to taste

2 cups water chestnuts, blanched in boiling water for 10 seconds, refreshed in cold water, drained, and coarsely chopped

Lightly chop the ground meat with a sharp knife until fluffy and place in a bowl. Add the Marinade ingredients and toss to mix.

Preheat the oven to 250°F. Spread the pine nuts on a cookie sheet and toast in the oven, shaking the pan occasionally so they color evenly, until golden, about 20 minutes. Let cool.

Combine the Sauce ingredients and blend well.

Slightly flatten each lettuce leaf with the flat side of a knife or a cleaver. Arrange on a platter and set aside.

Heat a wok or a deep skillet until hot, add 2 tablespoons of the oil, and heat until hot. Add the ground meat and stir-fry over high heat, mashing and breaking up the lumps of meat, until the meat loses its pink color. Remove and drain. Wipe out the pan.

Reheat the pan, add the remaining 2 tablespoons oil, and heat until very hot. Add the Minced Seasonings and hot chili paste, and stir-fry over high heat for about 10 seconds. Add the water chestnuts and stir-fry for about 10 seconds, until heated through. Add the sauce mixture and stir-fry until thickened. Add the meat and pine nuts and toss until lightly coated. Remove to a serving platter and serve warm or at room temperature. To eat, place some of the stir-fried meat on a lettuce leaf, roll up, and enjoy.

Variation: Substitute ground pork, chicken, or turkey for the lamb.

GLAZED BONELESS SPARERIBS

When I was studying in Taipei, I learned many simple yet unforgettable dishes from master chefs. One teacher, who hailed from Shanghai, had a delicious recipe for glazed spareribs, an eastern specialty, which gave me the inspiration for these. I substitute boneless ribs, which are easier to eat, and rather than deep-fry the meat as in the original version, I sear it in a hot oven. The saucy meat literally melts in your mouth. ● Serves 6

3¼ pounds boneless Chinese spareribs (see Note)

Marinade

2 tablespoons soy sauce

2 tablespoons rice wine or sake

1 teaspoon sesame oil

Braising Mixture

3 cups Chinese Chicken Broth (page 367) or water

3 tablespoons soy sauce

2 tablespoons rice wine or sake

1½ tablespoons sugar

1 star anise, smashed with a heavy knife or a cleaver

2 cinnamon sticks

6 scallions, trimmed and smashed with the flat side of a heavy knife or a cleaver

6 slices fresh ginger (about the size of a quarter), smashed with the flat side of a heavy knife or a cleaver

Trim any excess fat from the ribs. With a heavy knife or a cleaver, cut the ribs crosswise into sections about 1½ inches long. (You should have about 24 pieces.) Place the ribs in a bowl and add the Marinade ingredients. Toss lightly to coat, cover with plastic wrap, and let sit for about 30 minutes at room temperature.

Preheat the oven to 450°F.

Drain the marinade into a large pot, and place the ribs on a rack in a roasting pan. Add ½ inch water to the pan to prevent smoking. Bake the ribs for 7 to 8 minutes on each side, or until golden brown.

While the ribs are baking, add the Braising Mixture ingredients to the pot of marinade and heat until boiling.

Add the ribs to the braising mixture and bring back to a boil. Reduce the heat to low, partially cover, and cook for 30 minutes, turning the ribs occasionally. Uncover, turn up the heat, and boil the sauce until it is reduced to a syrupy glaze.

Discard the anise, cinnamon sticks, scallions, and ginger and transfer the ribs to a serving platter. Pierce with toothpicks, and serve warm or at room temperature.

Note: If boneless Chinese spareribs are unavailable, substitute country-style ribs. Trim any excess fat, cut through the bones into 1½-inch pieces, and proceed as directed.

SAUCY BARBECUED SPARERIBS

Everyone loves barbecued spareribs and this recipe has to be one of my favorites. Serve these garlicky hoisin-glazed ribs with plenty of ice-cold beer for a real treat. Pass plum sauce and hot mustard for dipping if you like. ● Serves 6

3 pounds country-style spareribs, cut into 3-inch-long ribs
  (have the butcher do this)

Marinade

½ cup hoisin sauce

2 tablespoons soy sauce

3 tablespoons rice wine or sake

2 tablespoons sugar

2 tablespoons ketchup

2 tablespoons minced garlic

Using a sharp knife, separate the ribs, cutting between the bones.

Bring a large pot of water to a boil. Add the spareribs and return to the boil, then reduce the heat to medium and simmer for about 20 minutes. Drain the spareribs, rinse briefly, and drain thoroughly. Place in a bowl.

Combine the Marinade ingredients and add to the ribs. Toss to coat, cover with plastic wrap, and let marinate for at least 4 hours, or overnight, in the refrigerator.

Preheat the oven to 350°F.

Arrange the spareribs on a baking sheet lined with aluminum foil, spooning the marinade on top. Bake for 35 to 45 minutes, until golden brown and crisp. Transfer to a serving platter and serve warm or at room temperature.

Variation: You can grill the blanched spareribs over a medium-hot fire, turning several times, for 20 minutes, or until brown.

PANCAKES,
DUMPLINGS,
AND
BREADS

heat-based delicacies such as pancakes, dumplings, and steamed breads make up another extensive category of Chinese finger foods. In this chapter I include old favorites like Scallion Pancakes, Steamed Shrimp Dumplings, Fried Wontons, and Spring Rolls, as well as new creations like Vegetarian Black Bean Turnovers and Curried Turkey Turnovers.

Many of the dishes are fairly traditional, although I've streamlined and adapted the more complicated procedures. Like the dishes in the preceding chapter, most of these call for ingredients found in most supermarkets. And again most of these can be prepared in advance and reheated just prior to serving.

Chinese pancakes require little introduction. Steamed tortillalike Mandarin pancakes are served with Peking duck and various stir-fries at most Chinese restaurants, and flaky scallion pancakes often appear as an appetizer or with stir-fries. Both of these are considered staples and may take the place of rice. Chinese pancakes signal a lighthearted informal meal, as they encourage diners to use their hands rather than chopsticks.

Dumplings come in a variety of forms. There are dainty, steamed dumplings like shrimp *shao mai* and crusty pan-fried potstickers stuffed with meat and vegetables. All dumplings are composed of a filling and a skin, or wrapper, which may vary in thickness and composition. Some are made simply of flour and water, others with an egg dough. Fillings consist of myriad combinations of meat, seafood, and vegetables. Dumplings please the eye as they pique the palate. In China, they are traditionally served as a light snack with tea or spirits, or in larger portions as lunch or dinner. They are especially appealing to busy cooks since they can be prepared ahead and reheated before serving.

Steamed breads, like pancakes, are served either instead of rice or as a snack. The yeast dough may be shaped into flowers or lotus leaves or formed into buns, stuffed, and steamed or baked. Like dumplings, Chinese breads can be conveniently prepared in advance and, like pancakes, they are informal delights that encourage a hands-on approach to eating.

SCALLION PANCAKES

Fried scallion pancakes, crisp and redolent of sesame oil and scallions, are a delicious snack or appetizer. They may also be served in place of rice with stir-fried meat and vegetable dishes. After endless testing, I discovered that all-purpose flour contains too much gluten and results in tough pancakes. Cake flour, and a little oil or shortening added to the dough, will ensure flaky, tender pancakes. ● Makes 16 pancakes

2 cups cake flour
1 teaspoon salt
2 tablespoons corn oil plus 1 cup corn or safflower oil
1 cup boiling water
All-purpose flour for kneading
¼ cup sesame oil
½ cup minced scallion greens

Combine the cake flour and salt in a bowl, and stir with a wooden spoon to combine. Stir in the 2 tablespoons oil and the boiling water until a rough dough forms. If the dough is soft, knead in about ¼ cup all-purpose flour. Turn the dough out onto a lightly floured surface and knead for 5 minutes, or until smooth, kneading in more all-purpose flour as necessary. Cover with a cloth or wrap in plastic wrap and let rest for 20 minutes.

On a floured work surface, roll the dough into a long snakelike roll about 1 inch thick. Cut the roll into 16 pieces. Keep the unused dough covered as you work. Place one piece of dough cut side down on the work surface and, using a rolling pin, roll out to a 5-inch circle. Brush the top with sesame oil and sprinkle with 1 teaspoon of the minced scallion greens. Roll up the circle like a jelly roll and pinch the ends to seal. Flatten the roll slightly with the rolling pin, and coil it into a snail shape, with the seam on the inside. Pinch the end to secure it and set aside on a lightly floured surface. Prepare the remaining pancakes, and let rest for 30 minutes. Reflour the work surface and roll each coiled pancake out to a 4-inch circle, placing them on a lightly floured tray. Let rest for 30 minutes.

Preheat the oven to 200°F.

Heat a heavy skillet or frying pan, add the 1 cup oil, and heat to 350°F. Add several pancakes and fry, turning once, until golden brown and crisp on both

(continued)

sides, about 3 minutes. Remove with a handled strainer and drain briefly in a colander, then transfer to absorbent paper. Transfer to a cookie sheet and keep warm in the oven while you fry the remaining pancakes, reheating the oil between each batch. Serve immediately. (The pancakes can be prepared ahead and reheated in a 350°F oven until piping hot, about 5 minutes.)

Note: To ensure that the pancakes are tender and flaky, allow the dough to rest after each step.

MANDARIN PANCAKES

Mandarin pancakes are a staple in northern China where they often are stuffed with a host of stir-fried mixtures to create spontaneous tortilla-like snacks. I like to prepare a double or triple recipe and freeze them. Allow frozen pancakes to come to room temperature before steaming them. When I'm too busy to prepare them from scratch, I've discovered that flour tortillas are a convenient substitute. ● Makes 16 pancakes

    2 cups all-purpose flour
    1 cup boiling water
    ¼ cup sesame oil

Place the flour in a mixing bowl and stir in the boiling water with a wooden spoon until a rough dough forms. Let cool slightly, then turn the dough out onto a lightly floured surface. Knead for several minutes, until smooth and elastic. Cut the dough in half. Cover one half with a kitchen towel, and roll out the other half to a long snakelike roll about 1½ inches thick. Cut the roll into 8 pieces, and cover the pieces with a towel. Repeat with the remaining dough.

Place one piece of dough, cut side down, on a lightly floured work surface and press to flatten to a 2-inch circle. Set aside. (Alternatively, you may flatten the dough in a tortilla press.) Flatten another piece of dough and brush the top with sesame oil. Place the first piece of flattened dough on top and press the 2 pieces together. Using a small, slender rolling pin, roll out to a 4-inch circle. Set aside on a lightly floured tray and cover with a cloth, while you prepare the remaining pancakes.

Heat a well-seasoned crêpe pan or a nonstick griddle until very hot. (A drop of water sprinkled on the surface should evaporate immediately.) Place one double pancake in the hot pan and fry, twirling the pancake in a circular motion with your fingertips so that it doesn't stick, and brown, for about 1 minute, or until it puffs in the middle. Flip over and cook, again twirling the pancake with your fingertips, for 1 minute longer. Remove from the pan and drop the pancake onto the work surface. Let cool slightly, then peel the 2 pancakes apart. Fold each one into quarters with the cooked surface inside. Repeat with the remaining pancakes, arrange them overlapping in a circle on a steamer tray or on a heatproof serving plate. Cover until ready to serve.

Fill a wok or a large pot with water for steaming and heat until boiling. Place the steamer tray or a plate over the boiling water, balancing the plate on a trivet or an empty tuna can (see page 9). Cover and steam over high heat for 5 minutes, or until cooked through. Serve immediately. (The steamed buns can be reheated by steaming over high heat.)

Note: The pan you use must have a well-seasoned surface to prevent the pancakes from sticking.

CURRIED TURKEY TURNOVERS

Spicy curry turnovers have long been one of my favorite Cantonese snacks or dim sum, but I substitute lean ground turkey for the more traditional pork. I usually prepare multiple batches and freeze them. Then, just before guests arrive, I quickly bake them and serve them piping hot as hors d'oeuvres. ● Makes about 30 turnovers

Turnover Dough

2 cups all-purpose flour

1 teaspoon salt

⅔ cup (10⅔ tablespoons) chilled unsalted butter, cut into 10 pieces

1 large egg, lightly beaten

5 to 6 tablespoons cold water

¾ pound ground turkey or chicken

Marinade

2 teaspoons soy sauce

1 teaspoon rice wine or sake

½ teaspoon sesame oil

Sauce

½ cup Chinese Chicken Broth (page 367) or water

1½ teaspoons sugar

1 teaspoon salt

1 tablespoon cornstarch

2 tablespoons corn or safflower oil

1 cup minced onions

1 tablespoon curry powder

Egg Wash

1 egg, lightly beaten

1 tablespoon water

¼ teaspoon salt

Combine the flour and salt in a food processor fitted with a steel blade and pulse to blend. Add the butter and pulse until the mixture resembles cornmeal. Combine the egg and 5 tablespoons cold water. With the machine running slowly add the egg mixture and process just until roughly combined. Add up to 1 tablespoon more water if the mixture is too dry. Turn out onto a lightly floured surface and, using the heels of your hands, lightly knead the mixture into a rough dough. Wrap in plastic wrap and refrigerate for 30 minutes.

Place the ground meat in a bowl, add the Marinade ingredients, toss lightly, and set aside briefly to marinate.

Combine the Sauce ingredients and blend well.

Heat a large skillet and add 1 tablespoon of the oil. Add the ground meat and cook over medium-high heat, breaking up any lumps with a spatula, until the meat loses its raw color. Remove with a handled strainer and drain in a colander.

Reheat the pan, add the remaining 1 tablespoon oil, and heat until hot. Add the onions and stir-fry over medium heat until soft and transparent. Add the curry powder and stir-fry for another 15 seconds, until fragrant. Add the Sauce mixture and cook, stirring constantly, until it thickens. Add the cooked meat, toss lightly, and remove from the heat. Spread the filling out on a cookie sheet and refrigerate until cool.

Divide the dough in half. On a lightly floured surface, roll the dough out to a circle about ⅙ inch thick. Using a 3-inch round cutter, cut out circles from the dough and place on a floured surface. Gather the dough scraps together into a ball, wrap in plastic wrap, and chill for about 10 to 15 minutes. Repeat with the remaining dough. Then roll out the chilled scraps and cut more circles; you should have about 30 in all.

Preheat the oven to 400°F.

Place a heaping teaspoon of the curry filling in the center of one dough circle. Lightly moisten the edges with water and fold over to form a half-circle, enclosing the filling. Press to seal. Crimp the edges to create a scalloped border or use the tines of a fork to create a decorative pattern, and place the turnover on an ungreased baking sheet. Repeat with the remaining dough and filling.

Combine all the Egg Wash ingredients and blend well. Brush the tops of the turnovers with the egg wash, and bake for 20 minutes, or until golden brown and flaky. Transfer to cooling racks and cool slightly before serving.

Note: The dough must be properly chilled before rolling out to relax the gluten and to make it easier to work with. If the dough becomes too warm as you roll it out, rewrap in plastic wrap and refrigerate for at least 30 minutes.

The unbaked turnovers will keep for several months in the freezer. Arrange them on a cookie sheet and freeze for 15 minutes, or until firm, then store in plastic bags. To bake, arrange the unthawed turnovers on a cookie sheet, brush with the egg wash, and bake as directed.

VEGETARIAN BLACK BEAN TURNOVERS

Turnovers used to be considered labor-intensive, but with a food processor, the dough can be prepared in minutes. In this meatless variation, the flaky dough encloses a pungent filling of diced peppers, onions, and mushrooms flavored with salted black beans, garlic, and ginger. These savory treats are ideal for serving with drinks. ● Makes about 24 turnovers

Turnover Dough

2 cups all-purpose flour

1 teaspoon salt

⅔ cup (10⅔ tablespoons) chilled unsalted butter, cut into 10 pieces

1 large egg, lightly beaten

5 to 6 tablespoons cold water

Sauce

1 tablespoon soy sauce

1 tablespoon rice wine or sake

¼ teaspoon sugar

½ teaspoon sesame oil

2 tablespoons corn or safflower oil

Minced Seasonings

1½ tablespoons fermented black beans, rinsed, drained, and minced

1 tablespoon minced garlic

1 tablespoon minced fresh ginger

1¼ cups coarsely chopped onions

1¼ cups rinsed, drained, and thinly sliced button mushrooms

1 red bell pepper, rinsed, cored, seeded, and cut into ⅛-inch dice

1 yellow bell pepper, rinsed, cored, seeded, and cut into ⅛-inch dice

Egg Wash

1 egg, lightly beaten

1 tablespoon water

¼ teaspoon salt

Combine the flour and salt in a food processor fitted with a steel blade and pulse to blend. Add the butter and pulse, until the mixture resembles cornmeal. Combine the egg and 5 tablespoons cold water. With the machine running, slowly add the egg mixture and process just until roughly combined. If the mixture seems dry, add up to 1 tablespoon more water. Turn out onto a lightly floured surface and, using the heels of your hands, lightly knead the mixture into a rough dough. Wrap in plastic wrap and refrigerate for 30 minutes.

Combine the Sauce ingredients.

Heat a skillet, add the oil, and heat until hot. Add the Minced Seasonings and stir-fry over high heat until fragrant, about 10 seconds. Add the onions and mushrooms, reduce the heat, and cook until the onions are soft and transparent and the mixture is almost dry. Increase the heat to high, add the peppers, and stir-fry for about 1 minute. Add the sauce mixture and toss to coat. Remove from the heat, spread the filling out on a platter or a tray, and refrigerate until cool.

On a lightly floured surface, roll out the dough to a circle that is approximately ⅛ inch thick. Using a 3-inch round cutter, cut out circles from the dough and place on a floured surface. Gather the dough scraps together into a ball, wrap in plastic wrap, and chill for about 10 to 15 minutes. Then roll out and cut more circles; you should have about 24 in all.

Preheat the oven to 400°F.

Place a tablespoon of the black bean filling in the center of one dough circle. Lightly moisten the edges with water and fold over to form a half-circle, enclosing the filling. Press to seal. Crimp the edges to create a scalloped border or press with the tines of a fork to create a decorative pattern, and place on a baking sheet. Repeat with the remaining dough and filling.

Combine the Egg Wash ingredients and blend well. Brush the tops of the turnovers with the egg wash. Bake for 20 minutes, or until golden brown and flaky. Transfer to cooling racks and cool slightly before serving.

Note: The dough must be properly chilled before rolling out to relax the gluten and make it easier to work with. If the dough becomes too warm as you roll it out, refrigerate for at least 30 minutes before continuing.

The unbaked turnovers will keep for several months in the freezer. Arrange them on a cookie sheet and freeze for 15 minutes, or until firm, then store in plastic bags. To bake, arrange the unthawed turnovers on a baking sheet, brush with the egg wash, and bake as directed.

FRIED WONTONS

I've received countless requests for this recipe. You can serve the fried wontons with the sweet-and-sour dipping sauce, or simply with plum sauce and hot mustard. There are endless possibilities for the filling for these wontons. Ground shrimp, turkey, or a combination of ground shrimp and pork all are delicious.　●　Makes 65 wontons

1½ pounds ground pork (butt or shoulder)
¾ cup water chestnuts, blanched in boiling water for 10 seconds, refreshed in cold water, drained, and chopped

Seasonings

2 tablespoons minced fresh ginger
1½ tablespoons minced scallions (white part only)
1½ tablespoons soy sauce
1 tablespoon rice wine or sake
1¼ teaspoons sesame oil
1½ tablespoons cornstarch

65 wonton skins

Sweet-and-Sour Dipping Sauce

¼ cup water
3 tablespoons ketchup
3 tablespoons sugar
1 tablespoon clear rice vinegar
1 teaspoon salt
1 teaspoon soy sauce
½ teaspoon sesame oil
1 teaspoon cornstarch

Corn or safflower oil for deep-frying

Using a sharp knife, lightly chop the meat until fluffy, and place in a bowl. Wrap the water chestnuts in a towel and squeeze out as much moisture as possible. Add to the pork, then add the Seasonings in the order listed and stir vigorously in one direction to combine evenly. The mixture should be stiff; if not, chill for about 1 hour, or until firm. Place a teaspoonful of the filling in the center of a wonton skin and fold the skin over diagonally to form a triangle.

Pinch the edges together to enclose the filling. Then dab a little water on the 2 opposite points of the triangle and press them together. Repeat with the remaining filling and skins, placing the wontons on a baking sheet dusted with cornstarch.

Combine the Sauce ingredients in a saucepan and heat until thickened, stirring constantly. Keep warm over low heat.

Preheat the oven to 200°F.

Heat a wok or a deep-fryer, add the oil, and heat to 350°F. Drop 8 or 9 of the wontons into the oil and deep-fry, turning constantly, until deep golden brown. Remove with a handled strainer or a slotted spoon, drain briefly in a colander, then transfer to absorbent paper. Fry the remaining wontons, keeping the fried wontons warm in the oven. Transfer the sauce to a serving dish, arrange the wontons on a platter, and serve.

Note: Fried wontons reheat beautifully in a moderate oven. They also can be frozen after they are deep-fried. Arrange them on cookie sheets and let cool, then freeze for 15 minutes, or until firm. Transfer to plastic bags and freeze. To reheat frozen wontons, arrange on a cookie sheet, defrost at room temperature, and bake in a preheated 350°F oven for 10 to 12 minutes, or until piping hot.

OPEN-FACED PORK DUMPLINGS

Teahouses that serve dim sum are among my favorite haunts in Taiwan and Hong Kong. Once settled at a table, I help myself to the dishes on an endless parade of carts bulging with sweet and savory dumplings. Although I relish almost every variety, I must admit a special fondness for "open-faced" dumplings, or *shao mai,* stuffed with ground pork, black mushrooms, and garlic chives. When I make this easy-to-prepare delicacy, I substitute leeks for the garlic chives. Serve with tea or beer as an appetizer or snack, or even as an entrée. ● Makes 32 dumplings

1 pound ground pork (butt or shoulder)
6 dried Chinese black mushrooms, softened in hot water for 20
    minutes, stems removed, and caps finely chopped
1½ cups minced leeks
1 tablespoon minced garlic

Seasonings

2 tablespoons minced fresh ginger
2 tablespoons soy sauce
2 teaspoons rice wine or sake
1½ teaspoons sesame oil
½ teaspoon sugar
¼ teaspoon freshly ground black pepper
1 egg white, lightly beaten
1½ teaspoons cornstarch

32 dumpling or gyoza skins
¼ cup minced scallion greens
Soy Dipping Sauce or Vinegar Dipping Sauce
    (recipes follow)

Lightly chop the ground pork until fluffy. Place in a bowl and add the black mushrooms, leeks, garlic, and the Seasonings. Stir vigorously in one direction to blend the ingredients evenly.

Line several steamer trays with damp cheesecloth or with parchment paper brushed with sesame oil; or use aluminum pie plates punched with holes and brushed with sesame oil (see page 7).

Place a heaping tablespoon of the filling in the middle of one dumpling skin and gather the edges of the skin around the filling. Holding the dumpling between your index finger and thumb, push the filling from the bottom up and then squeeze the dumpling in the middle to create a "waist." Dip the underside of a spoon in water and smooth the top of the filling. Repeat with the remaining filling and wrappers, placing the dumplings ¼ inch apart on the steamer trays or pie plates.

Fill a wok or a large pot with water for steaming and heat until boiling. Stack two steamer trays, or place one tray of dumplings on a pie plate over the boiling water, cover, and steam for 15 minutes over high heat, or until cooked through; reverse the steamer trays halfway through the cooking time. Remove, and steam the remaining dumplings. Sprinkle the cooked dumplings with the minced scallions and serve with either of the dipping sauces.

Note: The dumplings may be cooked in advance. To reheat before serving, steam for about 7 to 8 minutes over boiling water.

Soy Dipping Sauce

¼ cup soy sauce

2 teaspoons minced garlic

3 tablespoons water

Combine all the ingredients and place in a small bowl. For additional spice, add 1 teaspoon hot chili paste.

Vinegar Dipping Sauce

¼ cup soy sauce

2 teaspoons Chinese black vinegar or Worcestershire sauce

2 teaspoons finely shredded fresh ginger

3 tablespoons water

Combine all the ingredients and place in a serving bowl.

STEAMED SHRIMP DUMPLINGS

Dumplings are extraordinarily versatile. They can be steamed, deep-fried, or panfried, but their character is defined by their filling. The delicate dumplings in this recipe are almost ethereal with their stuffing of shrimp mousseline studded with bits of crisp water chestnuts. It is important to squeeze all the moisture from the shrimp and the water chestnuts as you prepare the filling so that the texture of the dumplings will be properly crisp and the filling will not leak through the dumpling skins.

● Makes 48 dumplings

1 pound medium shrimp, peeled, deveined, rinsed, and drained

½ cup water chestnuts, blanched in boiling water for 10 seconds, refreshed in cold water, drained, and coarsely chopped

Seasonings

1½ tablespoons minced fresh ginger

1 tablespoon minced scallions (white part only)

1 tablespoon rice wine or sake

2 teaspoons soy sauce

½ teaspoon salt

⅛ teaspoon freshly ground black pepper

1 egg white, lightly beaten

1½ tablespoons cornstarch

48 dumpling or gyoza skins

Wrap the shrimp in a dish towel or paper towels and squeeze out as much moisture as possible. Transfer to a food processor fitted with a steel blade and process to a paste; or chop by hand, using a sharp knife. Transfer to a bowl.

Wrap the water chestnuts in a dish towel or paper towels and squeeze out as much moisture as possible. Add to the shrimp. Add all the Seasonings except the cornstarch and stir vigorously in one direction to combine the ingredients evenly. Add the cornstarch and stir to blend. The mixture should be stiff; if necessary, chill for 1 hour, or until firm.

Line several steamer trays with parchment paper; or use aluminum pie plates punched with holes and lightly brushed with sesame oil (see page 7).

Place a heaping teaspoon of the shrimp filling in the center of one dumpling skin and fold over the skin to make a half-moon shape. Use your thumb and index finger to form small pleats along the top edge of the skin. Then, with your other hand, press the two edges of the skin together to seal, curving the bottom edge to conform with the pleated edge. Repeat with the remaining filling and skins, placing dumplings about ¼ inch apart on the steamer trays or pie plates.

Fill a wok or a large pot with water for steaming and heat until boiling. Stack the steamer trays on top of one another, place over the boiling water (or fit one pie plate in the pot), cover, and steam over high heat for 12 to 15 minutes, reversing the stacked trays after 8 minutes. Remove, and steam any remaining dumplings.

Serve with Soy Dipping Sauce (page 67) or Vinegar Dipping Sauce (page 67).

FRIED DUMPLINGS WITH HOT CHILI SAUCE

Panfried dumplings, or potstickers, have become a staple at Chinese-American restaurants. One can easily understand their popularity: The crusty skins contrast beautifully with the hearty meat filling. I like to serve these with a spicy dipping sauce seasoned with hot chili paste, black vinegar, and ginger, followed by chasers of ice-cold beer. ● Makes 40 dumplings

1 pound ground pork (butt or shoulder)

⅓ pound medium shrimp, peeled, deveined, rinsed, and drained

½ cup water chestnuts, blanched in boiling water for 10 seconds, refreshed in cold water, and thoroughly drained

Seasonings

2½ tablespoons minced fresh ginger

2 tablespoons minced scallions (white part only)

2 tablespoons soy sauce

1 tablespoon rice wine or sake

1½ teaspoons sesame oil

⅛ teaspoon freshly ground black pepper

1½ tablespoons cornstarch

Hot Chili Sauce

3 tablespoons soy sauce

1 tablespoon Chinese black vinegar or Worcestershire sauce

1 tablespoon sugar

2 tablespoons water

½ teaspoon hot chili paste

1 teaspoon minced fresh ginger

40 dumpling or gyoza skins

1 cup corn or safflower oil

Using a sharp knife or a cleaver, chop the ground pork until fluffy. Place in a bowl.

Wrap the shrimp in a dish towel or paper towels and squeeze out as much moisture as possible. Cut into small dice, and add to the pork.

Wrap the water chestnuts in a dish towel or paper towels and squeeze out as much moisture as possible. Transfer to a food processor fitted with a steel blade and coarsely chop. Add to the pork and shrimp. Add all the Seasonings except the cornstarch and stir vigorously in one direction to combine thoroughly. Add the cornstarch and stir to blend. The mixture should be stiff. Refrigerate until ready to use.

Combine the chili sauce ingredients and place in a serving bowl.

Place a heaping tablespoon of the shrimp filling in the center of one dumpling skin. Moisten the edges with water, fold over in half to enclose the filling, and press the edges to seal. Repeat with the remaining filling and skins, and arrange the dumplings on a tray lightly dusted with cornstarch.

Preheat the oven to 200°F.

Heat a wok or a skillet, add the oil, and heat to 350°F. Add 8 or 9 of the dumplings and fry, turning constantly, until a deep golden brown, about 7 to 8 minutes. Remove with a handled strainer, and drain briefly in a colander, then transfer to absorbent paper. Place on a baking sheet and keep warm in the oven. Fry the remaining dumplings, reheating the oil between each batch. Arrange the dumplings on a serving platter and serve with the Hot Chili Sauce.

Note: Chilling the filling makes it easier to handle when stuffing the dumplings.

CLASSIC DUMPLINGS

In Beijing, where these dumplings originated, there are stalls filled from dawn to dusk with customers who stop in briefly to consume mountains of boiled or panfried dumplings filled with ground pork, fragrant garlic chives, and cabbage. In this recipe for that Beijing classic, I give both cooking methods. The water used for boiling the dumplings is often served as a simple broth along with the dumplings for a hearty, satisfying meal.

● **Makes 40 dumplings**

5 cups minced Chinese (Napa) cabbage
1 teaspoon salt
1½ cups chopped garlic chives or 1½ cups chopped leeks plus
    1 tablespoon minced garlic
¾ pound ground pork (butt or shoulder)

Seasonings

2 tablespoons soy sauce
1 tablespoon rice wine or sake
1½ teaspoons sesame oil
⅛ teaspoon freshly ground black pepper
1½ tablespoons cornstarch

40 dumpling or gyoza skins

Place the minced cabbage in a bowl, add the salt, and toss lightly. Let sit at room temperature for 1 hour to remove excess water from the cabbage.

Taking one handful of cabbage at a time, squeeze out as much water as possible, and place the cabbage in a large bowl. Add the garlic chives or leeks and garlic, the ground pork, and all the Seasonings except the cornstarch and vigorously stir the mixture in one direction to blend the ingredients. Add the cornstarch and stir to blend. The mixture should be fairly stiff.

Place 1 tablespoon of the filling in the center of one dumpling skin and fold the skin over to form a half-moon shape. Use your thumb and index finger to form small pleats along the top edge of the skin. Then, with your other hand, press the two edges together to seal, curving the bottom edge to conform with the pleated edge. Repeat with the remaining filling and skins, placing the dumplings on a baking sheet or tray lightly dusted with cornstarch.

Fill a large pot with 3 quarts of water and heat until boiling. Add half the dumplings, bring back to a boil, and simmer for about 5 to 7 minutes over medium heat, stirring the dumplings from time to time. Remove with a handled strainer and place on a serving platter. Cook the remaining dumplings and arrange on the serving platter.

Serve with Soy Dipping Sauce (page 67), Vinegar Dipping Sauce (page 67), or Hot Chili Sauce (page 70).

Variation: To panfry the dumplings: heat a wok or a well-seasoned skillet until very hot, add 1½ tablespoons corn or safflower oil, and heat over high heat until hot. Remove from the heat and arrange half the dumplings very close together in the pan. Return to the heat and fry the dumplings until golden brown on the bottom. Stir 1 cup water into 1 tablespoon of flour until smooth, add to the dumplings, partially cover, and heat until boiling. Reduce the heat to low and cook for 10 minutes. Drain off any liquid, drizzle 1 tablespoon corn or safflower oil around the dumplings, and cook over high heat until crisp, about 5 minutes. Use a spatula to dislodge the dumplings and invert onto a heatproof serving plate and keep warm in a low oven while you repeat the procedure with the remaining dumplings. (Or use two skillets and cook all the dumplings at one time.) Serve with any of the suggested sauces.

CRUSTY VEGETARIAN DUMPLINGS

Many Americans tend to dismiss vegetarian food as bland and boring, but Chinese vegetarian fare defies the cliché. Pungent seasonings such as black mushrooms, sesame oil, ginger, and garlic are used in generous proportions to enliven meatless dishes like these golden dumplings, which will please even the most discriminating palate. ● Makes 30 dumplings

5 cups finely minced Chinese or (Napa) cabbage

1 teaspoon salt

Seasonings

2 tablespoons soy sauce

1 tablespoon rice wine or sake

1 teaspoon sesame oil

⅛ teaspoon freshly ground black pepper

1½ teaspoons cornstarch

2 tablespoons minced garlic

2 tablespoons minced fresh ginger

1 tablespoon corn or safflower oil

8 dried Chinese black mushrooms, softened in hot water for 20
      minutes, stems removed, and caps minced

1½ cups minced garlic chives or 1½ cups minced leeks plus 1
      tablespoon minced garlic

1½ cups grated carrots

1 tablespoon rice wine or sake

30 dumpling or gyoza skins

Corn or safflower oil for deep-frying

Place the minced cabbage in a mixing bowl, add the salt, and toss lightly. Let sit for 1 hour to remove excess water.

Taking one handful of cabbage at a time, squeeze out as much water as possible, and place the cabbage in a bowl.

Combine all the Seasoning ingredients except the garlic and ginger in a small bowl.

Heat a wok or a skillet, add the 1 tablespoon oil, and heat until hot. Add the minced garlic and ginger and the black mushrooms, and stir-fry for about 10 seconds, until fragrant. Add the garlic chives or leeks and garlic and the carrots and stir-fry over high heat for 30 seconds. Add the rice wine or sake and stir-fry for 30 seconds, then add the soy sauce mixture and toss until thickened. Spread the filling mixture out on a platter to cool.

Place a heaping tablespoon of the cooled filling in the center of one dumpling skin and fold over the skin to form a half-moon shape. Moisten the top edge of the dumpling with a little water and use your thumb and index finger to form small pleats along this edge. Then press the edges together to seal. Arrange the dumplings on a tray lightly dusted with cornstarch.

Preheat the oven to 200°F.

Heat a wok or a heavy skillet, add an inch or so of oil, and heat to 350°F. Add 7 or 8 of the dumplings and fry over medium heat, turning constantly, until a deep, dark brown. Use a handled strainer or a slotted spoon to remove the dumplings and drain briefly in a colander, then transfer to absorbent paper. Keep warm in the oven while you fry the remaining dumplings, adding more oil if necessary. (To reheat the dumplings if prepared ahead, arrange on a rack in a baking pan and heat until piping hot in a preheated 375°F oven.)

SPRING ROLLS

Too many Americans know spring rolls only as dense, stodgy rolls stuffed with cabbage and celery. Real spring rolls are elegantly thin and crisp, and the filling is generously embellished with shredded pork, black mushrooms, and bean sprouts. The lacy wrappers, made of flour and water, become extraordinarily crisp when deep-fried. Here is my version of the dish as it was meant to be.   ●   Makes 20 spring rolls

1 pound boneless center-cut pork loin

Marinade

1½ tablespoons soy sauce

1 tablespoon rice wine or sake

1 teaspoon sesame oil

1 teaspoon cornstarch

Sauce

1 tablespoon soy sauce

1 tablespoon rice wine or sake

1 teaspoon sesame oil

¼ teaspoon freshly ground black pepper

1 teaspoon cornstarch

5 tablespoons corn or safflower oil

Seasonings

1½ tablespoons minced garlic

1½ tablespoons minced fresh ginger

8 dried Chinese black mushrooms, softened in hot water for
       20 minutes, stems removed, and caps finely shredded

2½ cups finely shredded leeks

2½ cups finely shredded Chinese (Napa) cabbage

1 tablespoon rice wine or sake

3 cups bean sprouts, rinsed and drained

1 egg, lightly beaten

3 tablespoons all-purpose flour

1 tablespoon water

20 Shanghai spring roll wrappers or lumpia skins

Corn or safflower oil for deep-frying

Using a sharp knife or a cleaver, trim any fat or gristle from the pork loin. Cut the meat across the grain into thin slices about ⅛ inch thick. Then cut the slices into fine julienne shreds. Place the pork in a bowl, add the Marinade ingredients, and toss lightly to coat. Cover with plastic wrap and let sit for 20 minutes.

Combine the Sauce ingredients and blend well.

Heat a wok, add 3 tablespoons of the oil, and heat until very hot. Add the shredded pork and stir-fry over high heat, stirring constantly, until it loses its raw color and the shreds separate. Remove with a handled strainer or a slotted spoon and drain on paper towels.

Reheat the wok, add the remaining 2 tablespoons oil, and heat until very hot. Add the Seasonings and stir-fry for about 15 seconds, until fragrant. Add the leeks and stir-fry for about 1 minute over high heat. Add the cabbage and rice wine or sake and stir-fry for 1 minute. Add the bean sprouts and sauce mixture and stir-fry briefly, just until the sauce has thickened. Spread the filling out on a platter to cool, or refrigerate. Then drain the filling in a colander, pressing down on the mixture with the back of a spoon.

Combine the egg, flour, and water and blend to a smooth paste. Separate the wrappers or skins and cover with a damp cloth to keep from drying out.

Place a wrapper on a work surface with one of the corners facing you. Put about 2 tablespoons of the filling in a log shape in a straight line just below the center of the wrapper. (If the filling is still very wet, squeeze out any excess liquid as you work.) Brush some of the egg paste along the top of the wrapper. Starting at the bottom edge, roll up the spring roll one or two turns, then fold over the sides and roll up to completely enclose the filling. Press the seam to seal. Repeat with the remaining wrappers and filling.

Heat a wok, a deep-fryer, or a skillet, add enough oil for deep-frying, and heat to 375°F. Add 4 or 5 spring rolls and fry, turning occasionally, until a deep golden brown. Remove with a handled strainer or a slotted spoon and drain briefly in a colander, then transfer to paper towels. Deep-fry the remaining spring rolls. Serve. (To reheat the spring rolls if prepared ahead, arrange on a rack in a baking pan and heat in a 375°F oven until piping hot.)

Serve with plum sauce or duck sauce and hot mustard.

Note: It's important to remove as much liquid as possible from the filling so that it does not leak through the wrappers. For the same reason, deep-fry the spring rolls soon after forming them.

CHINESE YEAST DOUGH

Since Chinese breads are usually steamed, one might assume that they are heavy and soggy. In fact, the combination of yeast in the basic dough and baking powder added as the breads are shaped makes for incredibly light and springy bread. The long rising period also helps. Use this basic dough to make all types of rolls and stuffed buns.

● Makes enough for 16 to 18 buns or rolls

2 tablespoons sugar
1 cup warm water
½ tablespoon active dry yeast
3 cups all-purpose flour
1 tablespoon corn or safflower oil

Dissolve the sugar in the warm water. Add the yeast, mix gently, and let stand for about 10 minutes, until the mixture foams and forms a head.

Place the flour in a large bowl. Add the yeast mixture and the oil and, using a wooden spoon or your hands, slowly incorporate the liquid into the flour, mixing to a rough dough. Turn the dough out onto a lightly floured surface and knead until smooth and elastic, adding a little more flour if the dough is sticky. Grease a large bowl with the oil, place the dough in the bowl, and cover with a damp cloth. Let rise in a warm draft-free place, for 3 to 4 hours, or until tripled in bulk.

Note: The lengthy rising time gives the steamed dough a full, slightly yeasty flavor.

STEAMED FLOWER BUNS

In northern China, where wheat rather than rice is the staple grain, steamed buns in myriad shapes are eaten with stir-fried, steamed, and braised dishes. The dough can be fashioned into snails, lotus buns, and peaches, as well as these flower rolls. The buns can be shaped and cooked in advance, then reheated briefly in the steamer before serving.

● **Makes 18 buns**

> 1 recipe Chinese Yeast Dough (page 78)
> 1 teaspoon baking powder
> 3 tablespoons sesame oil

Place the dough on a lightly floured surface. Make a well in the center and add the baking powder. Knead lightly until smooth. Then cut the dough in half. Place one half on a floured work surface, and cover the remaining dough to prevent it from drying out. Roll the dough out to a rectangle about 18 inches long and 8 inches wide. Brush the surface of the rectangle liberally with sesame oil. Starting at one of the long edges, roll up the dough jelly-roll style. Pinch the ends to seal. Lightly flatten the roll with your hands and cut into pieces about 2 inches wide. With a chopstick or the tip of a blunt knife, make an indentation in the center of each bun. Repeat with the remaining dough.

Line two steamer trays with parchment, or use aluminum pie plates punched with holes and lightly brushed with sesame oil (see page 7). Arrange the buns about 1 inch apart on the steamer trays or pie plates. Cover with towels and let rise for 15 minutes in a warm draft-free place.

Fill a wok or a large pot with water for steaming and heat until boiling. Place the steamer trays, or one pie plate over the boiling water, cover, and steam over high heat for 15 minutes, or until the buns are light and springy. Transfer to a platter and cover with a towel or foil to keep warm while you steam any remaining buns. Arrange on the platter, and serve.

STEAMED BARBECUED PORK BUNS

One of my all-time favorite snacks is barbecued pork buns. I love the contrast of the fluffy steamed dough and the roasted meat drenched in a rich oyster sauce. These buns are one of the most popular items in any dim sum parlor, but they are easily prepared at home. You can make several batches at a time to appease even the most voracious appetites.

● Makes 16 buns

1 pound center-cut boneless pork loin

Barbecue Sauce

¼ cup hoisin sauce

2 tablespoons ketchup

1½ tablespoons rice wine or sake

1 tablespoon minced garlic

1 tablespoon soy sauce

Rich Oyster Sauce

2 tablespoons oyster sauce

1 tablespoon soy sauce

1 tablespoon sugar

½ tablespoon ketchup

1 teaspoon sesame oil

1 teaspoon cornstarch

1 recipe Chinese Yeast Dough (page 78)

1 teaspoon baking powder

To make the barbecued pork filling, trim any fat or gristle from the pork with a sharp knife or a cleaver. Combine the Barbecue Sauce ingredients in a bowl. Add the pork and turn to coat. Cover with plastic wrap and refrigerate for at least 1 hour, or overnight.

Preheat the oven to 350°F.

Place the pork in a baking pan lined with aluminum foil and roast for 30 to 45 minutes, until cooked through. Let cool. Pour off the cooking juices and reserve ¼ cup; skim off any fat. Cut the pork into ¼-inch dice.

Combine the Oyster Sauce ingredients in a bowl, add the reserved meat juices, and blend well.

Heat a wok or a skillet, add the sauce mixture, and heat until thickened, stirring constantly to prevent lumps. Add the diced pork and toss lightly to coat. Transfer to a platter, and refrigerate until thoroughly chilled.

Turn the Yeast Dough out onto a lightly floured work surface. Make a well in the center of the dough, add the baking powder, and lightly knead until the baking powder is fully incorporated. Roll the dough into a long snakelike roll about 1½ inches in diameter. Cut the roll in 16 pieces. Cover the unused dough with a towel as you work to prevent it from drying out. Place one piece cut side down on the work surface and use your fingers to flatten it into a 3-inch round; the edges should be slightly thinner than the center. Place a heaping teaspoon of the barbecued pork filling in the center and gather up the edges of the dough over the filling, pressing to seal. Then twist the gathered edges to prevent them from opening. Repeat with the remaining dough and filling. Arrange the buns about 1 inch apart on steamer trays lined with parchment paper or on aluminum pie plates punched with holes (see page 7), and let rise in a warm draft-free place for 15 minutes.

Fill a wok or a large pot with water for steaming and heat until boiling. Place one steamer tray or pie plate over the water and steam the buns over high heat for 15 to 20 minutes, until puffed and springy to the touch. Steam the remaining buns in the same manner. Transfer to a platter and serve immediately, or cover with foil and set aside until serving time. To reheat the buns, steam over boiling water for 10 to 15 minutes, or until hot.

Note: The filling is much easier to handle if it is well chilled.

BAKED BARBECUED
PORK BUNS

For a delectable variation, pork buns can be baked rather than steamed. The baked dough has a crusty, slightly dense texture, reminiscent of an Italian peasant loaf. This baked dough differs slightly from the steamed version, since baking powder is not necessary. Serve with a light soup as a satisfying and unusual meal. ● Makes 16 buns

Dough

2 tablespoons sugar

1 cup warm water

1 package active dry yeast

3 cups all-purpose flour

1 tablespoon corn or safflower oil

1 egg, lightly beaten

3 tablespoons water

1 recipe barbecued pork filling (see Steamed Barbecued Pork Buns, page 80), thoroughly chilled

16 4-inch parchment paper squares

Dissolve the sugar in the warm water. Add the yeast, mix gently, and let stand for about 10 minutes, until the mixture foams and forms a head. Place the flour in a mixing bowl and add the yeast mixture, oil, and half the beaten egg. (Reserve the remaining egg for egg wash.) Using a wooden spoon or your hands, mix to a rough dough, then turn out onto a lightly floured surface and knead until smooth and elastic. Grease a large bowl with the oil, place the dough in the bowl, and cover with a damp cloth. Let rise in a warm draft-free place for 3 to 4 hours, or until tripled in bulk.

Turn the dough out onto a lightly floured work surface and roll into a long snakelike roll about 1½ inches in diameter. Cut the roll into 16 pieces. Cover the unused dough with a damp cloth as you work. Place one piece cut side down on the work surface and use your fingers to flatten it into a 3-inch round; the edges should be slightly thinner than the center. Place a heaping teaspoon of the barbecued pork mixture in the center of the dough, gather up the edges to enclose the filling, and pinch to seal. Then twist the gathered edges together to prevent them from opening. Place the bun upside down, in the center of a parchment paper square. Repeat with the remaining dough and filling, and place the shaped buns about 2 inches apart on a cookie sheet. Let rise for 1 hour.

Preheat the oven to 350°F.

Lightly beat the reserved egg with the 3 tablespoons water, and lightly brush the buns with the egg wash. Bake for about 25 minutes, or until golden brown. Serve hot or at room temperature.

MAIN-DISH SALADS, COLD-TOSSED VEGETABLES, AND PICKLES

In virtually any season, the shelves of Asian produce stalls are heaped high with fresh vegetables. These days, much of this exotic produce appears in our local supermarkets as well. And there's almost no better use for these ingredients than to serve them in multilayered salads or turn them into spicy pickles.

In winter, the humble cabbage is transformed into zesty hot-and-sour slaws. Summer's cucumbers become delicious sweet-and-sour pickles. Green beans may be "cold-tossed" with garlic and soy sauce for a simple yet satisfying vegetable side dish. And for an unusual light lunch or dinner, a rainbow of julienne vegetables is arranged over noodles and served with a spicy peanut dressing.

This chapter offers a glimpse of the lively and ever-expanding category of Chinese salads and pickles. Some of the recipes are traditional, others are my own invention, a reflection of the creative mood in the Far East, where young chefs are developing their own masterpieces with a wealth of new ingredients.

Although fresh vegetables have long been relished in China, because of hygienic reasons, most have been served cooked. Consequently, the favored techniques have been those like stir-frying and steaming, quick-cooking methods that preserve the flavors and crisp textures of the fresh ingredients. And because refrigeration was scarce, myriad pickles, which preserve vegetables in a tart brine, have been another popular alternative.

Pickle dishes have not lost their appeal in modern times, and they are served year-round. Their irresistibly crunchy textures are perfect nibbles before a meal and a piquant complement to rice and a variety of other dishes.

Composed or layered salads of assorted meats, seafoods, and vegetables arranged on a bed of cooked noodles or rice now appear with some regularity on Chinese tables. Traditionally, the Chinese may have fancied them only as snacks, but now many feel—as I do—that they make a delightfully satisfying lunch or dinner.

SUMMER RICE SALAD

Rice salads studded with seasonal vegetables such as asparagus, tomatoes, corn, snow or snap peas, and peppers are a natural accompaniment to grilled meats and seafood. With the addition of leftover cooked ham, chicken, or seafood, this one would make a light yet satisfying simple lunch or dinner. ● Serves 6

1½ cups long-grain white rice

½ pound asparagus, tough ends trimmed

1 cup cherry tomatoes, rinsed, drained, and stems removed

1 small red onion, cut into ¼-inch dice

1 yellow bell pepper, rinsed, cored, seeded, and cut into ¼-inch dice

1½ tablespoons minced scallion greens or fresh chives (optional)

Dressing

6 tablespoons soy sauce

¼ cup freshly squeezed lemon juice

3 tablespoons minced cilantro (fresh coriander) or parsley

2 tablespoons sesame oil

½ teaspoon salt

1½ teaspoons sugar

¼ teaspoon freshly ground black pepper

Place the rice in a colander. Using your hands as a rake, rinse under cold running water until the water runs clear; drain thoroughly. Place in a saucepan with a tight-fitting lid, add 3 cups cold water, and bring to a boil. Reduce the heat to low, cover, and simmer for 20 minutes, or until all the water has been absorbed and craters appear on the surface of the rice. Remove from the heat and fluff with a fork. Let cool completely, then transfer to a serving bowl, fluffing and separating the grains with the fork.

Add 1 cup water to a frying pan or a sauté pan and heat until boiling. Add the asparagus, cover, and cook for 3 to 4 minutes, until just tender. Remove and refresh under cold running water. Drain thoroughly and cut into 1-inch lengths. Add the asparagus, tomatoes, red onion, yellow pepper, and scallion greens or chives (if using) to the rice. Whisk together the Dressing ingredients in a small bowl. Add to the rice mixture and toss to coat. Serve at room temperature or chilled.

WARM CRAB
AND SPINACH SALAD

My passion for spinach salads inspired me to create this recipe. Nuggets of fresh lump crabmeat paired with sweet red peppers dot shiny green spinach leaves, which are lightly wilted by a tangy warm soy dressing.

● Serves 6

1 pound (or two 10-ounce packages) fresh spinach, stems removed, rinsed thoroughly and drained

Spicy Dressing

6 tablespoons soy sauce

1½ tablespoons sugar

3 tablespoons clear rice vinegar

2 tablespoons rice wine or sake

1 pound lump crabmeat, picked through to remove any shells and cartilage

1 tablespoon rice wine or sake

1 tablespoon corn or safflower oil

3 tablespoons minced scallions (white part only)

1 tablespoon minced garlic

1 tablespoon minced fresh ginger

2 red bell peppers, rinsed, cored, seeded, and cut into ¼-inch dice

Cut the spinach roughly into large pieces and arrange in a serving bowl. For the Spicy Dressing combine the soy sauce, sugar, rice vinegar, and rice wine or sake in a small bowl, and set aside.

Heat a wok or a skillet until hot. Add the crabmeat and rice wine or sake and toss lightly over high heat for about 1 minute. Remove from the heat and scatter over the spinach leaves.

Reheat the pan until hot, add the corn or safflower oil, and heat until hot. Add the scallions, garlic, and ginger and stir-fry over high heat for about 15 seconds, until fragrant. Add the diced red peppers and stir-fry for 1 minute. Add the soy sauce mixture and cook for about 1 minute, stirring. Pour the hot dressing over the spinach and toss lightly. Serve immediately.

Variation: Substitute thinly sliced sea scallops or butterflied shrimp for the crabmeat. To cook the shellfish, heat 1 teaspoon corn or safflower oil, add the seafood and the rice wine or sake, and stir-fry for about 2 minutes, or until cooked. Scatter over the spinach leaves and proceed as directed.

HOT-AND-SOUR SEAFOOD SALAD

Lo mein noodles, egg-rich and delicate, are an ideal foil for a sumptuous stir-fry of scallops and shrimp garnished with water chestnuts and snow peas. The dressing is enlivened by the liberal use of chile flakes and black vinegar. ● Serves 6

½ pound sea scallops, lightly rinsed and drained

½ pound medium shrimp, peeled

Seafood Marinade

6 slices fresh ginger (about the size of a quarter), lightly smashed with the flat side of a knife or a cleaver

¼ cup rice wine or sake

1 teaspoon sesame oil

1 teaspoon salt

½ pound lo mein noodles or thin flat noodles such as fettucine or linguine

1 cup thinly sliced water chestnuts, blanched in boiling water for 10 seconds, refreshed in cold water, and drained

½ pound snow peas, ends trimmed, veiny strings removed, and sliced lengthwise in half

½ cup minced scallion greens

Hot-and-Sour Dressing

¼ cup sesame oil

1 teaspoon chile pepper flakes

2½ tablespoons minced fresh ginger

2 tablespoons minced garlic

6 tablespoons soy sauce

2 tablespoons rice wine or sake

1 tablespoon sugar

1½ tablespoons Chinese black vinegar or Worcestershire sauce

Slice each scallop horizontally in half and place in a bowl. Score each shrimp down the back and remove the dark vein. (The scoring will allow the shrimp to "butterfly" when cooked.) Rinse and drain. Place in another bowl.

Combine the Marinade ingredients and pinch the ginger slices in the mixture to bring out the flavor. Add half the marinade to the shrimp and half to the scallops. Toss lightly to coat, and let marinate for 20 minutes.

Heat a large pot of water until boiling. Add the shrimp with their marinade and cook, stirring occasionally, for about 3 minutes, or until they turn pink. Remove with a slotted spoon and drain. Reheat the water until boiling, add the scallops, and cook for about 1½ minutes, or until they are opaque. Remove with a slotted spoon and drain. Add the noodles to the boiling water and cook for about 7 to 8 minutes, or until just tender. Add the water chestnuts and snow peas and stir, then drain in a colander and cool under cold running water. Discard the ginger and drain thoroughly. Place the noodles, snow peas, scallops, shrimp, and scallion greens in a large bowl.

To prepare the Dressing, heat a wok or a skillet until hot, add the sesame oil, and heat until very hot. Add the chile flakes and cook for about 10 seconds. Remove from the heat, add the ginger, cover, and let sit for 15 to 20 minutes.

Stir the garlic, soy sauce, rice wine or sake, sugar, and Chinese black vinegar to the warm ginger oil and stir to dissolve the sugar. Pour over the seafood salad and toss lightly to coat. Serve warm, at room temperature, or cold.

Variation: Substitute cooked boneless chicken breasts or boneless pork loin for the seafood. Cook the noodles as directed, and add 1 cup slivered red bell peppers to the salad.

PEKING CHICKEN SALAD

This dish was inspired by a traditional northern Chinese recipe, but the combination of the delicate vinaigrette and the chopped peanuts gives it a slight Vietnamese or Thai flavor. Refreshing yet subtle, the colorful salad is superb as a main dish or an appetizer. ● Serves 6

1 boneless skinless chicken breast (about 1 pound)

1 tablespoon rice wine or sake

2 slices fresh ginger (about the size of a quarter), smashed with the flat side of a knife or a cleaver

2 scallions, trimmed and smashed with the flat side of a knife or a cleaver

6 carrots, peeled and trimmed

1 seedless cucumber or 4 gherkin or Kirby cucumbers, ends trimmed, halved, and seeded

½ pound bean sprouts, rinsed and drained

1 tablespoon minced scallion greens

Vinaigrette

5 tablespoons soy sauce

1½ tablespoons sugar

2 tablespoons sesame oil

3 tablespoons clear rice vinegar

¼ cup chopped dry-roasted peanuts

Place the chicken in a saucepan with water to cover and add the rice wine, ginger, and whole scallions. Heat until boiling, then reduce the heat to low and simmer uncovered for 10 minutes. Remove from the heat and let cool slightly, and drain. Tear or cut the chicken into shreds.

With a food processor fitted with a shredding blade or with a hand grater, shred or grate the carrots and cucumber. Squeeze the cucumber to remove excess liquid. Arrange the carrots in a circle around the outer edge of a serving platter, following with concentric circles of the cucumbers and then the bean sprouts, leaving a space in the center for the chicken. Arrange the chicken shreds in the center of the platter and sprinkle with the minced scallions.

Combine the Vinaigrette ingredients and place in a sauceboat.

Serve the salad at room temperature or chilled. Just before serving, pour the vinaigrette over the top, or dress each serving individually.

Variation: Substitute cooked whole shrimp or shredded boneless pork loin or flank steak for the chicken.

COMPOSED CHICKEN SALAD

The French are great fans of composed salads, which provided the inspiration for this recipe. Stir-fried marinated slices of chicken are arranged over shredded Romaine lettuce and topped with a heady mixture of cooked diced tomatoes and scallions seasoned with wine vinegar and sesame oil. The result is a light, unique, and flavorful dish. ● Serves 6

2 boneless skinless chicken breasts (about 1½ pounds)

Marinade

1½ tablespoons soy sauce

1 tablespoon rice wine or sake

1 teaspoon sesame oil

½ tablespoon cornstarch

3 cups julienned Romaine lettuce (cut into strips about 3 inches long and ¼ inch wide)

¼ cup corn or safflower oil

¼ cup sesame oil

½ cup minced scallions (white part only)

4 ripe but firm tomatoes, peeled, seeded, and cut into ½-inch dice

⅓ cup red wine vinegar

¾ teaspoon salt

½ teaspoon freshly ground black pepper

½ cup ½-inch-wide slices scallion greens

Trim any fat or sinew from the chicken breasts. Cut the breasts in half lengthwise, and then cut across the grain into wide, thin slices about 1 inch wide and ⅛ inch thick. Place the slices in a bowl, add all the marinade ingredients, and toss lightly. Refrigerate for at least 20 minutes.

Arrange the lettuce on a large round serving platter or on individual salad plates.

Heat a wok or a deep skillet, add 2 tablespoons of the corn or safflower oil, and heat until very hot. Add half the chicken and stir-fry over high heat, stirring constantly, until the meat loses its pink color and separates. Remove with a handled strainer and drain in a colander. Reheat the pan, add the remaining 2 tablespoons oil, and stir-fry the remaining chicken; drain. Mound the chicken on top of the lettuce. Clean out the pan.

Reheat the wok or skillet, add the sesame oil, and heat until hot. Add the minced scallions and toss over high heat for about 10 seconds, until fragrant. Add the diced tomatoes and toss lightly for 10 seconds. Add the vinegar and cook, stirring constantly, for about 1 minute, or until the liquid is reduced slightly. Add the salt, pepper, and scallion greens. Toss lightly and spoon over the chicken. Serve immediately.

Variation: Substitute turkey cutlets or boneless leg of lamb for the chicken.

WARM BEEF SALAD

In this layered salad, sliced flank steak is marinated in a pungent garlic and ginger sauce, then stir-fried and served over crisp-cooked green beans. The whole is then bathed in a spicy sesame oil and rice vinegar dressing. Bean threads or cellophane noodles may be added as a bed to soak up all the delicious flavors. ● Serves 6

1½ pounds flank steak or eye of round roast

Marinade

1 tablespoon minced garlic

1 tablespoon minced fresh ginger

3 tablespoons soy sauce

2 tablespoons rice wine

1 teaspoon sesame oil

1 teaspoon sugar

1 teaspoon cornstarch

1½ pounds green beans, rinsed, drained, ends trimmed, and cut into 2-inch lengths

¼ cup corn or safflower oil

2 tablespoons minced red onion (optional)

Dressing

2 tablespoons sesame oil

½ teaspoon chile pepper flakes

2 tablespoons minced scallions

¼ cup soy sauce

1 tablespoon sugar

2 tablespoons clear rice vinegar

2 tablespoons rice wine or sake

Using a sharp knife, trim the beef of any fat or gristle and cut with the grain into strips about 3 inches long. Cut the strips across the grain into ¼-inch-thick slices. Place in a bowl, add all the Marinade ingredients, and toss lightly to coat. Let marinate for 30 minutes at room temperature, cover with plastic wrap, and refrigerate overnight.

Heat a large pot of water until boiling. Add the green beans and cook for 4 to 5 minutes, until crisp-tender. Drain, refresh in cold water, and drain again. Arrange the beans on a serving platter, with a slight indentation in the center for the beef.

Heat a wok or a skillet, add 2 tablespoons of the corn or safflower oil, and heat until very hot. Add half the beef and stir-fry over high heat, tossing lightly, until the meat loses its raw color and separates. Remove with a handled strainer and drain. Reheat the pan, add the remaining 2 tablespoons oil, and heat until very hot. Add the remaining beef and stir-fry over high heat until cooked; drain. Arrange the beef over the green beans and sprinkle the minced red onion on top (if using).

To prepare the Dressing, heat a wok or a small skillet, add the sesame oil, and heat until hot. Add the chile flakes and scallions and stir-fry for 10 seconds, or until fragrant. Add the remaining ingredients and cook for about 1 minute. Adjust the seasonings, if necessary, and pour over the salad. Serve warm or at room temperature, tossing before serving.

Variation: Substitute boneless pork loin or boneless leg of lamb for the beef.

GRILLED
PEPPER STEAK SALAD

The appealing base of red and yellow peppers and fresh snow peas for this dish could easily be served by itself as a simple stir-fry. But add thin slices of anise-flavored steak seared over a charcoal fire and you have a unique salad that is delightful at any time of the year. ● Serves 6

1½ pounds flank steak or London broil

Marinade

6 slices fresh ginger (about the size of a quarter), lightly smashed with the flat side of a knife or a cleaver

6 cloves garlic, lightly smashed with the flat side of a knife or a cleaver and peeled

1 teaspoon aniseed

2½ cups water

¾ cup rice wine or sake

½ cup soy sauce

3 tablespoons sesame oil

2 tablespoons sugar

2 teaspoons corn or safflower oil

1 teaspoon sesame oil

1½ tablespoons minced garlic

1½ tablespoons minced fresh ginger

2 red bell peppers, rinsed, cored, seeded, and cut into thin julienne strips

2 yellow bell peppers, rinsed, cored, seeded, and cut into thin julienne strips

⅓ pound snow peas, ends trimmed and veiny strings removed

1 tablespoon rice wine or sake

¼ teaspoon salt

Using a sharp knife, trim the meat of any fat or gristle. Holding the knife at a 45° angle, score the steak lengthwise and crosswise at 1-inch intervals, making ½-inch-deep cuts. Place the steak in a deep nonreactive pan.

Combine the Marinade ingredients in a saucepan and heat until boiling. Reduce the heat to low and simmer for 20 minutes. Pour the hot marinade over the steak and turn to coat. Let cool to room temperature, cover with plastic wrap, and refrigerate for at least 3 hours, or overnight if possible, turning occasionally.

Prepare a fire in a charcoal grill or preheat the broiler.

Remove the steak from the pan, reserving the marinade. Grill or broil the meat about 3 inches from the heat source, brushing frequently with the marinade, until medium-rare, about 5 to 7 minutes on each side. Let sit. Strain the marinade and reserve 1 cup.

Heat a wok or a skillet, add the corn or safflower oil and the sesame oil, and heat until hot. Add the garlic, ginger, and red and yellow peppers and toss lightly over high heat for about 1 minute. Add the snow peas, rice wine, and salt and stir-fry over high heat for about 1½ minutes, until the snow peas are just tender. Remove and arrange the vegetables on a large round serving platter. With a sharp knife, cut the meat across the grain into ⅛-inch-thick slices. Mound the beef in the center of the vegetables.

Meanwhile, heat the reserved marinade in a saucepan until boiling. Remove from the heat.

Serve the salad warm, at room temperature, or cold, pouring the marinade over it just before serving.

SHREDDED BARBECUED PORK AND LEEK SALAD

Barbecued pork flavored with rich hoisin sauce is a delectable complement to stir-fried leeks and bean sprouts. To make the dish more substantial, serve over a layer of crisp panfried noodles. ● Serves 6

Barbecue Sauce

¼ cup hoisin sauce

2 tablespoons ketchup

1 tablespoon minced garlic

1½ tablespoons soy sauce

2 tablespoons rice wine or sake

1 tablespoon sugar

1½ pounds boneless center-cut pork loin, trimmed of fat and cut into chops about 1½ inches thick

Dressing

⅓ cup soy sauce

3 tablespoons clear rice vinegar

1 tablespoon sugar

2 tablespoons sesame oil

1 tablespoon corn or safflower oil

1 tablespoon minced fresh ginger

1 tablespoon minced garlic

3 cups leeks cut into thin julienne shreds

1½ tablespoons rice wine or sake

4 cups bean sprouts, rinsed and drained

Preheat the oven to 350°F.

Combine Barbecue Sauce ingredients in a bowl. Add the pork loin and toss lightly to coat.

Arrange the pork chops on a baking sheet lined with aluminum foil and bake for 30 to 35 minutes. Remove the pork and let cool. Pour the cooking juices into a large bowl and skim off any fat. Cut the barbecued pork against the grain into ¼-inch-thick slices, then cut into julienne shreds. Add to the cooking juices and set aside.

Combine the Dressing ingredients and stir until the sugar is dissolved.

Heat a wok or a large skillet, add the corn or safflower oil, and heat until very hot. Add the ginger, garlic, and leeks and stir-fry over high heat for 1 minute. Add the rice wine or sake, then add the bean sprouts and the dressing and stir-fry over high heat for 1 minute. Remove from the heat. Using a slotted spoon or a handled strainer, transfer the vegetables to a serving platter, making a slight indentation in the center. Arrange the barbecued pork shreds in the center and drizzle the warm dressing and cooking juices over all. Serve warm, at room temperature, or cold.

HAM SALAD WITH
SPICY MUSTARD DRESSING

Sweet-and-sour plum sauce and spicy ground mustard form the base for an unusual dressing that contrasts nicely with the smoky ham. For a more substantial dish, serve the salad in steamed Mandarin pancakes or spring roll wrappers. ● Serves 6

2 cups bean sprouts, rinsed and drained
2 cups julienned red bell pepper (cut into matchstick-size shreds)
2 cups julienned celery (cut into matchstick-size shreds)
2 cups julienned peeled carrots (cut into matchstick-size shreds)
2 cups julienned cooked ham (cut into matchstick-size shreds)

Mustard Dressing

1 tablespoon mustard powder
2 tablespoons hot water
½ cup plum sauce
2½ tablespoons clear rice vinegar
1 tablespoon sesame oil
2 teaspoons soy sauce

Arrange the bean sprouts in a circle around the outer edge of a serving platter, following with concentric circles of the red pepper, celery, carrots, and then the ham.

To prepare the Dressing, combine the mustard and hot water in a medium bowl and blend to a smooth paste. Add the remaining ingredients and stir until smooth. Transfer to a serving dish.

To serve, pour the dressing over the salad, or spoon some of the dressing over each individual serving.

WILTED CABBAGE SALAD

I've discovered that American cabbage works as nicely as (if not even better than) Chinese cabbage in this recipe. The firm leaves absorb the pungent sesame–black vinegar dressing but retain their pleasant crunch. Don't be timid about heating the pan and oil until *really* hot: The cabbage will pick up a smoky flavor that complements the tart dressing beautifully.

● Serves 6

> 1 medium head green cabbage or Chinese (Napa) cabbage
> (about 1¼ pounds)
> 3 tablespoons soy sauce
> 2 teaspoons sugar
> 2 teaspoons Chinese black vinegar or Worcestershire sauce
> 2 tablespoons sesame oil
> 1 teaspoon chile pepper flakes
> 2 tablespoons finely shredded fresh ginger
> 1 tablespoon rice wine

Cut the cabbage in half. With a sharp knife, cut out the core. Separate the leaves, rinse lightly, and drain. Cut into 1-inch pieces, keeping the harder stem sections and the more tender leafier sections separate.

Combine the soy sauce, sugar, and black vinegar or Worcestershire sauce in a small bowl.

Heat a wok or a skillet, add the sesame oil, and heat until almost smoking hot. Add the chile flakes and ginger and stir-fry for about 10 seconds, until fragrant. Add the harder cabbage pieces and stir-fry over high heat for about 1 minute, stirring constantly. Add the rice wine and then the leafier cabbage pieces and stir-fry for about 30 seconds. Add the soy sauce mixture, toss lightly to coat, and transfer to a serving bowl. Let cool slightly before serving. Serve warm, at room temperature, or cold.

SWEET-AND-SOUR CHINESE PICKLES

Asian cooks are masters of pickling, and they prepare an infinite variety of preserved vegetables. Cucumbers and cabbage are particular favorites. This sweet-and-sour pickle with carrots, cucumbers, and icicle radishes is one of the easiest and tastiest. Sugar, rice vinegar, and a generous sprinkling of shredded ginger enhance the flavor of the crunchy vegetables. Serve as a vegetable side dish or a snack. ● Serves 6

6 carrots, peeled, trimmed, and cut on the diagonal into 1-inch lengths

2 seedless cucumbers or 6 Kirby pickling cucumbers, rinsed and ends trimmed

½ pound icicle radishes, peeled and trimmed (see Note)

2 teaspoons salt

1½ tablespoons finely shredded fresh ginger

¾ cup clear rice vinegar

½ cup plus 2 tablespoons sugar

Cut the carrots lengthwise in half, then cut them on the diagonal into 1-inch sections. Place in a large bowl. Cut the cucumbers lengthwise in half. Using a spoon, scrape out the seeds. Cut the cucumber halves lengthwise into 3 or 4 strips about ¾ inch wide, then cut the strips on the diagonal into 1-inch lengths. Place the cucumbers in a large bowl, add the carrots, radishes, and salt, and toss lightly to coat. Let sit at room temperature for 2 hours to remove excess liquid from the vegetables.

Transfer the vegetables to a colander and rinse lightly under cold running water. Drain thoroughly, and return to the bowl. Add the ginger, vinegar, and sugar and toss to coat. Cover with plastic wrap and refrigerate for at least 3 hours, or overnight if possible, tossing occasionally. Serve chilled. These pickles will keep for at least 1 week in the refrigerator; the longer the vegetables marinate, the more flavor they will have.

Note: If icicle radishes are unavailable, substitute red radishes or omit the radishes entirely.

Salting the vegetables removes their natural moisture so that the sweet-and-sour marinade will be better absorbed and flavor them more fully.

SPICY CUCUMBER SPEARS

There are few pickles as irresistible as these piquant, crunchy, and juicy cucumber spears, redolent of garlic, ginger, and sweet rice vinegar. They have become so popular with my friends that I make them in large batches and give them away at holiday time. Their vibrant flavor becomes even better with the passage of time. ● Serves 6

2 pounds gherkins or Kirby cucumbers or 2 seedless cucumbers, rinsed

1 tablespoon salt

Spicy Dressing

2 tablespoons sesame oil

1 teaspoon chile pepper flakes or 6 dried red chile peppers, cut lengthwise into ¼-inch strips and seeded

2 tablespoons minced fresh ginger

6 cloves garlic, peeled and thinly sliced

¼ cup clear rice vinegar

3 tablespoons sugar

Trim the ends of the cucumbers and cut each one in half lengthwise. Using a spoon, scrape out the seeds. Cut each half into 3-inch pieces and then cut each piece lengthwise into ¼-inch-thick slices. Place in a bowl, add the salt, and toss to coat. Let stand for 1 hour at room temperature. Transfer to a colander, rinse lightly under cold running water, drain, and place in a bowl.

To prepare the Spicy Dressing, heat a wok or a heavy saucepan, add the sesame oil, and heat until very hot. Add the chile flakes and heat for about 10 seconds, stirring constantly. Remove from the heat, cover, and let stand for 10 minutes.

Stir the ginger, garlic, rice vinegar, and sugar into the chile oil. Add to the cucumbers and toss lightly to coat. Cover with plastic wrap and refrigerate for at least 3 hours, or overnight if possible, tossing occasionally. The cucumbers will keep for up to a week, becoming even more flavorful over time.

Variation: Substitute 1 medium green or red cabbage, cored and cut into julienne shreds (about 7 cups), for the cucumber. Place the cabbage in a large bowl and toss with the salt. Place a plate with a heavy weight on top on the cabbage and let sit for 2 to 3 hours. Drain and proceed as directed above.

HOT-AND-SOUR CABBAGE SLAW

I first tasted this feisty cabbage slaw on a sultry summer day at a little restaurant in eastern China. The hot chile peppers made my mouth tingle, while the finely shredded cabbage and carrots were pleasantly crunchy and tart. Since then I've re-created and savored this slaw many times, and its luscious flavor makes it equally appealing as a side dish or a snack year-round. ● Serves 6

1 medium head green cabbage (about 1¼ pounds)
1 tablespoon salt
1 cup finely shredded carrots

Sweet-and-Sour Dressing

1 cup sugar
1 cup clear rice vinegar
2 tablespoons minced fresh ginger
2 tablespoons finely shredded hot red chile peppers or 1½ teaspoons
    chile pepper flakes

Cut the cabbage in half. With a sharp knife, cut out the core. Separate the leaves, rinse in cold water, and drain thoroughly. Cut the leaves into very fine julienne shreds. Place in a bowl, add the salt, and toss lightly. Place a plate with a weight on top on the cabbage and let sit for 2 to 3 hours at room temperature. Transfer the cabbage to a colander and drain thoroughly.

Place the cabbage in a bowl and add the shredded carrots. Add all the Dressing ingredients, toss lightly to coat, and cover with plastic wrap. Refrigerate for at least 3 hours, or overnight if possible, tossing occasionally. Serve chilled or at room temperature. This slaw will keep for up to a week in the refrigerator; its flavor will become more intense as it sits.

Note: Cabbage contains a great deal of water. The salt brings out the excess liquid, allowing the dressing to be absorbed and keeping the vegetable crisp.

ZUCCHINI AND SQUASH IN LEMON-CILANTRO DRESSING

Some vegetables require little seasoning to bring out their inherent sweetness. Such is the case with tender zucchini and squash. In this recipe, the lemon juice and minced ginger and cilantro in the dressing underscore the fresh flavors of the lightly cooked, still-crisp vegetables.

● Serves 6

3 zucchini (about 1 pound), rinsed and drained

3 yellow summer squash (about 1¼ pounds), rinsed and drained

Lemon-Cilantro Dressing

¼ cup freshly squeezed lemon juice

2 tablespoons soy sauce

2 tablespoons sugar

2 tablespoons minced cilantro (fresh coriander)

1½ tablespoons minced fresh ginger

1½ tablespoons sesame oil

1 teaspoon chile pepper flakes

Trim the ends of the zucchini and the yellow squash and cut in half lengthwise. Cut each half into pieces about 3 inches long, then cut each piece lengthwise into thin slices about ¼ inch thick. Line two steamer trays with parchment paper (see page 7), and arrange the zucchini in one tray and the squash in the other.

Fill a wok or a large pot with water for steaming and heat until boiling. Set the tray of zucchini over the water, cover, and steam for 6 to 7 minutes, or until just tender. Remove. Place the tray of yellow squash over the boiling water, cover, and steam for 5 to 6 minutes, or until just tender. Arrange the vegetables on a serving platter.

Combine all the Dressing ingredients in a small bowl, and stir to dissolve the sugar. Pour over the steamed vegetables and toss to coat. Cover with plastic wrap and refrigerate for 1 hour. Serve cold or bring to room temperature.

Note: Steamed foods continue cooking after they have been removed from the heat. To prevent overcooking, steam vegetables just until barely tender.

RAINBOW CORN SALAD

Sweet corn, red bell peppers, water chestnuts, and a sprinkling of roasted pine nuts are combined in a colorful stir-fry that's delicious warm or cold. Serve over shredded lettuce as a side dish, or add cooked crabmeat or shrimp for a light summery entrée. ● Serves 6

6 ears corn, husked

1½ cups water chestnuts, preferably fresh

2 cups iceberg or Romaine lettuce cut into fine julienne shreds

Dressing

3½ teaspoons soy sauce

1½ tablespoons rice wine or sake

1½ tablespoons sugar

1½ tablespoons Chinese black vinegar or Worcestershire sauce

1 tablespoon corn or safflower oil

2 tablespoons sesame oil

2½ tablespoons minced fresh ginger

1 teaspoon hot chili paste or ¾ teaspoon chile pepper flakes

2 medium red bell peppers, rinsed, cored, seeded, and cut into
1-inch dice

¾ cup roasted pine nuts (optional)

¾ cup minced scallion greens

Cook the corn in a large pot of boiling salted water until just tender, about 3 to 4 minutes. Drain and cool under cold running water. Cut off the kernels and set aside. (There should be about 6 cups.)

If using fresh water chestnuts, blanch for 5 minutes in boiling water, refresh in cold water, and drain. If using canned chestnuts, plunge into boiling water for 5 seconds, then refresh under cold running water and drain thoroughly. Coarsely chop the water chestnuts in a food processor fitted with a steel blade.

Arrange the shredded lettuce on a serving platter, making a slight indentation in the center.

For the Dressing, combine the soy sauce, rice wine or sake, sugar, and vinegar or Worcestershire sauce in a small bowl and stir to dissolve the sugar.

Heat a wok or a skillet, add the corn or safflower oil and the sesame oil, and heat until hot. Add the ginger and chili paste or chile flakes and stir-fry for about 15 seconds, until fragrant. Add the red bell peppers and stir-fry for 20 seconds over high heat, tossing lightly. Add the corn, water chestnuts, pine nuts (if using), and scallion greens and stir-fry for 15 seconds. Add the soy sauce mixture and toss lightly to coat. Mound the salad over the shredded lettuce. Serve warm, at room temperature, or cold.

You can also serve this salad wrapped in steamed lumpia wrappers or in Mandarin Pancakes (page 58).

Variation: If fresh corn is not in season, substitute 6 cups thawed frozen corn kernels.

"NEW" POTATO SALAD
WITH SCALLION-OIL DRESSING

Normally I am a purist about potato salad, preferring a classic combination of mayonnaise, onions, and potatoes. Here tender red potatoes are tossed in a vibrant sesame-oil dressing, infused with scallions and sparked by a dousing of rice vinegar and a sprinkling of black pepper.

● Serves 6

Scallion-Oil Dressing

½ cup corn or safflower oil

¼ cup sesame oil

10 scallions, trimmed, and lightly smashed with the flat side of a knife or cleaver

¼ cup clear rice vinegar

½ teaspoon salt, or to taste

¾ teaspoon freshly ground black pepper

2 pounds red or white new potatoes, rinsed

5 tablespoons minced prosciutto (optional)

¼ cup minced scallion greens

To prepare the Dressing, combine the corn or safflower oil and the sesame oil in a heavy saucepan and heat until the oil begins to smoke. Add the scallions, cover, and remove from the heat. Let stand for about 20 minutes, until cool. Strain the oil through a fine-meshed strainer, pressing on the scallions to remove as much oil as possible; discard the scallions. Add the rice vinegar, salt, and black pepper and stir to blend.

Place the potatoes in a large pot with water to cover and heat until boiling. Reduce the heat to medium and cook uncovered for 20 to 25 minutes, until tender. Drain and cool slightly.

Peel the potatoes, cut into slices about ½ inch thick, and place in a bowl. Add the dressing, prosciutto (if using), and 3 tablespoons of the scallion greens. Toss to coat, cover with plastic wrap, and let sit at room temperature for 2 hours. Serve at room temperature or cold. Just before serving, sprinkle the top with the remaining 1 tablespoon scallion greens.

Variation: Add ½ cup diced red bell pepper or thinly sliced celery for additional flavor and crunch.

SPICY COLD-TOS[   ]I

B roccoli is not the only vegetable [   ] [   ] garlic
sauce. Cauliflower, green beans, [   ] until
barely tender and tossed while still warm in the pungent dressing make an
intoxicatingly good vegetable side dish. ● Serves 6

   1 bunch broccoli (about 1 pound)

   ¼ cup soy sauce

   1 tablespoon sugar

   2 tablespoons clear rice vinegar

   2 tablespoons sesame oil

   1 tablespoon minced fresh ginger

   1 tablespoon minced garlic

   ¾ teaspoon chile pepper flakes

With a sharp knife, peel off the tough skin from the broccoli stalks. Cut off
the florets and cut the larger ones into small florets. Cut the stalks on the
diagonal into 1-inch pieces.

Heat a large pot of water until boiling. Add the broccoli and boil for about 3
minutes, or until just tender. Drain in a colander, cool under cold running
water, and drain again. Place in a bowl.

Combine the soy sauce, sugar, and rice vinegar in a small bowl and stir to
dissolve the sugar.

Heat a wok or a skillet, add the sesame oil, and heat until hot. Add the ginger, garlic, and chile flakes and stir-fry for about 10 seconds, or until fragrant.
Add the soy sauce mixture and cook for about 30 seconds, stirring constantly.
Pour over the broccoli and toss to coat. Let sit for at least 30 minutes at room
temperature or cover with plastic wrap and chill for several hours before
serving.

COLD-TOSSED
GARLICKY GREEN BEANS

[G]reen beans are an ideal vegetable for a "cold-tossed" salad—especially if they are glazed with a light sauce made with scallions, garlic, soy sauce, and a hint of sugar. After cooking the beans until just tender, immediately refresh them in cold water so that they retain their vibrant green color.
● Serves 6

2 pounds green beans, ends trimmed and cut into 2-inch lengths

1 tablespoon corn or safflower oil

¼ cup minced scallions (white part only)

1½ tablespoons minced garlic

2 tablespoons rice wine or sake

3½ tablespoons soy sauce

2 tablespoons sugar

3 tablespoons water

Heat a large pot of water until boiling. Add the green beans and cook for 4 minutes, or until crisp-tender. Drain in a colander, immerse in cold water until cool, and drain again.

Heat a wok or a large skillet, add the oil, and heat until hot. Add the scallions and garlic and stir-fry over high heat for about 10 seconds. Add the green beans and rice wine or sake and stir-fry for about 30 seconds. Add the soy sauce, sugar, and water, stirring to dissolve the sugar. Cook until the beans are tender and the sauce has reduced to a glaze, about 1½ minutes. Transfer to a serving platter. Serve warm, at room temperature, or cold.

SEAFOOD

China's seas offer unlimited culinary treasures, and the Chinese relish shrimp, crab, scallops, and all types of fish. Freshwater fish from the country's lakes and ponds are held in even higher regard as their flavor is considered more delicate than that of their saltwater counterparts. Freshly caught and briefly cooked, Chinese seafood is infinitely appealing, from a steamed fish seasoned with a whisper of scallions and ginger to whole shrimp tossed in a spicy hot-and-sour sauce.

An emphasis on freshness and delicacy characterizes Chinese seafood cookery, and a high priority is set on highlighting and preserving the inherent sweetness of the food. Accordingly, seasonings such as fresh ginger and rice wine or sake are used to marinate seafood. Like lemons, they remove any fishy flavor, while imparting a unique taste of their own.

Simplicity figures prominently in Chinese seafood dishes as well. Cooking methods that are characterized by high heat and brief cooking times, such as stir-frying, steaming, and blanching, are most popular. Complementary ingredients like garlic, oyster sauce, fermented black beans, and smoky shiitake mushrooms are used in subtle blendings that enhance the flavors of the seafood rather than overwhelm them.

In the last few years, fish and seafood have assumed an even more conspicuous role on the Chinese-American restaurant scene thanks to the burgeoning numbers of Hong Kong–style eateries that specialize in meticulously cooked fresh seafood. These restaurants often feature tanks stocked with the "catch of the day," and their storefronts, with eye-catching displays of gleaming fish and live shrimp and crab, resemble outdoor fish markets.

Seafood has also recently gained a broader appeal as more Americans are reducing their meat intake and turning to lighter main-course alternatives. It seems that American cooks have finally discovered the key to successful seafood cooking: Use only the freshest fish and seafood, and keep cooking times to a minimum.

With their light sauces and almost effortless preparation, the seafood dishes in this chapter should appeal to any cook, Chinese or American, master chef or novice.

CANTONESE-STYLE STEAMED FILLETS

This dish exemplifies the simplicity and refinement of classic Chinese cooking. Fresh fillets are steamed until just cooked, sprinkled with ginger and scallions, and drizzled with hot sesame oil. The sizzling topping adds a delectable flavor that enhances the sweetness of the delicate fish.

● Serves 6

2 pounds firm-fleshed fish fillets, such as flounder, sole, pickerel, or lake trout, skin removed

Marinade

2 tablespoons rice wine or sake

½ teaspoon salt

3 slices fresh ginger (about the size of a quarter), smashed with the flat side of a heavy knife or a cleaver

Seasonings

1 tablespoon soy sauce

2 tablespoons Chinese Chicken Broth (page 367)

2 tablespoons corn or safflower oil

2 teaspoons sesame oil

3 tablespoons finely shredded scallions (white part only)

2½ tablespoons finely shredded fresh ginger

¼ teaspoon freshly ground black pepper

Rinse the fish fillets lightly and pat dry. Place in a bowl. Combine all the Marinade ingredients and lightly pinch the ginger slices in the rice wine to impart their flavor. Add to the fillets and toss lightly to coat. Cover with plastic wrap and let marinate in the refrigerator for 20 minutes.

Place the fillets skinned side down on a heatproof plate with a rim and place in a steamer tray (see page 9). Combine the soy sauce and chicken broth and pour over the fish.

Fill a wok or a large pot with water for steaming and heat until boiling. Place the steamer tray of fish over the boiling water and steam until the fish flakes when prodded with a knife, about 6 to 7 minutes for flounder or sole, 10 to

(continued)

12 minutes for pickerel or lake trout. Meanwhile, combine the corn or safflower oil and the sesame oil in a heavy pan and heat until smoking.

Sprinkle the steamed fillets with the scallions, ginger, and pepper, and slowly pour the hot oil over the seasonings. Serve immediately.

Serve with Roasted Black Bean Peppers (page 303) and/or Hot-and-Sour Cabbage Slaw (page 108).

Note: Alternatively, the fish can be baked, covered with aluminum foil, for 12 minutes in a preheated 450°F oven.

BAKED FISH FILLETS WITH BLACK BEAN SAUCE

lmost any firm-fleshed fish fillet is outstanding served in this sauce. Smothered with a pungent topping of black beans and garlic, the fish bakes until flaky in a hot oven, releasing its sweet juices. Serve with plenty of steamed rice. ● Serves 6

> 2 pounds firm-fleshed fish fillets, such as haddock, cod, pickerel, or orange roughy, skin removed

Marinade

2 tablespoons rice wine or sake
3 slices fresh ginger (about the size of a quarter), smashed with the flat side of a heavy knife or a cleaver

Sauce

½   cup Chinese Chicken Broth (page 367)
2 tablespoons rice wine or sake
1½   tablespoons soy sauce
1½   teaspoons sugar
1¼   teaspoons cornstarch

1   tablespoon corn or safflower oil

Seasonings

1½ tablespoons fermented black beans, rinsed, drained, and minced

2 tablespoons minced scallions (white part only)

1 tablespoon minced garlic

2 tablespoons minced scallion greens or chopped cilantro (fresh coriander)

Rinse the fish fillets lightly and pat dry. Place in a bowl. Combine all the Marinade ingredients and lightly pinch the ginger slices in the rice wine to impart their flavor. Add to the fillets and toss lightly to coat. Cover with plastic wrap and refrigerate for 20 minutes.

Preheat the oven to 450°F.

Combine all the Sauce ingredients and blend well. Arrange the fish skinned side down in a baking pan.

Heat a wok or a skillet, add the oil, and heat until very hot. Add the Seasonings and stir-fry for about 10 seconds, until fragrant. Add the sauce mixture and cook, stirring to prevent lumps, until thickened. Spoon the sauce over the fish and cover with aluminum foil. Bake for about 12 minutes, or until the fish flakes when prodded with a knife. Sprinkle with the scallion greens or cilantro, and serve immediately.

Serve with Stir-Fried Spinach (page 308) and/or Cold-Tossed Garlicky Green Beans (page 114).

PANFRIED SWEET-AND-SOUR FISH

Sweet-and-sour is a popular theme in Chinese cooking, but it is at its most appealing in this dish. The fillets are first dusted with a fragrant coating of flour that has been lightly seasoned with five-spice powder. Panfried until crisp, the fish is a superb foil for the tart, slightly sweet sauce.

● Serves 6

2 pounds flounder or sole fillets (about 5 ounces each)

Marinade

3 tablespoons rice wine or sake

3 slices fresh ginger (about the size of a quarter), smashed with the flat side of a heavy knife or a cleaver

3 scallions, trimmed and smashed with the flat side of a heavy knife or a cleaver

Coating

1 cup cornstarch

1 teaspoon five-spice powder (see page 5)

¼ teaspoon freshly ground black pepper

Sweet-and-Sour Sauce

2 tablespoons ketchup

½ cup water

1½ tablespoons clear rice vinegar

1½ tablespoons sugar

1 teaspoon soy sauce

½ teaspoon salt

½ teaspoon sesame oil

1 teaspoon cornstarch

About ¼ cup corn or safflower oil

Minced Seasonings

1 tablespoon minced garlic

1 tablespoon minced fresh ginger

1 tablespoon minced scallions (white part only)

Rinse the fish fillets lightly and pat dry. Place in a bowl. Combine all the Marinade ingredients and lightly pinch the ginger and scallions in the rice wine to impart their flavor. Add to the fillets and toss lightly to coat. Cover with plastic wrap and refrigerate for 20 minutes.

Mix the Coating ingredients together and spread on a plate. Combine the Sauce ingredients and blend well.

Preheat the oven to 200°F.

Dredge the fish fillets in the coating and place on a cookie sheet lightly dusted with cornstarch.

Heat a small skillet or a wok, add 1 tablespoon corn or safflower oil, and heat until hot. Add the Minced Seasonings and stir-fry for 10 seconds or until fragrant. Add the sauce mixture and cook until thickened, stirring to prevent lumps. Cover and remove from the heat.

Heat a nonstick skillet, add 3 tablespoons corn or safflower oil, and heat until very hot. Add only as many of the fillets as will fit without crowding and fry over moderately high heat for about 2 to 3 minutes, until golden brown and crisp on the bottom. Flip over and cook until golden brown and crisp on both sides. Remove with a slotted spatula to paper towels, drain briefly, and arrange on a cookie sheet lined with aluminum foil to keep warm in the oven. Reheat the oil, adding more if necessary, and fry the remaining fillets.

Arrange the fish fillets on a serving platter. Reheat the sauce, if necessary, and pour into a serving bowl. Serve the sauce on the side for dipping or drizzle over the fish. Serve immediately.

Serve with Garlic Broccoli (page 296) and/or Rainbow Corn Salad (page 110).

SPICY BRAISED HALIBUT

The Sichuanese are justly renowned for their spicy sauces, which bombard the palate with contrasting elements of hot, tart, sweet, and salty flavors. This sauce is a perfect example. Once you've felt the burn of the chiles, your sensitized palate will fully appreciate the combination of black vinegar, ginger, garlic, sugar, and sesame oil, and then finally the sweet flavor of the fish. Scrod and red snapper fillets are also delicious prepared this way.

● **Serves 6**

2½ pounds halibut steaks, about ¾ inch thick

Marinade

2 tablespoons rice wine or sake

½ teaspoon salt

3 slices fresh ginger (about the size of a quarter), smashed with the
flat side of a heavy knife or a cleaver

Sauce

1½ cups Chinese Chicken Broth (page 367)

2½ tablespoons soy sauce

1 tablespoon rice wine or sake

1½ tablespoons sugar

2 teaspoons Chinese black vinegar or Worcestershire sauce

1 tablespoon cornstarch

2 tablespoons water

2 tablespoons corn or safflower oil

Minced Seasonings

2 tablespoons minced scallions (white part only)

1½ tablespoons minced garlic

1 tablespoon minced fresh ginger

1 teaspoon hot chili paste or ½ teaspoon chile pepper flakes

2 tablespoons minced scallion greens

Rinse the fish steaks lightly and pat dry. Place in a bowl. Combine the Marinade ingredients and lightly pinch the ginger slices in the rice wine to impart their flavor. Add the fish and toss lightly to coat. Cover with plastic wrap and refrigerate for 20 minutes.

Combine the Sauce ingredients and set aside. Combine the cornstarch and water and blend well.

Heat a wok or a Dutch oven, add the oil, and heat until very hot. Add only as many steaks as will fit without crowding and fry briefly over high heat, until golden brown on the bottom. Remove with a slotted spatula, and fry the remaining steaks.

Drain off all but 1 tablespoon of the oil and reheat the pan. Add the Minced Seasonings and chili paste or chile flakes and stir-fry for about 10 seconds, until fragrant. Add the sauce mixture and heat until boiling. Arrange the fish steaks in the sauce, golden side up, partially cover, and bring back to a boil. Reduce the heat to medium high and cook for 8 to 10 minutes, or until the fish flakes when prodded with a knife. Using a slotted spatula, transfer the fish to a platter. Add the cornstarch thickener to the sauce and cook, stirring constantly to prevent lumps, until thickened. Pour enough sauce over the fish to cover, and pour the rest into a bowl to serve on the side. Sprinkle the fish with the minced scallions. Serve immediately.

Serve with Saucy Eggplant (page 300) and/or Pickled Carrots (page 299).

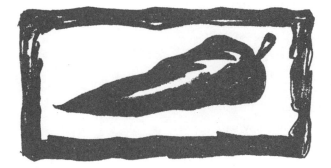

HOT-AND-SOUR POACHED SALMON

The Chinese method of poaching fish is even simpler than the Western technique. Rice wine, water, and a few smashed scallions and ginger slices are simmered together briefly to allow the flavors to marry, then the fish is added and poached until tender. In this recipe, the flavorful "court bouillon" becomes the base for a spicy sauce that is enlivened by the addition of red bell pepper, chile flakes, and shredded ginger and scallions.

● Serves 6

2½ pounds salmon steaks, about ¾ inch thick

Marinade

3 tablespoons rice wine or sake

4 slices fresh ginger (about the size of a quarter), smashed with the flat side of a heavy knife or a cleaver

4 scallions, trimmed and smashed with the flat side of a heavy knife or a cleaver

½ teaspoon salt

1 tablespoon cornstarch

2 tablespoons water

¼ cup rice wine or sake

3 quarts water

Sauce

1 cup reserved Poaching Liquid

2 tablespoons soy sauce

1½ tablespoons sugar

1 tablespoon plus 1 teaspoon Chinese black vinegar or Worcestershire sauce

¼ teaspoon freshly ground black pepper

1 tablespoon corn or safflower oil

1 cup finely shredded scallion greens

¼ cup finely shredded fresh ginger

¼ cup finely shredded red bell pepper

½ teaspoon chile pepper flakes

2 tablespoons coarsely chopped cilantro (fresh coriander)

Lightly rinse the salmon steaks and pat dry. Place in a bowl. Combine the Marinade ingredients and lightly pinch the ginger and scallions in the rice wine to impart their flavor. Add to the salmon steaks and toss lightly to coat. Cover with plastic wrap and refrigerate for 20 minutes.

Combine the cornstarch and the 2 tablespoons water and blend until smooth.

Heat a wok or a Dutch oven, add the rice wine and water, cover, and heat until boiling. Add the salmon steaks with their marinade, arranging them in a single layer, and bring back to a boil. (If necessary, cook the salmon in two batches.) Turn off the heat, cover, and let the steaks sit in the poaching liquid for 10 to 12 minutes, or until the fish flakes when prodded with a knife. (If they are not completely cooked after 12 minutes, cook over low heat until done.) Remove the fish steaks with a slotted spatula, arrange on a deep serving platter, and cover to keep warm. Reserve 1 cup of the poaching liquid, discarding the seasonings, and place in a bowl. Add the remaining Sauce ingredients.

Heat a skillet, add the oil, and heat until hot. Add the shredded scallions, ginger, red bell pepper, and chile flakes and stir-fry until fragrant. Add the sauce mixture and heat until boiling. Slowly add the cornstarch thickener and cook, stirring constantly to prevent lumps, until thickened. Pour the sauce over the fish, sprinkle with the cilantro, and serve immediately.

Serve with Vegetarian Roll-Ups (page 306) and/or Northern-Style Tofu (page 320).

Variation: Substitute halibut steaks for the salmon.

BRAISED FISH FILLETS WITH GARLIC AND BLACK MUSHROOMS

This has long been one of my favorite Chinese dishes. The classic recipe calls for a whole fish, but I like to simplify the procedure by using fillets. The fish is cooked until sweet and tender in a mellow sauce enriched with generous amounts of finely sliced garlic and slivers of Chinese black mushrooms. ● Serves 6

2½ pounds firm-fleshed fish fillets, such as haddock, scrod, red snapper, or orange roughy, skin removed

Marinade

2 tablespoons rice wine or sake

½ teaspoon salt

3 slices fresh ginger (about the size of a quarter), smashed with the flat side of a heavy knife or a cleaver

Braising Liquid

1½ cups Chinese Chicken Broth (page 367)

¼ cup soy sauce

2 tablespoons rice wine or sake

1½ tablespoons sugar

1 tablespoon cornstarch

2 tablespoons water

2 tablespoons corn or safflower oil

Seasonings

6 dried Chinese black mushrooms, softened in hot water for 20 minutes, stems removed, and caps shredded

1½ tablespoons thinly sliced garlic

2 tablespoons shredded scallion greens

Rinse the fish fillets lightly and pat dry. Place in a bowl. Combine the Marinade ingredients and lightly pinch the ginger slices in the rice wine to impart their flavor. Add to the fillets and toss lightly to coat. Cover with plastic wrap and refrigerate for 20 minutes.

Combine the Braising Liquid ingredients and set aside. Combine the cornstarch and water and blend until smooth.

Heat a wok or a heavy skillet large enough to hold the fish in a single layer, add the corn or safflower oil, and heat until hot. Add half the fillets, skinned side down, to the pan and fry over high heat until golden brown on the bottom. Remove with a slotted spatula and fry the remaining fillets; remove from the pan. Reheat the oil, add the Seasonings, and stir-fry for 10 to 15 seconds, until fragrant. Add the braising mixture and bring to a boil. Arrange the fillets golden brown side up in the pan, partially cover, and simmer for 8 to 10 minutes, until the fish flakes when prodded with a knife. With a slotted spatula, remove the fish fillets to a serving platter. Add the cornstarch thickener to the sauce and cook, stirring constantly, until thickened. Pour some of the sauce over the fillets, and pour the remainder into a serving dish. Sprinkle the fish with the shredded scallions. Serve immediately.

Serve with Tossed Bean Sprouts (page 294) and/or Wilted Cabbage Salad (page 105).

BAKED FISH PACKAGES

This simple but elegant dish is ideally suited to entertaining, as it may be prepared in advance and baked at the last minute. Fillets are coated with a delicate ginger-and-scallion sauce and wrapped in parchment paper, and baked in a hot oven. The fish steams in its own juices, causing the packages to puff up and creating a dramatic presentation. ● Serves 6

12 thin firm-fleshed fish fillets, such as flounder, sole, or trout
(about 3 to 4 ounces each), skin removed

Marinade

2 tablespoons rice wine or sake
3 slices fresh ginger (about the size of a quarter), smashed with the
flat side of a heavy knife or a cleaver

Sauce

1 cup Chinese Chicken Broth (page 367)
2 teaspoons soy sauce
2 tablespoons rice wine or sake
1 teaspoon sugar
1 teaspoon cornstarch

1 tablespoon corn or safflower oil

Seasonings

½ cup finely shredded scallions
¼ cup finely shredded fresh ginger
¼ cup finely shredded shiitake mushrooms (caps only)

12 twelve-inch squares parchment paper or aluminum foil

Rinse the fish fillets lightly, pat dry, and place in a bowl. Combine the Marinade ingredients and lightly pinch the ginger slices in the rice wine to impart their flavor. Add to the fillets and toss lightly to coat. Cover with plastic wrap and refrigerate for 20 minutes.

Combine the Sauce ingredients and blend well.

Preheat the oven to 450°F.

Heat a wok or a skillet, add the oil, and heat until very hot. Add the Seasonings and stir-fry for about 15 seconds, until fragrant. Add the sauce mixture and heat until it boils. Add the cornstarch thickener and cook, stirring constantly to prevent lumps, until thickened. Remove from the heat and let cool slightly.

Fold each of the parchment paper or aluminum foil squares in half on the diagonal to create a crease; unfold. Arrange 1 fish fillet just below the fold on each sheet of paper. Spoon the sauce mixture over the fish and fold the paper over to enclose the fish completely. Fold and crimp the edges of the packages to seal. Arrange the packages on cookie sheets and bake for 8 minutes, or until the packages puff up (the fish should flake when prodded with a knife). To serve, cut open the packages with scissors, trimming the paper around the fish, or let everyone open the packages at the table. Serve immediately.

Serve with Stir-Fried Asparagus with Crabmeat (page 291) and/or Cold-Tossed Garlicky Green Beans (page 114).

CRISPY GARLIC SHRIMP

At the King Neptune Restaurant in Taipei, Taiwan, shrimp in the shell are fried until crisp in hot oil, then tossed while still sizzling with salt and minced garlic. I make a simplified version, frying shelled shrimp and adding a little five-spice powder for additional flavor. My Chinese friends, I'm pleased to say, claim my recipe rivals the original. ● **Serves 6**

2 pounds medium shrimp, peeled

Marinade

3 tablespoons rice wine or sake

3 slices fresh ginger (about the size of a quarter), smashed with the flat side of a heavy knife or a cleaver

1 teaspoon five-spice powder (see page 5)

6 tablespoons cornstarch

2 cups corn or safflower oil

Seasonings

3 tablespoons minced garlic

1 teaspoon salt

Score each shrimp down the length of the back and remove the dark vein. (The scoring will cause the shrimp to butterfly when cooked.) Rinse the shrimp lightly, pat dry, and place in a bowl. Combine the Marinade ingredients and lightly pinch the ginger slices in the rice wine to impart their flavor. Add to the shrimp and toss lightly to coat. Cover with plastic wrap and refrigerate for 20 minutes.

Discard the ginger and add the cornstarch to the shrimp, tossing lightly to coat.

Add the oil to a wok or a deep skillet and heat to 400°F. Add half the shrimp and fry, turning constantly, until crisp and golden, about 3 to 4 minutes. Remove with a handled strainer and drain briefly in a colander, then blot on paper towels. Reheat the oil if necessary and fry the remaining shrimp. Remove and drain.

Drain off the oil from the pan and wipe out with paper towels. Reheat the pan, add the fried shrimp and the Seasonings, and toss lightly over high heat for 1 minute. Serve immediately.

Serve with Saucy Eggplant (page 300) and/or Zucchini and Squash in Lemon-Cilantro Dressing (page 109).

SPICY SHRIMP WITH CASHEWS

The appealing contrast of flavors and textures in this dish makes it a family favorite. Plump shrimp, crisp water chestnuts, and crunchy cashews are tossed in a spicy hot-and-sour sauce for a light yet satisfying main course. ● Serves 6

1½ pounds medium shrimp, peeled

Marinade

2 tablespoons rice wine or sake

2 slices fresh ginger (about the size of a quarter), smashed with the flat side of a heavy knife or a cleaver

½ teaspoon salt

1 teaspoon sesame oil

1 tablespoon cornstarch

Spicy Sauce

½ cup Chinese Chicken Broth (page 367) or water

2½ tablespoons soy sauce

2 tablespoons rice wine

2 tablespoons sugar

1 teaspoon sesame oil

1 tablespoon Chinese black vinegar or Worcestershire sauce

1¼ teaspoons cornstarch

6 tablespoons corn or safflower oil

Minced Seasonings

2 tablespoons minced scallions

1½ tablespoons minced fresh ginger

1 tablespoon minced garlic

1 teaspoon hot chili paste or ½ teaspoon chile pepper flakes

1½ cups thinly sliced water chestnuts, blanched in boiling water for 10 seconds, refreshed in cold water, and drained

1½ cups dry-roasted cashews or peanuts

Score each shrimp down the back and remove the dark vein. Rinse the shrimp lightly, drain, and pat dry. Place in a bowl. Combine the Marinade ingredients and lightly squeeze the ginger slices in the liquid to impart their flavor. Add to the shrimp and toss lightly to coat. Cover with plastic wrap and refrigerate for 20 minutes.

Combine the Spicy Sauce ingredients and blend well.

Drain the shrimp and discard the ginger.

Heat a wok or a skillet, add 2 tablespoons of the oil, and heat until hot. Add half the shrimp and toss lightly over high heat until the shrimp turn pink and curl, about 1½ minutes. Remove with a slotted spatula or a handled strainer and drain. Reheat the pan, add 2 tablespoons of the oil, and heat until hot. Fry the remaining shrimp; drain. Wipe out the pan.

Reheat the pan, add the remaining 2 tablespoons oil, and heat until hot. Add the Minced Seasonings and the chili paste or chile flakes and stir-fry for about 15 seconds, until fragrant. Add the sliced water chestnuts and stir-fry for about 1 minute, until heated through. Add the sauce mixture and cook, stirring constantly to prevent lumps, until thickened. Add the cooked shrimp and the cashews or peanuts and toss lightly to coat. Remove to a serving platter and serve immediately.

Serve with Broccoli in Oyster Sauce (page 295) and/or Spicy Cucumber Spears (page 107).

Variation: Substitute scallops for the shrimp and add ½ pound blanched snow peas (ends snapped off and veiny strings removed) to the recipe; add the snow peas to the sauce along with the scallops.

STEAMED GARLIC SHRIMP

Simplicity is the hallmark of Chinese seafood cooking and nowhere is that more evident than in this dish. Shrimp in the shell are split open and sprinkled with minced garlic, chicken broth, and soy sauce. Then, after a brief steaming, they are drizzled with hot sesame oil and fresh cilantro. The result is stunning and delicious. ● Serves 6

2 pounds large shrimp in the shell

Marinade

2 tablespoons rice wine or sake

4 slices fresh ginger (about the size of a quarter), smashed with the flat side of a heavy knife or a cleaver

6 scallions, trimmed and smashed with the flat side of a heavy knife or a cleaver

About 6 large cabbage or lettuce leaves, blanched in boiling water for 10 seconds, refreshed in cold water, and drained

Seasonings

2½ tablespoons minced garlic

1 tablespoon soy sauce

½ cup Chinese Chicken Broth (page 367)

2 tablespoons sesame oil

2 tablespoons coarsely chopped cilantro (fresh coriander)

Using a sharp knife, score the shrimp down the back and open out to butterfly. Rinse lightly and pat dry. Place in a bowl. Combine the Marinade ingredients and lightly pinch the ginger and scallions in the rice wine or sake to impart their flavor. Add to the shrimp and toss lightly to coat. Cover with plastic wrap and refrigerate for 20 minutes.

Line two steamer trays with the blanched cabbage leaves, making certain that there are no holes, or use aluminum pie plates punched with holes (see page 7). Lay the butterflied shrimp out flat on the cabbage leaves. Combine the Seasonings and drizzle over the shrimp.

Heat a wok or a large pot with water for steaming and heat until boiling. Place the steamer trays or pie pans over the boiling water, cover, and steam for 4 to 5 minutes, until the shrimp turn pink and are cooked through. While the shrimp are cooking, heat the sesame oil in a small heavy saucepan until almost smoking.

Remove the shrimp from the heat and carefully pour the hot oil on top. Sprinkle with the chopped cilantro and serve right from the steamer trays, making certain that each person dips the shrimp liberally in the sauce in the bottom of the tray.

Serve with Braised Tofu with Mushrooms (page 314) and/or Sweet-and-Sour Chinese Pickles (page 106).

Variation: You can use medium shrimp, but steam for only 3 to 4 minutes.

The shrimp can also be baked, covered with aluminum foil, in a 450°F oven for 5 to 6 minutes, or until cooked.

SHRIMP IN LOBSTER SAUCE

I have special feelings for this dish, since it was one of the first to arouse my passion for Chinese food. To this day it remains a favorite. The shrimp are bathed in a garlicky sauce embellished with pungent black beans and ground pork. Almost any type of seafood, including scallops, squid, lobster, and even fish fillets, can be substituted for the shrimp. ● Serves 6

2 pounds medium shrimp, peeled

Marinade

2 tablespoons rice wine or sake

3 slices fresh ginger (about the size of a quarter), lightly smashed with the flat side of a heavy knife or a cleaver

1 tablespoon cornstarch

½ pound ground pork

1 tablespoon soy sauce

1 tablespoon rice wine or sake

1 teaspoon sesame oil

Lobster Sauce

1 cup Chinese Chicken Broth (page 367)

1½ tablespoons soy sauce

2 tablespoons rice wine or sake

1 tablespoon sugar

1½ teaspoons sesame oil

¼ teaspoon freshly ground black pepper

1½ teaspoons cornstarch

3 tablespoons corn or safflower oil

Minced Seasonings

2 tablespoons fermented black beans, rinsed thoroughly, drained, and minced

1½ tablespoons minced garlic

1 tablespoon minced scallions (white part only)

1 egg, lightly beaten with 3 tablespoons water (optional)

2 tablespoons minced scallion greens

Score each shrimp down the back and remove the dark vein. (The scoring will allow the shrimp to butterfly when cooked.) Rinse, drain, and pat dry. Combine the Marinade ingredients and squeeze the ginger slices in the rice wine to impart their flavor. Add to the shrimp and toss lightly to coat. Cover with plastic wrap and refrigerate for 20 minutes.

Place the ground pork in a bowl and add the soy sauce, rice wine, and sesame oil. Stir to blend. Combine the Lobster Sauce ingredients and blend well.

Drain the shrimp and discard the ginger.

Heat a wok or a skillet, add 1½ tablespoons of the oil, and heat until very hot. Add half the shrimp and toss lightly over high heat until they turn pink and curl, about 1½ minutes. Remove with a handled strainer and drain. Wipe out the pan, reheat, add 1 tablespoon of the remaining oil, and heat until very hot. Add the remaining shrimp and cook over high heat; drain.

Drain the oil from the pan and wipe it out.

Reheat the pan, add the remaining ½ tablespoon oil, and heat until hot. Add the Minced Seasonings and stir-fry for about 10 seconds, until fragrant. Add the ground pork and stir-fry, mashing and breaking up any lumps of meat, until it loses its raw color. Add the sauce mixture and heat, stirring constantly, until boiling and thickened. Add the shrimp and toss lightly to coat. Slowly add the beaten egg (if using), pouring it in a thin stream around the sides of the wok. Stir once or twice, until cooked, and transfer the shrimp to a platter. Sprinkle with the minced scallion greens and serve immediately.

Serve with Tossed Bean Sprouts (page 294) and/or Spicy Cold-Tossed Broccoli (page 113).

SWEET-AND-SOUR SHRIMP

The classic rendition of sweet-and-sour shrimp is justifiably popular, but this streamlined version is much easier and no less delicious. The delicate flavor of the crisp panfried shrimp contrasts perfectly with the pungent sauce. ● Serves 6

1½ pounds medium shrimp, peeled

Marinade

2 tablespoons rice wine or sake

3 slices fresh ginger (about the size of a quarter), smashed lightly
    with the flat side of a heavy knife or a cleaver

1½ tablespoons cornstarch

Sweet-and-Sour Sauce

2½ tablespoons ketchup

½ cup water

2 tablespoons clear rice vinegar

2 tablespoons sugar

1 teaspoon soy sauce

½ teaspoon salt

1 teaspoon sesame oil

1½ teaspoons cornstarch

¼ cup corn or safflower oil

Minced Seasonings

2 tablespoons minced scallions (white part only)

1 tablespoon minced garlic

1 tablespoon minced fresh ginger

1 red bell pepper, rinsed, cored, seeded, and diced

1 green bell pepper, rinsed, cored, seeded, and diced

Score each shrimp down the back and remove the dark vein. The scoring will allow the shrimp to butterfly when cooked. Rinse, drain, and pat dry. Combine the Marinade ingredients and squeeze the ginger slices in the rice wine to impart their flavor. Add to the shrimp and toss lightly to coat. Cover with plastic wrap and refrigerate for 20 minutes.

Combine the Sauce ingredients and blend well.

Drain the shrimp and discard the ginger.

Heat a wok or a skillet, add 2 tablespoons of oil, and heat until very hot. Add half the shrimp and toss lightly over high heat until they turn pink and curl, about 1½ minutes. Remove with a handled strainer and drain. Wipe out the pan, reheat, add 1½ tablespoons of the remaining oil, and heat. Add the remaining shrimp and cook over high heat; drain.

Drain off the oil and wipe out the pan.

Heat the pan, add the remaining ½ tablespoon oil, and heat until very hot. Add the Minced Seasonings and stir-fry for about 10 seconds, until fragrant. Add the bell peppers and stir-fry for about 1 minute over high heat. Add the sauce mixture and cook, stirring constantly to prevent lumps, until thickened. Add the shrimp, toss lightly to coat, and transfer to a serving platter. Serve immediately.

Serve with Stir-Fried Chinese Cabbage (page 297) and/or Garlic Broccoli (page 296).

Variation: Substitute sea scallops for the shrimp, cooking them just until they are opaque.

STIR-FRIED SCALLOPS
WITH ASPARAGUS

Quickly tossed in a delicate ginger-flavored sauce, fresh scallops are superb paired with crisp-cooked asparagus. Other vegetables such as broccoli, snow peas, and peppers would shine here as well. For a satisfying, easy meal, serve with bowls of steamed rice. ● Serves 6

2 pounds sea scallops

Marinade

3 tablespoons rice wine or sake

3 slices fresh ginger (about the size of a quarter), smashed with the flat side of a heavy knife or a cleaver

3 scallions, trimmed and smashed with the flat side of a heavy knife or a cleaver

1½ pounds asparagus, trimmed, peeled, and cut into 1-inch pieces

Sauce

½ cup Chinese Chicken Broth (page 367)

2 tablespoons rice wine or sake

¾ teaspoon salt

½ teaspoon sugar

1¼ teaspoons sesame oil

⅛ teaspoon ground white pepper

1½ teaspoons cornstarch

2 tablespoons corn or safflower oil

Minced Seasonings

1½ tablespoons minced scallions

1½ tablespoons minced fresh ginger

Rinse the scallops lightly and drain thoroughly. Slice each scallop horizontally in half. Place in a bowl. Combine the Marinade ingredients and squeeze the ginger and scallions in the rice wine to impart their flavor. Add to the scallops and toss lightly to coat. Cover with plastic wrap and refrigerate for 20 minutes.

Meanwhile, heat 1½ cups of water in a large skillet until boiling. Add the asparagus pieces and cook for 5 minutes, or until just tender. Drain and immediately refresh in cold water; drain again.

Combine the Sauce ingredients and blend well.

Heat a large pot of water until boiling. Add the scallops in their marinade and cook for about 30 seconds, until they become opaque. Drain thoroughly and discard the ginger and scallions.

Heat a wok or a skillet, add the corn or safflower oil, and heat until hot. Add the Minced Seasonings and stir-fry over high heat for about 10 seconds, until fragrant. Add the sauce mixture and cook, stirring constantly to prevent lumps, until thickened. Add the asparagus and scallops, toss lightly to coat, and transfer to a serving platter. Serve immediately.

PANFRIED LEMON SCALLOPS

Like most bay scallop lovers I am a purist, believing they should be cooked simply, to allow their sweet flavor to come through. Crisp-fried in a bread crumb coating and dipped in a fresh lemon sauce, these scallops will win the favor of any bay scallop addict. Serve as a main dish or an appetizer. ● Serves 6

2 pounds bay scallops

Marinade

3 tablespoons rice wine or sake
3 slices fresh ginger (about the size of a quarter), smashed with the
    flat side of a knife or a cleaver

2 large eggs, lightly beaten
2 cups dried bread crumbs

Fresh Lemon Sauce

3½ tablespoons freshly squeezed lemon juice
1½ tablespoons sugar
¾ teaspoon salt
¾ teaspoon sesame oil
½ cup Chinese Chicken Broth (page 367)
1½ teaspoons cornstarch

18 six-inch skewers, soaked in water for 1 hour
1 cup corn or safflower oil

Rinse the scallops lightly and drain thoroughly. Combine the Marinade ingredients and squeeze the ginger slices in the rice wine to impart their flavor. Add to the scallops and toss lightly to coat. Cover with plastic wrap and refrigerate for 20 minutes.

Pour the eggs into a pie pan or a shallow plate and spread the bread crumbs on a plate. Combine the Lemon Sauce ingredients in a nonreactive saucepan and set aside.

Thread the scallops onto the skewers. Dip the scallops into the eggs, then dredge in the bread crumbs, turning to coat on all sides. Lightly press the scallop coating so the bread crumbs adhere. Arrange the skewers on a cookie sheet lined with aluminum foil.

Preheat the oven to 200°F.

Heat a deep skillet, add the oil, and heat to about 375°F. Add several of the scallop skewers and fry over medium-high heat until golden brown on the bottom, about 3 to 4 minutes. Turn over and fry until golden brown. Remove with a slotted spatula and drain briefly in a colander, then transfer to paper towels. Fry the remaining scallops, keeping the cooked ones warm in the oven.

Meanwhile, place the lemon sauce mixture over medium heat and cook until thickened, stirring occasionally. Transfer to a serving bowl.

Arrange the fried scallops on a serving platter and place the bowl of sauce in the center. Serve immediately, either spooning the sauce over the scallops or letting your guests dip their scallops in it.

Serve with Glazed Green Beans (page 301) and/or Pickled Carrots (page 299).

SCALLOPS IN CHILE-OIL DRESSING

Served on a bed of sliced cucumbers and topped with a pungent hot-and-sour dressing, these scallops are perfect for a light summer lunch or dinner. For a more substantial dish, arrange the scallops on a mound of spinach or egg noodles. ● Serves 6

3 seedless cucumbers or 8 to 10 small gherkins or Kirby cucumbers, rinsed and drained
½ teaspoon salt
1½ pounds sea scallops

Marinade

2 tablespoons rice wine or sake
3 slices fresh ginger (about the size of a quarter), smashed with the flat side of a heavy knife or a cleaver
3 scallions, trimmed and smashed with the flat side of a heavy knife or a cleaver

Chile-Oil Dressing

¼ cup sesame oil
1 teaspoon chile pepper flakes
2½ tablespoons minced fresh ginger
2 tablespoons minced garlic
6 tablespoons soy sauce
2 tablespoons rice wine or sake
1 tablespoon sugar
1½ tablespoons Chinese black vinegar or Worcestershire sauce

2 tablespoons sesame oil
1 tablespoon minced scallion greens

Slice the cucumbers lengthwise in half and scoop out the seeds. If using seedless cucumbers, cut each half into 3- to 4-inch pieces; if using gherkins or Kirbys, cut each half into 2 pieces. Then cut each piece lengthwise into ⅛-inch-thick slices. Place in a bowl, add the salt, and toss lightly. Let sit for 30 minutes.

Meanwhile, rinse the scallops lightly and drain thoroughly. Slice each scallop horizontally in half. Place in a bowl. Combine the Marinade ingredients and squeeze the ginger slices in the rice wine to impart their flavor. Add to the scallops and toss lightly to coat. Cover with plastic wrap and refrigerate for 20 minutes.

To prepare the Dressing, heat a wok or a deep skillet, add the sesame oil, and heat until very hot. Add the chile flakes and ginger, cover, and remove from the heat. Let sit for 15 to 20 minutes. Add the garlic, soy sauce, rice wine or sake, sugar, and Chinese black vinegar or Worcestershire sauce and stir to dissolve the sugar.

Heat a large pot of water until boiling. Add the scallops with the marinade and cook for 1 minute, or until they turn opaque. Drain, and discard the ginger. Set aside.

Drain the cucumbers. Add the sesame oil and toss lightly. Arrange the cucumber slices on a platter, making a slight indentation in the center. Place the scallops in the center, pour the dressing over the scallops, and sprinkle with the scallion greens. Serve immediately.

Serve with Stir-Fried Spinach (page 308) and/or Potato Pancakes (page 302).

Variation: Substitute shrimp for the scallops, and cook for 3 to 4 minutes, until they turn pink.

SPICY SCALLOPS
WITH SNOW PEAS

Surrounded by a colorful border of crisp-fried snow peas, these tender scallops are irresistible in their spicy sauce. The snow peas may be cooked in advance if desired and served at room temperature, making the dish ideal for entertaining. ● Serves 6

2 pounds sea scallops

Marinade

2 tablespoons rice wine or sake

3 slices fresh ginger (about the size of a quarter), smashed with the flat side of a heavy knife or a cleaver

Spicy Sauce

½ cup Chinese Chicken Broth (page 367)

2½ tablespoons soy sauce

2 tablespoons rice wine or sake

1 tablespoon Chinese black vinegar or Worcestershire sauce

1½ teaspoons sugar

1 teaspoon sesame oil

1¼ teaspoons cornstarch

1 tablespoon sesame oil

1 pound snow peas, ends trimmed and veiny strings removed

1 tablespoon minced garlic

1½ tablespoons rice wine or sake

½ teaspoon salt

1 tablespoon corn or safflower oil

Minced Seasonings

2 tablespoons minced scallions

1½ tablespoons minced fresh ginger

1 tablespoon minced garlic

1 teaspoon hot chili paste or ½ teaspoon chile pepper flakes

1 red bell pepper, rinsed, cored, seeded, and diced

2 tablespoons minced scallion greens

Rinse the scallops lightly and drain thoroughly. Slice each scallop horizontally in half. Place in a bowl. Combine the Marinade ingredients and squeeze the ginger slices in the rice wine to impart their flavor. Add to the scallops and toss lightly to coat. Cover with plastic wrap and refrigerate for 20 minutes.

Combine the Sauce ingredients and blend well.

Heat a large pot of water until boiling. Add the scallops in the marinade and cook for about 30 seconds, until they become opaque. Drain thoroughly and discard the ginger.

Heat a wok or a skillet, add the sesame oil, and heat until almost smoking. Add the snow peas and garlic and toss lightly over high heat for 10 seconds. Add the rice wine and salt and cook for about 1 minute, until the snow peas are crisp-tender. Remove and arrange around the outside of a serving platter.

Reheat the wok or skillet, add the corn or safflower oil, and heat until very hot. Add the Minced Seasonings, the chili paste or chile flakes, and bell pepper and stir-fry over high heat for about 10 seconds, until fragrant. Add the sauce mixture and cook, stirring constantly to prevent lumps, until thickened. Add the cooked scallops and toss lightly to coat. Mound the scallops in the center of the platter, sprinkle with the minced scallion greens, and serve immediately.

BOILED CRABS WITH GINGER DIPPING SAUCE

Whenever I find live crabs at the market I can't resist bringing out my trusty crab bibs, lining the dinner table with newspapers, and digging in to a real feast. My spicy Chinese "crab boil" mixture, with smashed scallions and ginger, rice wine, and chile flakes, underlines the sweet flavor of the succulent crabmeat. ● Serves 6

Chinese Crab Boil

10 cups water

⅓ cup rice wine or sake

6 slices fresh ginger (about the size of a quarter), lightly smashed with the flat side of a heavy knife or a cleaver

6 scallions, trimmed and lightly smashed with the flat side of a heavy knife or a cleaver

1 teaspoon chile pepper flakes

Ginger Dipping Sauce

⅓ cup soy sauce

2½ tablespoons clear rice vinegar

3 tablespoons water

1 tablespoon sugar

1½ tablespoons finely shredded fresh ginger

6 medium live blue crabs (5 to 7 ounces each), preferably female (check the underside of the crab—the tail should be an oval shape)

Combine the Crab Boil ingredients in a large stockpot and heat until boiling. Reduce the heat to low and simmer uncovered for 10 minutes.

Meanwhile, combine the Dipping Sauce ingredients and place in a serving bowl.

Add the live crabs to the crab boil, cover, and bring back to a boil. Reduce the heat to medium and cook, partially covered, for 15 to 17 minutes, until the shells have turned a bright red and the crabs are cooked through. Drain and let cool slightly.

With a sharp knife or a cleaver, cut away the first two hairy joints of each leg. Twist off and discard the apron from the underside. Pry off and discard the top shell. Remove and discard the spongy tissue (the gills) that covers the cartilage. Using a sharp knife, cut the bodies in half to expose the meat. Lightly tap the claws with the blunt edge of a heavy knife or a mallet to crack them. Arrange the crabs on a platter, and serve with the dipping sauce. Be sure to provide small forks for prying out the crabmeat.

Serve with Spicy Snow Peas and Water Chestnuts (page 304) and/or Braised Tofu with Mushrooms (page 314).

Variation: Substitute live lobsters for the crabs, revising the boiling time accordingly (about 8 to 9 minutes for 1½-pound lobsters).

CRABMEAT OMELET

This seafood omelet with a delicate ginger sauce is a perfect entrée for a light dinner. Try substituting cooked shrimp, lobster meat, or scallops for the crabmeat. ● Serves 6

Sauce
1 cup Chinese Chicken Broth (page 367)
2 tablespoons soy sauce
1½ tablespoons rice wine or sake
½ teaspoon sesame oil
1 teaspoon sugar
1½ tablespoons cornstarch

½ pound lump crabmeat, picked over to remove any cartilage or shells, rinsed, and thoroughly drained
2 tablespoons rice wine or sake
3 tablespoons corn or safflower oil
½ cup finely shredded leeks or scallions
1 tablespoon minced fresh ginger
8 large eggs, lightly beaten
½ teaspoon salt

(continued)

Combine the Sauce ingredients in a saucepan and set aside.

Heat a wok or a nonstick skillet until hot, add the crabmeat, and toss lightly over high heat for about 1 minute. Add the rice wine or sake, toss briefly, then remove and drain.

Reheat the pan, add 1 tablespoon of the oil, and heat until hot. Add the leeks or scallions and ginger and stir-fry for 10 seconds, or until fragrant. Push the seasonings to one side of the pan, add the remaining 2 tablespoons oil, and heat until hot. Add the beaten eggs, crabmeat, and salt and stir to distribute the seasonings evenly, then tilt the pan to make an even layer of eggs. Cook for about 1 minute over medium heat to brown the bottom of the omelet, then reduce the heat to low, cover, and cook for 5 to 7 minutes, or until the eggs are set. Using a spatula, flip the omelet over, and cook for 1 to 2 minutes until golden brown. Meanwhile, heat the sauce mixture over medium heat until thickened, stirring to prevent lumps.

Slide the omelet out onto a serving platter and cut into wedges. Serve with the sauce on the side.

Serve with Spicy Bean Sprouts (page 292) and/or Hot-and-Sour Cabbage Slaw (page 108).

CRAB WITH BROCCOLI

This dish is a masterful study of complementary colors, flavors, and textures. Nuggets of tender crabmeat and crisp-tender broccoli are a delectable combination. Or substitute asparagus, snow peas, cucumbers, and hearts of baby cabbage—all are excellent paired with fresh crabmeat.

● Serves 6

1 large bunch broccoli (about 1½ pounds)

Sauce

1 cup Chinese Chicken Broth (page 367)

2½ tablespoons rice wine or sake

¾ teaspoon salt

1 teaspoon sugar

1½ teaspoons sesame oil

⅛ teaspoon ground white pepper

1½ teaspoons cornstarch

1 pound lump crabmeat, picked over to remove any cartilage or shells, rinsed, and thoroughly drained

2 tablespoons rice wine or sake

1½ tablespoons corn or safflower oil

Minced Seasonings

3 tablespoons minced scallions (white part only)

2 tablespoons minced fresh ginger

Peel the tough skin from the broccoli stems and cut off the florets. Cut the stalks on the diagonal into 1-inch pieces. Heat a large pot of water until boiling, add the broccoli stems and florets, and cook for 3 minutes, or until just tender. Drain, refresh under cold running water, and drain thoroughly.

Combine the Sauce ingredients and blend well.

Heat a wok or a skillet until hot, add the crabmeat, and stir-fry over high heat for about 30 seconds. Add the rice wine or sake and cook for about 30 seconds longer. Remove the crab, and reheat the pan. Add the corn or safflower oil and heat until hot. Add the Minced Seasonings and stir-fry over high heat for about 10 seconds, until fragrant. Add the sauce mixture and cook, stirring constantly to prevent lumps, until thickened. Add the broccoli and crabmeat, toss lightly, and transfer to a platter. Serve immediately.

SPICY CLAMS
IN BLACK BEAN SAUCE

At a recent gathering, I watched my guests polish off this dish in record time and, in a slightly unorthodox manner, mop up the garlicky sauce with chunks of French bread. Make certain to cook the clams only until they just begin to open. If overcooked, littleneck clams become tough and rubbery.

● Serves 6

48 littleneck or small cherrystone clams

Sauce

½ cup Chinese Chicken Broth (page 367) or water

1 tablespoon soy sauce

1½ tablespoons rice wine or sake

1 teaspoon sugar

¼ teaspoon freshly ground black pepper

1 teaspoon cornstarch

1 tablespoon water

1 tablespoon corn or safflower oil

Minced Seasonings

2 tablespoons fermented black beans, rinsed, drained, and coarsely chopped

2 tablespoons minced scallions (white part only)

1½ tablespoons minced garlic

1 tablespoon minced fresh ginger

½ teaspoon chile pepper flakes

2 tablespoons minced scallion greens

Lightly scrub the clam shells with a vegetable brush. Place the clams in a bowl with water to cover and soak for 1 hour.

Combine the Sauce ingredients and set aside. Combine the cornstarch and water and blend until smooth.

Drain the clams.

Heat a wok or a large pot, add the corn or safflower oil, and heat until hot. Add the Minced Seasonings and stir-fry for about 10 seconds, until fragrant. Add the sauce mixture and heat until boiling. Add the clams, cover, and cook, shaking the pot occasionally, until they just begin to open, about 3 to 4 minutes. Using a slotted spoon, transfer the clams to a serving bowl. Slowly add the cornstarch thickener to the sauce, stirring to prevent lumps. Pour the sauce over the clams, sprinkle the top with the minced scallions, and serve.

Serve with Garlic Broccoli (page 296) and/or Rainbow Corn Salad (page 110).

Variation: Substitute medium shrimp in the shell for the clams, and cook until the shrimp turn pink.

STEAMED CLAM POT

For an unusual variation on the classic steamed clam recipe, I spice up the cooking liquid with smashed garlic, ginger, scallions, and rice wine. The resulting broth is so flavorful that once the clams have been eaten, we drink it down as well. ● Serves 6

1½ quarts steamers or softshell clams (about 60)

½ cup rice wine or sake

6 slices fresh ginger (about the size of a quarter), smashed with the flat side of a heavy knife or a cleaver

6 scallions, trimmed and smashed with the flat side of a heavy knife or a cleaver

6 cloves garlic, smashed with the flat side of a heavy knife or a cleaver and peeled

Lightly scrub the clam shells with a vegetable brush and rinse thoroughly under cold running water to remove any sand. Place the clams in a bowl with cold water to cover and soak for 1 hour.

Thoroughly drain the clams and place them in a large heavy pot. Add the rice wine or sake, ginger, scallions, and garlic, cover, and heat until boiling. Reduce the heat to medium and cook, shaking the pot from time to time to allow the clams to cook evenly, for 5 minutes or until the clams are open. With a slotted spoon, portion the clams into serving bowls. Discard the seasonings, and serve cups of the broth on the side for dipping the clams and for drinking, if desired.

Serve with Vegetarian Roll-Ups (page 306) and/or Cold-Tossed Garlicky Green Beans (page 114).

Variation: Substitute mussels for the clams.

LOBSTER CANTONESE

Few dishes compare in flavor to this unforgettable delicacy, a classic on Cantonese-American menus. Chunks of lobster are bathed in a pungent black bean–garlic sauce, which is garnished with bits of ground pork. Serve this easy dish, with plenty of steamed rice, as the centerpiece for a truly memorable meal. ● Serves 6

3 live chicken lobsters (about 1¼ to 1½ pounds each)
½ pound lean ground pork
1 tablespoon soy sauce
1 tablespoon rice wine or sake
1 teaspoon sesame oil

Sauce

1 cup Chinese Chicken Broth (page 367)
1½ tablespoons soy sauce
2 tablespoons rice wine or sake
1 tablespoon sugar
1 teaspoon sesame oil

1½ teaspoons cornstarch
2 tablespoons water
2 tablespoons corn or safflower oil

Minced Seasonings

2 tablespoons fermented black beans, rinsed thoroughly and drained
1½ tablespoons minced garlic
2 tablespoons minced scallions (white part only)

1½ tablespoons rice wine or sake
2 tablespoons minced scallion greens

Using a heavy knife or a cleaver, cut each lobster in half crosswise at the point near the head where there is a pale cross on its back (see Note, page 158). Cut away the pincer claws and cut apart at the joints. Using the back of the knife or a mallet, crack the claws slightly. Cut away the legs. Cut each lobster body in half and then crosswise in two, through the shell. Split the tails in half, removing the intestinal tract that runs up the back. Cut each tail crosswise in half. Remove the sand sacs and veins from the heads and discard. Carefully remove the coral and tomalley from each lobster and set aside.

Place the ground pork in a bowl, add the soy sauce, rice wine or sake, and sesame oil, and stir to blend. Combine the Sauce ingredients and set aside. Combine the cornstarch and water and blend well.

Heat a wok or a large skillet, add the oil, and heat until hot. Add the Minced Seasonings and stir-fry for about 10 seconds, until fragrant. Add the ground pork and stir-fry, mashing and breaking up any lumps of meat, until it loses its raw color. Add the lobster pieces and rice wine or sake and stir-fry over high heat for about 1 minute. Add the sauce mixture and heat until boiling. Cover and cook for about 4 to 5 minutes, then add the tomalley and coral and cook for 1 minute. Using a slotted spoon, transfer the lobster pieces to a platter. Slowly add the cornstarch thickener to the sauce, stirring constantly to prevent lumps, and cook until thickened. Spoon the sauce over the lobster, sprinkle the minced scallion greens on top, and serve immediately.

Serve with Spicy Bean Sprouts (page 292) and/or Zucchini and Squash in Lemon-Cilantro Dressing (page 109).

GARLIC LOBSTER

At the New House of Toy in Boston, the chefs prepare dishes that reflect both Eastern and Western influences. Inspired by their innovative approach, I developed this simple recipe for chunks of lobster in the shell cooked until tender in a Western-style garlic and butter sauce. I serve it with steamed asparagus and, in a continued departure from tradition, with slices of crusty French bread for mopping up the sauce. ● Serves 6

    3 live chicken lobsters (about 1¼ to 1½ pounds each)
    4 tablespoons unsalted butter
    1½ tablespoons minced garlic
    ¼ cup rice wine or sake

Using a heavy knife or a cleaver, cut each lobster in half crosswise at the point near the head where there is a pale cross on its back (see Note). Cut away the pincer claws and cut apart at the joints. Using the back of the knife or a mallet, crack the claws slightly. Cut away the legs. Cut each lobster body in half and then crosswise in two, through the shell. Split each tail in half, removing the intestinal tract that runs up the back. Cut the tails crosswise in half. Remove the sand sacs and veins from the heads and discard. Remove the coral and tomalley from each lobster and set aside.

Heat a large skillet or a wok, add the butter, and heat until it foams. Add the garlic and toss for about 5 seconds, then add the lobster pieces and cook over high heat for about 1 minute. Add the rice wine or sake, reduce the heat to medium, cover, and cook for about 5 minutes. Add the reserved tomalley and coral and cook for 1 minute. Transfer to a serving platter and serve immediately.

Note: Splitting the lobsters like this kills them instantly. However, if you prefer to temporarily lull lobsters before cutting them, place them on a rack in a pot filled with cold water and gradually heat to lukewarm (about 104°F).

Serve with Hot-and-Sour Bok Choy (page 298) and/or Spicy Cold-Tossed Broccoli (page 113).

CHICKEN

Visit any Chinese restaurant and, as the menu will attest, you'll see that chicken is a very popular item. Chicken dishes may well be the lengthiest and most varied category on the menu. Visit any well-stocked Chinese market and, inevitably, there will be an impressive poultry section with an ample area devoted to freshly killed whole chickens (heads intact), artfully arrayed near a full range of chicken parts, including the feet. Or stroll by any Chinese delicatessen and you will see glistening barbecued and roasted chickens hanging invitingly in the window. Braised chicken feet, livers, and gizzards are artfully displayed. The Chinese savor and relish every part of the chicken.

It is no wonder that chicken enjoys such popularity. The meat is lean, flavorful, and full of vitamins, and the bird is a versatile medium that is amenable to almost every cooking technique employed in the Chinese kitchen. Whole chickens are braised in a soy sauce—based cooking liquid that transforms the skin and meat to a rich, burnished copper color, or they are seasoned with five-spice powder and stuffed with ginger, then roasted to a crispy doneness in a hot oven. The breasts are steamed and tea-smoked, imbuing the meat with a delicate smoky fragrance that may be further enhanced with orange peel and cinnamon. Cut-up chicken, seasoned with pungent black bean sauce or curry, appears in casseroles. And boneless chicken meat is stir-fried with almost any vegetable and tossed in a fragrant sauce that may be sweet-and-sour, hot-and-sour, or deliciously light and delicate.

For American cooks, chicken is equally appealing. Although it has long been popular, it has gained a wider audience as more Americans shun beef for leaner meats. Its versatility makes it even more attractive.

Chinese chicken dishes, as the recipes in this chapter show, are tailor-made for the modern American kitchen. The preparation time of almost all of these dishes is minimal and the majority need only a simple vegetable and steamed rice or bread to make a complete meal. Another advantage for the time-pressed cook is that most of these dishes can be prepared in advance—and they taste even better the second time around.

CHINESE BARBECUED CHICKEN

Ever since I can remember, I've loved barbecued chicken. Heavy with garlic and hoisin sauce, this barbecue sauce will fill your house with a rich, appetizing aroma. The all-purpose sauce is great on pork and country-style spareribs too. ● Serves 6

1 split fryer or broiler chicken (about 3½ pounds)

Barbecue Sauce

½ cup hoisin sauce

3 tablespoons soy sauce

3 tablespoons rice wine or sake

2 tablespoons sugar

2 tablespoons ketchup

2 tablespoons minced garlic

Rinse the chicken and drain thoroughly. Remove any fat deposits from the neck and the inside and place the chicken halves in a bowl. Combine the Barbecue Sauce ingredients and pour over the chicken. Toss lightly to coat, and spread the mixture all over the outside and inside of the chicken. Cover with plastic wrap and refrigerate for at least 1 hour, or overnight if possible.

Preheat the oven to 375°F.

Arrange the chicken halves skin side down on a baking sheet lined with aluminum foil. Bake for 30 minutes, turn over, and bake for another 30 minutes, until crisp and brown. Let the chicken cool slightly, and remove to a cutting board.

Using a sharp knife, cut away the wings. Cut off the legs and thighs and split them in half at the joint. Cut the thighs into 2 to 3 pieces. Cut the breast into thin slices and arrange on a serving platter. Arrange the remaining pieces on the platter and serve.

Serve with Broccoli in Oyster Sauce (page 295) and/or Rainbow Corn Salad (page 110).

ROASTED FIVE-SPICE CHICKEN

Roasted chicken, with its crispy skin and juicy meat, is an appealing dish in any cuisine. The aromatic dry-rub of Chinese five-spice powder and salt in this recipe infuses the chicken meat with such seasonings as anise, cinnamon, ground ginger, and pepper. Then, in the final stage of cooking, plum sauce is brushed over the skin to produce a lacquerlike glaze. ● Serves 6

1 teaspoon five-spice powder (see page 5)

1 teaspoon salt

1 roasting chicken (about 4 to 5 pounds)

1 lemon

4 slices fresh ginger (about the size of a quarter), smashed lightly with the flat side of a heavy knife or a cleaver

¼ cup plum sauce

½ tablespoon soy sauce

Preheat the oven to 400°F.

Heat a wok or a skillet until very hot. Add the five-spice powder and salt and toast over high heat, tossing lightly with a spatula, for 3 minutes, or until very fragrant. Remove and let cool.

Rinse the chicken and drain thoroughly. Remove any fat deposits at the neck and around the cavity, and pat dry.

Cut the lemon in half. Squeeze the juice over the outside and inside of the chicken, and rub the surface with the cut edge. Rub the five-spice mixture evenly over the outside and inside of the chicken. Place the smashed ginger inside the chicken. Arrange the chicken breast side up in a roasting pan or on a baking sheet.

Roast the chicken for 45 minutes, until brown and slightly crisp. Then combine the plum sauce and soy sauce, brush liberally over the skin, and bake for an additional 15 minutes, or until deep golden and crisp. Let cool slightly.

Remove the ginger from the cavity of the chicken. Carve the breast meat into thin slices and cut up the chicken, cutting off the wings, cutting away the legs and thighs, and splitting them at the joint. Arrange the breast slices and chicken pieces on a serving platter and serve warm or at room temperature.

Variation: Substitute 2½ to 3 pounds chicken breasts, thighs, or drumsticks for the whole chicken. Bake for 25 to 30 minutes at 375°F, brush with the plum sauce, and bake for an additional 10 minutes.

Serve with Spicy Snow Peas and Water Chestnuts (page 304) and/or Sweet-and-Sour Chinese Pickles (page 106).

SPICED BRAISED CHICKEN

Soy sauce is merely the base of the sumptuous braising mixture in this dish, as it also contains a heady portion of rice wine, orange peel, ginger, and cinnamon. As it simmers until tender, the chicken turns a rich burnished brown. Turkey, Cornish game hens—even brisket—are delicious cooked in this flavorful brew. ● Serves 6

Braising Mixture

1 cup soy sauce

4 cups water

½ cup rice wine or sake

⅓ cup sugar

1 teaspoon aniseed

1 cinnamon stick

Zest of 1 orange, removed in strips with a vegetable peeler

4 slices fresh ginger (about the size of a quarter), smashed with the flat side of a heavy knife or a cleaver

4 scallions, trimmed and smashed with the flat side of a heavy knife or a cleaver

1 roasting chicken (about 4 to 5 pounds)

Combine the Braising Mixture ingredients in a stockpot or a Dutch oven and heat until boiling. Reduce the heat to low and simmer for 15 minutes to combine the flavors.

Meanwhile, rinse the chicken and drain thoroughly. Remove any fat deposits from the neck and the cavity.

Add the chicken breast side down to the braising mixture, partially cover, and gently simmer for 45 minutes. Turn the chicken over and cook for 30 minutes longer. Remove from the heat and let the chicken sit, covered, for 15 minutes in the braising mixture.

Drain the chicken and cut into serving pieces with a heavy knife or a cleaver; cut off the wings. Cut away the legs and thighs and split them in half at the joint, then cut the thighs in half. Split the carcass lengthwise in half, separating the back from the breast, and remove the "oysters" and any other meat from the back. Discard the back and place the chicken breast skin side up on a cutting board. Using the heel of your hand, press down on the chicken breast to separate the bones from the meat. Remove the bones and cut the chicken breast lengthwise in half, then cut each breast half crosswise into 1-inch-thick pieces. Arrange the pieces on a serving platter, placing the breast pieces in the center and the other pieces around so that you are "reconstructing" the whole chicken. Spoon about ½ cup of the cooking liquid over the chicken, and serve additional sauce on the side in a serving bowl if you like.

Serve with Stir-Fried Asparagus with Crabmeat (page 291) and/or Wilted Cabbage Salad (page 105).

BRAISED GARLIC CHICKEN

Garlic, smoky black mushrooms, and soy sauce are the dominant flavorings in this hearty casserole. As with many braised dishes, the flavor improves with reheating. Serve this simple yet incredibly satisfying dish with steamed or stir-fried vegetables and bowls of steamed rice. ● Serves 6

1 roasting chicken (about 4 to 5 pounds)

2 tablespoons soy sauce

1½ teaspoons cornstarch

2 tablespoons water

1 tablespoon corn or safflower oil

12 cloves garlic, smashed with the flat side of a heavy knife or a cleaver and peeled

6 scallions (white part only), cut into 1-inch sections

6 dried Chinese black mushrooms, softened in hot water for 20 minutes, drained, stems removed, and caps cut in half (optional)

Braising Mixture

3 cups Chinese Chicken Broth (page 367)

¼ cup soy sauce

2 tablespoons rice wine or sake

2 teaspoons sugar

1 teaspoon sesame oil

Rinse the chicken, drain thoroughly, and pat dry with paper towels. Remove any fat deposits from the neck and cavity opening. Using a sharp knife or a cleaver, cut the chicken into serving pieces. Cut away the wings. Cut off the legs and thighs, then separate the legs from the thighs at the joint. Cut the thighs in half. Cut the carcass in half, separating the back from the breast. Cut the back section crosswise into 4 pieces. Cut the breast lengthwise in half and cut each half crosswise into 1½-inch-wide pieces. Place the chicken in a bowl and add the soy sauce, tossing to coat. Combine the cornstarch and water and blend until smooth.

Heat a flameproof casserole or a Dutch oven, add the oil, and heat until very hot. Add only as many of the chicken pieces, skin side down, as will fit comfortably in the pan and sear the skin to a golden brown over high heat. Turn over and brown on the other side. Remove with a slotted spoon, reheat the oil, and fry the remaining chicken. Drain off all but 2 teaspoons of the oil from the pan.

Reheat the oil, add the garlic cloves, scallions, and black mushrooms (if using), and toss over medium heat until lightly golden. Add all the Braising Mixture ingredients and heat until boiling. Add the chicken, partially cover, and cook for about 45 minutes over medium-low heat, turning the chicken several times, until very tender. Remove the chicken with a slotted spoon, and skim the sauce to remove any fat. Heat the sauce until boiling, add the cornstarch thickener, and cook, stirring constantly to prevent lumps, until thickened. Return the chicken to the sauce, and serve directly from the pot.

Serve with Hot-and-Sour Bok Choy (page 298) and/or Tossed Bean Sprouts (page 294).

SAUCY BLACK BEAN CHICKEN

My friends call this dish "Chinese mommy food," perhaps because it brings to mind the gutsy black bean sauce we've enjoyed since childhood at Chinese restaurants. ● Serves 6

1 fryer or broiler chicken (about 3½ pounds)

Marinade

2 tablespoons soy sauce

1½ tablespoons rice wine or sake

1 teaspoon sesame oil

Sauce

¾ cup Chinese Chicken Broth (page 367)

2½ tablespoons soy sauce

2 tablespoons rice wine or sake

1 tablespoon sugar

1½ teaspoons cornstarch

1 tablespoon corn or safflower oil

Minced Seasonings

2 tablespoons fermented black beans, rinsed and drained

2 tablespoons minced scallions (white part only)

1 tablespoon minced fresh ginger

1 tablespoon minced garlic

1 teaspoon chile pepper flakes

2 tablespoons minced scallion greens

Rinse the chicken and drain thoroughly. Remove any fat deposits around the neck and cavity. With a heavy knife or a cleaver, cut the chicken into pieces. Cut away the wings. Cut off the legs and thighs, split them at the joint, and cut the thighs crosswise into 2 or 3 pieces. Cut the carcass lengthwise in half, separating the back from the breast. Cut the back section crosswise into 4 pieces. Cut the breast lengthwise in half and cut each half crosswise into 1½-inch-thick pieces. Place the chicken in a bowl, add the Marinade ingredients, and toss lightly to coat. Cover with plastic wrap and refrigerate for at least 1 hour, or overnight if possible.

Combine the Sauce ingredients and blend well.

Preheat the oven to 375°F.

Drain the chicken, adding the marinade to the sauce. Heat a heavy flameproof casserole or a Dutch oven, add the oil, and heat until very hot. Add only as many chicken pieces, skin side down, as will fit comfortably in the pan and sear to a golden brown over high heat. Turn over and brown on the other side. Remove with a slotted spoon, reheat the oil, and fry the remaining pieces. Drain off all but 1 tablespoon of the oil from the pot.

Heat the oil until hot, add the Minced Seasonings, and stir-fry over high heat for about 15 seconds, until fragrant. Add the sauce mixture and heat until thickened, stirring constantly to prevent lumps. Add the chicken pieces and toss to coat. Cover the pot and reinforce the lid with aluminum foil, crimping the edges to prevent any steam from escaping. Bake for 45 minutes, until the chicken is very tender.

Skim the sauce to remove any fat, and turn the chicken pieces to coat well. Sprinkle with the minced scallion greens, and serve directly from the pot.

Serve with Garlic Broccoli (page 296) and/or Hot-and-Sour Cabbage Slaw (page 108).

BAKED ORANGE CHICKEN

Like French cooks, Chinese chefs are fond of pairing poultry with citrus fruits. The slices of navel orange in this tart sauce impart a juicy sweetness that complements the tender chunks of chicken meat. This dish offers a refreshing, yet subtle, departure from classic Chinese cuisine.

● Serves 6

> 1 roasting chicken (about 4 to 5 pounds)
> 2 tablespoons soy sauce

Sauce

> ⅔ cup Chinese Chicken Broth (page 367)
> 3 tablespoons ketchup
> 2 tablespoons rice wine or sake
> 2 tablespoons sugar
> 1 teaspoon salt
> ¼ teaspoon freshly ground black pepper
>
> 1½ teaspoons cornstarch
> 1½ tablespoons water
> 1 tablespoon corn or safflower oil
> 1 cup thinly sliced onions
> 1 tablespoon minced garlic
> 2 teaspoons minced fresh ginger
> 2 navel oranges, peeled and sectioned

Rinse the chicken, drain thoroughly, and pat dry. Remove any fat deposits around the neck and cavity. Using a sharp knife or a cleaver, cut the chicken into serving pieces. Cut away the wings. Cut the legs and thighs from the carcass, then separate the legs from the thighs at the joint. Cut the thighs in half. Cut the carcass in half, separating the back from the breast, and cut the back section crosswise into 4 pieces. Cut the breast lengthwise in half and cut each half crosswise into 1½-inch-thick pieces. Place the chicken in a bowl and add the soy sauce, tossing to coat.

Combine the Sauce ingredients and set aside. Combine the cornstarch and water and blend until smooth.

Preheat the oven to 375°F.

Heat a flameproof casserole or a Dutch oven until hot, add the oil, and heat until hot. Add as much of the chicken pieces, skin side down, as will fit comfortably in the pan and sear the skin to a golden brown over high heat. Turn over and brown on the other side. Remove with a slotted spoon, reheat the oil, and fry the remaining pieces. Drain off all but 1 tablespoon of the oil from the pan.

Heat the oil until hot. Add the onions and cook for 4 to 5 minutes over medium heat, until soft and transparent. Add the garlic and ginger and stir-fry for about 10 seconds, until fragrant. Add the orange sections and toss for 5 seconds. Add the sauce mixture and heat until boiling, then add the cornstarch thickener and cook until thickened, stirring constantly to prevent lumps. Add the chicken pieces and toss to coat. Cover the pot and reinforce the lid with aluminum foil, crimping the edges to prevent steam from escaping. Bake for 45 minutes, until the chicken is very tender.

Using a spoon or a ladle, skim off any fat from the sauce, and toss the chicken to coat well. Serve directly from the pot, or transfer to a serving platter and pour the sauce on top.

Serve with Saucy Eggplant (page 300) and/or Cold-Tossed Garlicky Green Beans (page 114).

SPICY CHICKEN CURRY

If the truth be known, I was not a big fan of curries until I traveled to the Far East. There I sampled Chinese curry dishes, which are milder and somewhat mellower than the traditional Indian versions. In my Chinese household, we often would cook a meat-and-vegetable curry for Sunday lunch for a satisfying meal-in-one casserole. Now I do the same in my own kitchen and am delighted to have the flavorful leftovers. Try substituting pork, beef, or lamb for the chicken in this recipe, and serve the curry with plenty of steamed rice. ● Serves 6

1 fryer or broiler chicken (about 3½ pounds)
1½ tablespoons soy sauce
½ cup all-purpose flour
2 medium onions, peeled

Sauce

2½ cups Chinese Chicken Broth (page 367)
2 tablespoons soy sauce
3 tablespoons rice wine or sake
1½ tablespoons sugar

1 tablespoon corn or safflower oil
1½ tablespoons imported curry powder
½ teaspoon chile pepper flakes
1 tablespoon minced garlic
4 carrots, peeled and cut on the diagonal into 1-inch pieces
4 medium red potatoes (about 1½ pounds), peeled and cut into 1-inch chunks

Rinse the chicken and drain thoroughly. Pat dry with paper towels and remove any fat deposits from the neck and cavity opening. Using a sharp knife or a cleaver, cut the chicken into serving pieces. Cut away the wings. Cut off the legs and thighs, then split the legs and thighs at the joint. Cut the thighs in half. Cut the carcass in half, separating the back from the breast, and cut the back section crosswise into 4 pieces. Cut the breast section lengthwise in half and cut each half into 1½-wide pieces. Place the chicken in a bowl, add the soy sauce, and toss lightly to coat. Spread the flour on a plate and dredge the pieces of chicken in the flour to coat lightly. Set aside.

Cut the onions in half, then cut each half in half crosswise, and cut into 1-inch cubes. Combine the Sauce ingredients.

Heat a flameproof casserole or a Dutch oven, add the oil, and heat until hot. Add as many of the chicken pieces, skin side down, as will fit comfortably in the pan and sear the skin to a golden brown over high heat. Turn over and brown on the other side. Remove with a slotted spoon, reheat the oil, and fry the remaining pieces. Drain off all but 1 tablespoon of the oil from the pan. Heat the oil until hot, add the onions, and stir-fry for about 1 minute over medium heat. Add the curry powder, chile flakes, and garlic and stir-fry for about 10 seconds, until fragrant. Add the sauce mixture and heat until boiling. Add the chicken and carrots and bring back to a boil, then partially cover and cook for 35 minutes over medium-low heat, stirring from time to time. Add the potatoes and cook for 20 minutes longer, or until the potatoes are tender and the sauce has thickened to a coating consistency. Skim away any fat from the surface with a spoon or a ladle and serve directly from the casserole.

Serve with Stir-Fried Spinach (page 308) and/or Spicy Cucumber Spears (page 107).

SWEET-AND-SOUR GLAZED CHICKEN WINGS

In my neighborhood, I am known as the chicken wing queen since I make them once a week. Their popularity in our household has a great deal to do with my young son, who shuns all other meat dishes. As a result, I have developed a slew of chicken wing sauces. This is one of our favorites. The sweet-and-sour glaze, which combines brown sugar, ketchup, garlic, soy sauce, and rice vinegar, could be described as a fusion of American and Chinese barbecue sauces. ● Serves 6

3 pounds chicken wings (about 16)

Sweet-and-Sour Glaze

½ cup ketchup

½ cup brown sugar

¼ cup clear rice vinegar

3 tablespoons soy sauce

2 tablespoons sesame oil

2 tablespoons minced garlic

(continued)

Rinse the chicken wings and drain thoroughly. Combine the Glaze ingredients in a large bowl. Add the chicken wings and toss lightly to coat. Cover with plastic wrap and refrigerate for at least 1 hour, turning occasionally.

Preheat the oven to 375°F.

Arrange the chicken wings skin side down on a baking pan lined with aluminum foil. Bake for 25 minutes, turn over, and bake for another 25 minutes, or until a deep golden brown. Transfer to a serving platter and serve immediately.

Serve with Stir-Fried Chinese Cabbage (page 297) and/or Spicy Cold-Tossed Broccoli (page 113).

Variation: Substitute a whole chicken (about 2½ to 3 pounds) for the wings. Roast at 400°F for about 50 minutes.

FRIED LEMON CHICKEN

Despite my aversion to deep-frying, I can't resist occasionally preparing what I call Chinese fried chicken. The chicken pieces are marinated in a heady mixture of soy sauce, rice wine, and sesame oil, with a healthy dose of garlic. Then the chicken is coated in egg and cornstarch (which produces a light, crisp coating) and fried until golden brown. Serve the crusty chicken hot, at room temperature, or cold with a tart lemon dipping sauce for a truly memorable dish. ● Serves 6

1 fryer or broiler chicken (about 3½ pounds)

Marinade

2½ tablespoons soy sauce
1½ tablespoons rice wine or sake
1 teaspoon sesame oil
1½ tablespoons minced garlic

1 cup cornstarch
1 egg, lightly beaten

Lemon Sauce

5 tablespoons freshly squeezed lemon juice

1 cup Chinese Chicken Broth (page 367)

3 tablespoons sugar

¾ teaspoon salt

1 teaspoon sesame oil

1½ teaspoons cornstarch

Corn or safflower oil for deep-frying

Rinse the chicken and drain thoroughly. Remove any fat deposits around the cavity and neck. Using a heavy knife or a cleaver, cut the chicken into serving pieces. Cut away the wings. Cut off the legs and thighs and split them at the joint. Cut the thighs in half. Cut the carcass in half, separating the back from the breast, and cut the back section crosswise into 4 pieces. Cut the breast section lengthwise in half and cut each half crosswise into 1½-inch-wide pieces. Place the chicken in a bowl, add the Marinade ingredients, and toss lightly to coat. Cover with plastic wrap and refrigerate for at least 1 hour.

Spread the cornstarch on a plate. Add the beaten egg to the chicken and toss to coat. Dredge the chicken pieces in the cornstarch, coating them evenly, and press lightly so the cornstarch adheres.

Combine the Lemon Sauce ingredients in a nonreactive saucepan and blend well. Set aside.

Preheat the oven to 200°F.

Heat a wok or a deep-fryer, add the oil, and heat it to 375°F. Add 4 or 5 pieces of chicken and fry for about 3½ minutes, turning constantly, until crisp and golden brown. Remove with a handled strainer, drain briefly in a colander, and transfer to paper towels. Then arrange the chicken on a cookie sheet lined with aluminum foil and keep warm in the oven while you fry the remaining chicken; reheat the oil and remove any debris with a fine-meshed strainer before you add each batch. Meanwhile, heat the sauce mixture, stirring to prevent lumps, until thickened.

Arrange the fried chicken on a serving platter. Pour the sauce into a bowl for dipping.

Serve with Roasted Black Bean Peppers (page 303) and/or Vegetarian Roll-Ups (page 306).

SMOKED CHICKEN SALAD

Whereas Western chefs smoke with wood chips, Chinese cooks combine brown sugar and fragrant black tea with such seasonings as cinnamon, aniseed, fennel, and orange peel to impart a unique smoky flavor to a variety of dishes. In this recipe, smoked boneless chicken is served on a bed of flash-cooked bean sprouts and bathed in a cilantro vinaigrette. A superb choice for a light summer lunch or dinner. ● Serves 6

2 whole chicken breasts (about 1½ pounds each)

Marinade

6 slices fresh ginger (about the size of a quarter), lightly smashed with the flat side of a knife or a cleaver

6 scallions, trimmed and smashed with the flat side of a knife or a cleaver

¼ cup rice wine or sake

½ teaspoon salt

Tea-Smoking Mixture

6 tablespoons loose black tea

¼ cup light brown sugar

2 teaspoons ground cinnamon

1½ teaspoons sesame oil

Vinaigrette

6 tablespoons soy sauce

¼ cup clear rice vinegar

2½ tablespoons sesame oil

1½ tablespoons sugar

3 heaping tablespoons minced cilantro (fresh coriander)

1 tablespoon corn or safflower oil

4 cups bean sprouts, rinsed lightly and drained

1 cup 1-inch pieces scallion greens

1 tablespoon rice wine or sake

Rinse the chicken breasts, drain thoroughly, and pat dry with paper towels. Remove any fat deposits. Place in a bowl. Combine the Marinade ingredients and pinch the ginger slices and scallions in the rice wine for several minutes to impart their flavor. Add to the chicken and toss lightly to coat. Cover with plastic wrap and refrigerate for at least 1 hour.

Fill a wok or a pot with water for steaming and heat until boiling. Arrange the chicken breasts skin side up on a steamer tray (see page 7). Place over the boiling water, cover, and steam for 20 to 25 minutes, or until just cooked. (To test for doneness, pierce the thickest section of one breast with a knife; the juices should run clear.)

Meanwhile, line a wok or a large pot and its lid with heavy-duty aluminum foil. Combine the Smoking Mixture ingredients in the bottom of the wok or pot. Arrange 6 crisscrossed chopsticks or a rack to suspend the chicken over the smoking mixture.

Place the chicken breasts skin side up over the smoking mixture and cover, crimping the edges of the foil so that no smoke will escape. Place over high heat and cook for about 15 minutes from the time a smoky smell is first apparent. Remove from the heat and let stand, covered, for 10 minutes. Remove the chicken breasts and cool slightly, then brush generously with the sesame oil and let cool to room temperature.

With the heel of your hand, press down on the central cartilage of each breastbone, turn the breast skin side down, and remove the breastbone. Using a sharp knife, cut each breast lengthwise in half, then cut each half crosswise into ½-inch-thick slices.

Combine the Vinaigrette ingredients and blend well.

Heat a wok or a skillet, add the corn or safflower oil, and heat until very hot. Add the bean sprouts and scallion pieces and toss lightly over high heat. Add the rice wine or sake and stir-fry for about 1½ minutes, until crisp-tender. Using a slotted spoon, remove the vegetables and arrange on a serving platter, making a slight indentation in the center.

Reheat the pan, add the vinaigrette, and bring to a boil. Add the smoked chicken pieces and heat through. Arrange over the bean sprouts, and spoon the vinaigrette on top. Serve warm.

CITRUS CHICKEN

Pungent fresh orange zest, crushed red pepper, garlic, and ginger provide contrasting flavors for this hot-and-sour Sichuanese sauce. I often prepare the sauce using tangerines or clementines instead of oranges. With its contrasting textures of crunchy water chestnuts and tender chicken slices, the dish is sure to become a family favorite. Serve with plenty of steamed rice.

● Serves 6

1½ pounds boneless skinless chicken breasts

Marinade

2 tablespoons soy sauce

1½ tablespoons rice wine or sake

1 teaspoon sesame oil

1 tablespoon cornstarch

1 navel orange

1½ cups thinly sliced water chestnuts

Sauce

¾ cup Chinese Chicken Broth (page 367) or water

3½ tablespoons soy sauce

3 tablespoons rice wine or sake

1½ tablespoons clear rice vinegar

1 teaspoon Oriental sesame oil

2 teaspoons sugar

¼ teaspoon freshly ground black pepper

1¼ teaspoons cornstarch

5 tablespoons corn or safflower oil

Seasonings

1 teaspoon chile pepper flakes

1 tablespoon minced fresh ginger

1½ tablespoons minced garlic

With a sharp knife or a cleaver, trim away any fat or sinew from the chicken, and cut the breasts in half. Cut the chicken breasts on an angle into very thin, wide slices about ⅛ inch thick and about 1½ inches long by 1½ inches wide.

Place the slices in a bowl, add the Marinade ingredients, and toss lightly to coat. Cover with plastic wrap and refrigerate for at least 30 minutes.

Using a vegetable peeler, remove the zest from the orange in long strips and cut into thin julienne shreds. Heat a small pan of water until boiling, add the orange shreds, and boil for 1 minute. Remove with a slotted spoon and refresh in cold water, then drain and squeeze dry in paper towels. Blanch the water chestnuts in the boiling water for 20 seconds, drain, refresh in cold water, and drain again. Combine the Sauce ingredients and blend well.

Heat a wok or a skillet, add 3½ tablespoons of the oil, and heat until very hot. Add the chicken slices and stir-fry over high heat, stirring constantly, until the meat loses its pink color and separates. Remove with a handled strainer or a slotted spoon and drain in a colander. Clean out the pan.

Reheat the pan, add the remaining 1½ tablespoons oil, and heat until very hot. Add the orange shreds and Seasonings and stir-fry for about 10 seconds over high heat, until fragrant. Add the water chestnuts and toss lightly for 30 seconds, or until heated through. Add the sauce mixture and cook, stirring constantly to prevent lumps, until thickened. Add the cooked chicken, toss lightly to coat, and transfer to a serving platter. Serve immediately.

Serve with Glazed Green Beans (page 301) and/or Pickled Carrots (page 299).

CHICKEN AND
BROCCOLI IN OYSTER SAUCE

While oyster sauce and broccoli are often paired with beef, I like to substitute chicken or turkey meat for a flavorful, healthy alternative. Both are admirable foils for the garlicky sauce. ● Serves 6

1½ pounds boneless skinless chicken breasts

Marinade

2 tablespoons soy sauce

1½ tablespoons rice wine or sake

1½ tablespoons minced garlic

1 teaspoon sesame oil

1 tablespoon cornstarch

1 large bunch broccoli (about 1¾ pounds)

Sauce

½ cup Chinese Chicken Broth (page 367) or water

5 tablespoons oyster sauce

1 tablespoon rice wine or sake

1½ teaspoons sugar

1 teaspoon soy sauce

1 teaspoon sesame oil

1½ teaspoons cornstarch

5 tablespoons corn or safflower oil

Seasonings

1½ tablespoons minced fresh ginger

2 tablespoons minced scallions (white part only)

With a sharp knife or a cleaver, trim away any fat or sinew from the chicken, and cut the breasts in half. Cut the breasts on an angle into very thin, wide slices, about ⅛ inch thick and about 1½ inches long by 1½ inches wide. Place in a bowl, add the Marinade ingredients, and toss lightly to coat. Cover with plastic wrap and refrigerate for at least 30 minutes.

Peel the tough outer skin from the broccoli stalks, trim the ends, and cut the stalks on the diagonal into 1-inch pieces. Cut the florets into bite-size pieces. Heat a large pot of water until boiling, add the broccoli, and boil for 3 minutes. Drain, refresh in cold water, and drain again.

Combine the Sauce ingredients and blend well.

Heat a wok or a skillet, add 3½ tablespoons of the oil, and heat until very hot. Add the chicken and stir-fry over high heat, stirring constantly, until the meat loses its pink color and separates. Remove with a handled strainer or a slotted spoon and drain in a colander. Clean out the pan.

Reheat the pan, add the remaining 1½ tablespoons oil, and heat until very hot. Add the Seasonings and stir-fry over high heat for about 15 seconds, until fragrant. Add the sauce mixture and cook, stirring constantly to prevent lumps, until thickened. Add the broccoli and chicken and stir-fry until heated through. Transfer to a serving platter, and serve immediately.

Variation: Substitute ¾ pound snow peas, ends trimmed and veiny strings removed, for the broccoli, adding them to the pan with the seasonings and cooking for 30 seconds, or until crisp-tender. Or substitute 2 pounds fresh asparagus, peeled and cut into 1-inch lengths: Precook the asparagus in boiling water for 5 minutes, drain, refresh in cold water, and drain again. Add to the sauce with the chicken, and stir-fry until heated through.

SPICY CHICKEN WITH PEANUTS

Spicy, crunchy, and simply delicious, this Sichuanese classic embodies all the best qualities of western Chinese cooking. In my recipe, nuggets of chicken meat, crisp water chestnut slices, and peanuts are tossed in a fiery sauce enriched with a dousing of black vinegar. ● Serves 6

1½ pounds boneless skinless chicken breasts

Marinade

2 tablespoons soy sauce

1 tablespoon rice wine or sake

1 teaspoon sesame oil

2 teaspoons minced fresh ginger

1 tablespoon cornstarch

Spicy Sauce

¾ cup Chinese Chicken Broth (page 367) or water

3 tablespoons soy sauce

2½ tablespoons rice wine or sake

2½ tablespoons sugar

1 tablespoon Chinese black vinegar or Worcestershire sauce

1 teaspoon sesame oil

1¼ teaspoons cornstarch

5 tablespoons corn or safflower oil

Seasonings

1 tablespoon minced scallions

1 tablespoon minced fresh ginger

1 tablespoon minced garlic

1 teaspoon chile pepper flakes or hot chili paste

2 cups thinly sliced water chestnuts, blanched in boiling water for 10 seconds, refreshed in cold water, and drained

1½ cups unsalted dry-roasted peanuts

With a sharp knife, remove any fat or sinew from the chicken, and cut the chicken breasts in half. Cut the chicken into ½-inch cubes and place in a bowl. Add the Marinade ingredients and toss lightly to coat. Cover with plastic wrap and refrigerate for at least 30 minutes.

Combine the Spicy Sauce ingredients and blend well.

Heat a wok or a skillet, add 3½ tablespoons of the oil, and heat until very hot. Add the chicken and stir-fry over high heat, until the meat loses its pink color and separates. Remove with a handled strainer or a slotted spoon and drain in a colander. Clean out the pan.

Reheat the pan, add the remaining 1½ tablespoons oil, and heat until very hot. Add the Seasonings and stir-fry over high heat for about 10 seconds, until fragrant. Add the water chestnuts and toss lightly for 30 seconds, or until heated through. Add the sauce mixture and cook, stirring continuously to prevent lumps, until thickened. Add the chicken and peanuts and toss lightly until heated through. Transfer to a serving platter and serve immediately.

Serve with Stir-Fried Spinach (page 308) and/or Sweet-and-Sour Chinese Pickles (page 106).

Variation: Substitute turkey cutlets for the chicken meat and dry-roasted cashews for the peanuts.

CHICKEN ROLL-UPS

Inspired by mu shu pork, this delicious dish combines shredded chicken with leeks, fresh and dried mushrooms, and bean sprouts, all tossed in a delicate sauce. Serve the fragrant mixture rolled up in crisp lettuce leaves or Mandarin pancakes. Or, for a convenient substitute for the pancakes, use flour tortillas, steamed and then brushed with sesame oil. Serve this dish as an entrée or as an appetizer. ● Serves 6

1½ pounds boneless skinless chicken breasts

Marinade

2 tablespoons soy sauce

2 tablespoons rice wine or sake

1 tablespoon sugar

1 teaspoon sesame oil

1 tablespoon cornstarch

Sauce

½ cup Chinese Chicken Broth (page 367)

3 tablespoons soy sauce

2½ tablespoons rice wine or sake

1½ teaspoons sugar

1½ teaspoons sesame oil

¼ teaspoon freshly ground black pepper

1 teaspoon cornstarch

½ cup hoisin sauce

2 small heads Bibb or Boston lettuce, cored, rinsed, and drained, or
    1 recipe Mandarin Pancakes (page 58) or 18 flour tortillas,
    steamed until piping hot

5 tablespoons corn or safflower oil

1½ tablespoons minced fresh ginger

8 cloves garlic, peeled and very thinly sliced

2 cups leeks (white part only) cut into fine julienne shreds about
    1½ inches long

10 dried Chinese black mushrooms, softened in hot water for 20
    minutes, stems removed, and caps cut into fine julienne shreds

1 tablespoon rice wine or sake

½ pound button mushrooms, trimmed and cut into thin slices

4 cups bean sprouts, rinsed lightly and drained

Using a sharp knife or a cleaver, trim away any fat or sinew from the chicken, and cut the chicken breasts in half. Cut the chicken across the grain into thin, wide slices about 1½ inches long, 1½ inches wide, and ⅛ inch thick. Then cut along the grain into matchstick-size shreds. Place in a bowl, add the Marinade ingredients, and toss lightly to coat. Cover with plastic wrap and refrigerate for at least 30 minutes.

Combine the Sauce ingredients and blend well. Spoon the hoisin sauce into a serving bowl. Arrange the lettuce leaves in a basket, if using.

Heat a wok or a skillet, add 3½ tablespoons of the oil, and heat until very hot. Add the chicken shreds and stir-fry over high heat, stirring constantly, until the meat loses its pink color and separates. Remove with a handled strainer or a slotted spoon and drain in a colander. Clean out the pan.

Reheat the pan, add the remaining 1½ tablespoons oil, and heat until very hot. Add the ginger, garlic, leeks, and black mushrooms and stir-fry over high heat for about 1 minute, stirring constantly. Add the rice wine or sake and toss. Add the button mushrooms, reduce the heat slightly, and stir-fry for about 1½ minutes. Add the sauce mixture and bean sprouts and toss lightly over high heat for about 1 minute, until the bean sprouts are just wilted. Add the chicken shreds and stir-fry briefly to mix. Transfer to a serving platter.

To serve, brush about ½ teaspoon of the hoisin sauce over a lettuce leaf, or a warm pancake or tortilla, spoon some of the stir-fried chicken mixture into the center, and roll up.

SAUCY CHICKEN
WITH PEPPERS

The contrasting textures and flavors of the chicken, red peppers, water chestnuts, hoisin sauce, and garlic make this simple stir-fry a memorable feast. Serve with plenty of steamed rice or buns, and don't let a drop of the rich sauce escape. ● Serves 6

1½ pounds boneless skinless chicken breasts

Marinade

2 tablespoons soy sauce

1½ tablespoons rice wine or sake

1 teaspoon sesame oil

1 tablespoon cornstarch

Sauce

3 tablespoons hoisin sauce

2 tablespoons soy sauce

1½ tablespoons rice wine or sake

1½ tablespoons sugar

5 tablespoons water

5 tablespoons corn or safflower oil

Seasonings

1½ tablespoons minced garlic

1 tablespoon minced fresh ginger

2 medium red bell peppers, rinsed, cored, seeded, and cut into
1-inch squares

1 tablespoon rice wine or sake

1 cup thinly sliced water chestnuts, blanched in boiling water for 20
seconds, refreshed in cold water, and drained

½ cup ½-inch pieces scallion greens

With a sharp knife or a heavy cleaver, trim away any fat or sinew from the chicken, and cut the chicken breasts in half. Cut the chicken into ½-inch cubes and place in a bowl. Add the Marinade ingredients and toss lightly to coat. Cover with plastic wrap and refrigerate for at least 30 minutes.

Combine the Sauce ingredients and stir to dissolve the sugar.

Heat a wok or a skillet, add 3½ tablespoons of the oil, and heat until very hot. Add the chicken pieces and stir-fry over high heat, stirring constantly, until the meat loses its pink color and separates. Remove with a handled strainer or a slotted spoon and drain in a colander. Clean out the pan.

Reheat the pan, add the remaining 1½ tablespoons oil, and heat until very hot. Add the Seasonings and stir-fry over high heat for about 10 seconds, until fragrant. Add the bell peppers and stir-fry for about 1½ minutes; toss until slightly softened. Add the rice wine or sake and toss. Add the water chestnuts and stir-fry for about 30 seconds, until heated through. Add the sauce mixture and cook, stirring constantly to prevent lumps, until thickened. Add the cooked chicken and the scallion greens, toss lightly to coat, and transfer to a serving platter. Serve immediately.

Serve with Tossed Bean Sprouts (page 294) and/or Wilted Cabbage Salad (page 105).

CORNISH HENS, DUCK, AND TURKEY

he poultry sections of American supermarkets used to be filled with nothing but chicken. Frozen ducks and turkeys might appear on occasion, but one had to wait for the holidays or resort to a specialty butcher for the fresh products.

These days, supermarket meat counters have been transformed and now routinely carry a wide array of poultry. Cornish hens and duck are widely available. And turkey has become a rising star as Americans have discovered its versatility.

Although turkey is still rare in the Far East, it is in fact naturally suited to Chinese recipes. Meaty turkey thighs can be marinated in a spicy blend of seasonings, then steamed or baked. Turkey cutlets, usually packaged in lean slices, are ideal for stir-frying. They can be shredded into julienne strips or cut into small cubes, paired with almost any vegetable, and tossed with a pungent sauce. Ground turkey is an excellent substitute for ground beef or pork in Chinese dishes, and it has a fraction of the fat. The only concession I make when cooking with turkey is to up the seasonings, since it is stronger in flavor than chicken.

Similarly, Cornish hens are admirably suited to Chinese cooking. They are a good substitute for quail, a Chinese favorite, in any recipe. Stuffed with a seasoned rice filling and simmered in a soy sauce–anise braising mixture, they become sumptuous fare. And coated in a tangy sweet-and-sour sauce or a crystallized ginger coating and roasted, they make an appealing alternative to chicken.

Duck, of course, is a Chinese staple, and in recent years, its popularity has broadened considerably in this country. Whereas frozen Long Island duckling was once the only option in most supermarkets, today many stores carry fresh whole ducks, as well as boneless duck breasts.

Chinese cooks favor longer cooking for duck than European chefs do, and with the fatty varieties most widely available in this country, I heartily agree. It's also imperative to prick the skin thoroughly before roasting to allow the fat to drain off. I favor a fairly hot oven and I turn the bird periodically, draining off the rendered fat from the pan as it accumulates.

Roasting duck may require some tending, but almost nothing compares to the flavor of the roasted meat. Try it topped with a dollop of pungent bean sauce and wrapped in a steamed pancake, or cut the meat into thin julienne strips and serve it atop a colorful bed of crisp stir-fried vegetables.

SMOTHERED CORNISH HENS

In this simple recipe, Cornish hens are "smothered" with a fragrant mixture of finely shredded ginger and scallions, soy sauce, and rice wine and steamed until tender. The juicy cooked meat is succulent in the delicate, natural broth. ● Serves 6

3 Cornish hens (about 1½ pounds each)

Marinade

¼ cup rice wine or sake

6 tablespoons soy sauce

1 cup very finely shredded fresh ginger

1¼ cups finely shredded scallions (white part only)

¼ teaspoon freshly ground black pepper

About 6 green cabbage leaves, blanched in boiling water for
20 seconds, refreshed in cold water, and drained

Remove any excess fat from the hens. Rinse lightly, drain, and pat dry. Place in a bowl. Combine the Marinade ingredients and rub the mixture all over the hens, inside and out; stuff the cavities with some of the ginger and scallion shreds. Cover with plastic wrap and refrigerate for 1 hour, turning occasionally.

Fill a wok or a pot with water for steaming and heat until boiling. Line a steamer tray or a pie plate (see page 7) with the blanched cabbage leaves and arrange the hens breast side up on the cabbage. Pour the marinade over, arranging the ginger and scallions on top of the hens. Place over the boiling water, cover, and steam for 35 minutes, or until the hens are cooked. (To test for doneness, prick the thigh of one hen with the tip of a sharp knife; the juices should run clear.)

Remove the hens, reserving the juices remaining in the tray. Using a sharp knife, split each hen in half. Arrange on serving plates, skim the sauce, removing fat, and spoon the sauce and shredded seasonings on top. Serve immediately.

Serve with Garlic Broccoli (page 296) and/or Wilted Cabbage Salad (page 105).

Variation: Substitute 3 whole chicken breasts for the Cornish hen.

ORANGE-GLAZED CORNISH HENS STUFFED WITH WILD RICE

Nutty wild rice and buttery pine nuts provide contrasting flavors in the delicious stuffing for these hens. There's also a hint of orange, which accentuates the orange juice in the glaze. The hens are baked in a hot oven, where they acquire a lacquerlike finish. This dish will transform any meal into a special occasion. ● Serves 6

3 Cornish hens (about 1½ pounds each)

1 teaspoon salt

¼ teaspoon fresh ground black pepper

3 cloves garlic, peeled and puréed with a garlic press

Wild Rice Stuffing

1 cup wild rice

1 teaspoon sesame oil

¼ cup minced scallions (white part only)

1 tablespoon soy sauce

2 tablespoons rice wine or sake

3 cups Chinese Chicken Broth (page 367), heated until boiling

1 cup toasted pine nuts

1 teaspoon minced orange zest

Glaze

½ cup orange juice

2 tablespoons honey

1 tablespoon soy sauce

½ cup dry sherry

Remove any excess fat from the game hens. Rinse, drain, and pat dry. Combine the salt, pepper, and garlic and rub the hens inside and out with the mixture. Set aside.

To prepare the stuffing, wash the wild rice in a colander under cold running water until the water runs clear. Heat the sesame oil in a saucepan with a tight-fitting lid until hot. Add the scallions and stir-fry for about 1 minute.

Add the wild rice and stir-fry briefly. Add the soy sauce, rice wine or sake, and chicken broth and bring to a boil. Cover tightly, reduce the heat to low, and simmer until the liquid has evaporated and the rice is fluffy, about 1 hour. Stir in the pine nuts and orange zest, remove from the heat, and let cool.

Preheat the oven to 400°F.

Stuff ½ cup of the cooled stuffing into the cavity of each hen. Secure with toothpicks or sew closed with kitchen twine or thread. Transfer the remaining rice to a heatproof casserole, cover with aluminum foil, and set aside. Arrange the hens breast side up on a baking sheet lined with aluminum foil. Combine the Glaze ingredients, and spoon some of the mixture over the hens. Bake for 45 to 50 minutes, basting the hens every 15 minutes with the remaining glaze mixture, until golden brown and crisp. Meanwhile, about 15 minutes before the hens are done, place the rice in the oven and reheat until hot.

Remove the hens from the oven, cool slightly, and then split each hen in half. Place on serving plates, dividing the stuffing equally. Skim off the fat from the pan juices and spoon the juices over the hens. Serve the extra rice on the side.

Serve with Stir-Fried Asparagus with Crabmeat (page 291) and/or Spicy Cucumber Spears (page 107).

Variation: Substitute 1 whole chicken (about 3½ pounds) for the game hens, and roast for 1 hour.

BRAISED STUFFED CORNISH HENS

Short-grain rice studded with bits of smoky black mushrooms, carrots, and peas is a delicious stuffing for any type of poultry, and Cornish hens are no exception. In this recipe, a rich soy sauce–aniseed braising mixture colors the skin and infuses the meat with additional flavor. You can prepare the dish in advance and heat before serving; the flavor deepens with reheating. ● Serves 6

3 Cornish hens (about 1½ pounds each)

2 tablespoons soy sauce

Rice Stuffing

1 cup glutinous, Arborio, or other short-grain white rice

1 tablespoon corn or safflower oil

1 tablespoon minced scallions (white part only)

6 dried Chinese black mushrooms, softened in hot water for 20 minutes, stems removed, and caps cut into ¼-inch dice

2 medium carrots, peeled and cut into ¼-inch dice

2 tablespoons soy sauce

1 tablespoon rice wine or sake

1 teaspoon sesame oil

2 cups Chinese Chicken Broth (page 367)

1 cup fresh or frozen peas

Braising Mixture

½ cup soy sauce

4½ cups water

¼ cup rice wine or sake

2 tablespoons sugar

1 teaspoon aniseed

6 slices fresh ginger (about the size of a quarter), smashed with the flat side of a knife or a cleaver

6 scallions, trimmed and smashed with the flat side of a knife or a cleaver

1 tablespoon corn or safflower oil

1 tablespoon cornstarch

3 tablespoons water

Remove any excess fat from the hens, rinse, drain, and pat dry. Rub the soy sauce all over the hens, inside and out. Refrigerate for 1 hour. Place the rice in a colander and rinse under cold running water. Transfer to a bowl and add warm water to cover. Let soak for 1 hour; drain.

Meanwhile, combine the Braising Mixture ingredients in a large pot and heat until boiling. Reduce the heat and simmer for 20 minutes to blend the flavorings. Remove from the heat and set aside.

To prepare the Stuffing, heat the oil in a skillet or a saucepan until hot. Add the minced scallions, black mushrooms, carrots, and drained rice and toss lightly over high heat for 15 seconds. Add the soy sauce, rice wine or sake, sesame oil, and chicken broth and heat until boiling. Reduce the heat to medium low and cook for about 10 minutes, stirring occasionally, until the mixture is dry. Add the peas and toss lightly. Remove from the heat and let cool.

Fill the cavity of each hen with 1 cup of the stuffing mixture. Secure with toothpicks or sew with a trussing needle and twine or thread. Place the remaining rice in a baking dish, cover with aluminum foil, and set aside.

Preheat the oven to 350°F.

Heat a skillet or a wok, add the corn or safflower oil, and heat until hot. Place the hens breast side down in the pan and fry over high heat until golden brown. Turn and fry until golden brown on the other side. Remove and drain. Add the hens to the braising mixture, breast side down, cover, and heat until boiling. Reduce the heat to medium low, cover, and cook for 45 minutes, turning the hens after 25 minutes. Meanwhile, cook the reserved rice stuffing in the oven for 20 minutes, or until cooked. Remove the hens from the braising mixture and let cool slightly. Set the braising liquid aside.

Combine the cornstarch and water and blend well.

Using a sharp knife, split the hens in half and arrange on serving plates, dividing the stuffing equally. Reheat the braising mixture until boiling, add the cornstarch thickener, and cook, stirring constantly to prevent lumps, until thickened. Spoon some of the sauce over the hens and pour the remaining sauce into a serving dish. Serve the extra hot rice on the stuffing side.

Serve with Hot-and-Sour Bok Choy (page 298) and/or Cold-Tossed Garlicky Green Beans (page 114).

CORNISH HENS GLAZED WITH CRYSTALLIZED GINGER

Crystallized ginger is often associated with sweet desserts, but I find that it adds a distinctive flavor to roasted meats. Mixed with plum sauce and maple syrup, as in the unique barbecue sauce in this recipe, it gives roasted birds an exquisite flavor and a rich brown color. Try it with a whole chicken, or chicken wings or parts, instead of the Cornish hens.

● Serves 6

3 Cornish game hens (about 1½ pounds each)
1 teaspoon salt
¼ teaspoon freshly ground black pepper
1 tablespoon minced fresh ginger

Ginger Barbecue Sauce

¼ cup finely minced crystallized ginger
½ cup plum sauce or duck sauce
¼ cup maple syrup
½ cup dry sherry
2½ tablespoons soy sauce
1 tablespoon minced fresh ginger

Preheat the oven to 375°F.

Remove any excess fat from the hens. Rinse, drain, and pat dry. Rub the hens inside and out with the salt and pepper. Stuff the cavity of each hen with 1 teaspoon of the minced ginger, rubbing the ginger all over the cavity. Place the hens on a rack in a roasting pan, place in the middle section of the oven, and roast for 15 minutes. Meanwhile, combine the Sauce ingredients.

Brush the hens generously with the sauce mixture and bake for about 45 minutes longer, brushing every 15 minutes with the sauce, until golden brown and crisp. (To test for doneness, pierce the thigh of one hen with the tip of a knife; the juices should run clear.)

Split the hens in half and arrange on individual plates. Serve immediately.

Serve with Spicy Snow Peas and Water Chestnuts (page 304) and/or Rainbow Corn Salad (page 110).

SWEET-AND-SOUR BARBECUED CORNISH HENS

This smoky barbecue sauce has just the right balance of sweet and sour.
● Serves 6

Sweet-and-Sour Glaze

1 cup pineapple juice

½ cup light brown sugar

½ cup ketchup

2½ tablespoons soy sauce

2 tablespoons sesame oil

½ teaspoon salt

2 teaspoons cornstarch

1 tablespoon corn or safflower oil

1 tablespoon minced fresh ginger

1 tablespoon minced garlic

3 Cornish game hens (about 1½ pounds each)

Combine the Glaze ingredients and blend well. Heat a skillet or a wok, add the oil, and heat until hot. Add the ginger and garlic and stir-fry for about 10 seconds, until fragrant. Add the glaze mixture and cook over high heat, stirring continuously to prevent lumps, until thickened. Transfer to a large nonreactive bowl and let cool.

Meanwhile, remove any excess fat from the hens. Rinse, drain, and pat dry. Using a sharp knife, split the hens in half.

Add the hens to the cooled glaze, turning to coat. Cover with plastic wrap and refrigerate for at least 1 hour, or overnight if possible.

Preheat the oven to 375°F.

Arrange the hens skin side down in a roasting pan lined with aluminum foil. Pour the remaining glaze on top. Roast for 30 minutes, or until golden brown. Turn over, spoon the pan juices on top, and roast for 30 minutes longer, or until golden brown. Transfer to a serving platter and serve immediately.

Serve with Potato Pancakes (page 302) and/or Spicy Cold-Tossed Broccoli (page 113).

CRISPY ORANGE DUCK

Inspired by a no-frills method for roasting duck mastered during my years in the Far East and by memories of my mother's duckling à l'orange, I created this "orange duck." It is a lighter, more accessible variation of the classic recipe. Serve with steamed bread or rice. ● Serves 6

1 duck (about 5½ to 6 pounds)
1 teaspoon salt
¼ teaspoon freshly ground black pepper
3 cloves garlic, peeled and puréed with a garlic press
1 orange, cut into 6 wedges

Glaze

1 cup orange juice
½ cup rice wine or sake
2 tablespoons soy sauce
2 tablespoons honey

Preheat the oven to 425°F.

Remove any fat deposits from the duckling. Rinse, drain, and pat dry. Cut off the wing tips and trim away the large skin flap at the neck. Rub the salt and pepper all over the duck, inside and out. Rub the cavity with the garlic purée and stuff with the orange wedges. Combine the Glaze ingredients.

Place the duck breast side up on a rack in a shallow roasting pan and prick the skin all over rather deeply with the tip of a paring knife or the tines of a carving fork. Pour 2 cups of water in the bottom of the pan to prevent the drippings from smoking. Roast for about 20 minutes, or until golden brown and crisp. Turn the duck over, spoon the glaze mixture liberally over it, and bake for 15 minutes. Then turn breast side up, baste again liberally with the glaze, and bake for 15 minutes. Drain the fat from the pan and add 2 more cups of water. Baste liberally and roast for about 1 hour, basting every 15 minutes, until the skin is very crisp. Let the duck rest for 10 minutes.

Carve the breast into thin slices and arrange on a platter. Cut off the legs and separate the legs and thighs. Remove the meaty sections and skin from the back of the carcass and add to the platter. Serve immediately.

Serve with Glazed Green Beans (page 301) and/or Hot-and-Sour Cabbage Slaw (page 108).

SIMPLIFIED PEKING DUCK

The traditional preparation for Peking duck is an arduous process, requiring a day's work. For those, like myself, who want an easier method, I offer the following simplified recipe. Purists will not be disappointed: the lacquerlike skin is crisp, and the meat is juicy and tender. Wrap both in a pancake with a healthy dollop of sweet bean sauce or hoisin sauce, and savor the exquisite flavors that give this dish its just reputation.

● Serves 6

1 duck (about 5½ to 6 pounds)

½ cup rice wine or sake

6 slices fresh ginger (about the size of a quarter), smashed with the flat side of a knife or a cleaver

¼ cup honey

3 tablespoons clear rice vinegar

3 tablespoons cornstarch

¼ cup water

6 to 8 thick scallions (white part only), trimmed and cut into 3-inch lengths

Dipping Sauce

½ cup sweet bean sauce or hoisin sauce

2 tablespoons sugar

1 tablespoon soy sauce

1 teaspoon sesame oil

Mandarin Pancakes (page 58) or flour tortillas, steamed until hot, or 2 heads Bibb lettuce, leaves separated, trimmed, rinsed, and drained

Remove any fat deposits from the duckling. Rinse, drain, and pat dry. Cut away the wing tips and trim away the large skin flap at the neck. Using a sharp paring knife or a carving fork, carefully prick the skin rather deeply all over.

Combine the rice wine, ginger, honey, and vinegar in a Dutch oven or a large skillet and heat until boiling. Reduce the heat to low and simmer for 15 minutes. Combine the cornstarch and water, blend well, and add to the rice wine mixture. Cook, stirring to prevent lumps, until thickened. Remove from

(continued)

the heat. Place the duck on its side in the hot liquid and, using a ladle, pour the liquid over the skin of the duck for several minutes. Carefully turn the duck over and ladle the liquid over the other side for several minutes. Drain the duck and suspend it in a cool, breezy place, preferably in front of a fan, to dry for 2 hours.

Preheat the oven to 425°F.

Place the duck breast side up on a rack in a shallow roasting pan lined with aluminum foil. Roast for 30 minutes, then drain off the fat in the pan and turn the duck over. Roast for 50 minutes, drain off the fat in the pan, and turn the duck over. Roast for 30 minutes longer, or until the skin is crisp and dark brown; if the wings and legs start to get too dark, cover with aluminum foil. Let rest for 10 minutes.

While the duck is cooking, cut the scallions into brushes: Make four 1½-inch slits in each scallion, starting at the root end, so the scallion end will curl up into thin frills. Place in a bowl of ice water and let sit for 1 hour. Combine the Dipping Sauce ingredients in a saucepan and heat until reduced and thickened. Transfer to a serving dish.

Cut away the legs and thighs from the duck and cut apart at the joint. Cut off the meat from the thighs and cut into very thin slices. Cut the breast meat on the diagonal into very thin slices, about ⅙ inch thick. Transfer the duck to a serving platter, and garnish with the scallion brushes. Spoon a dollop of the sauce onto each pancake or tortilla, or lettuce leaf, arrange a slice of duck on top, and roll up and eat.

Serve with Spicy Bean Sprouts (page 292) and/or Zucchini and Squash in Lemon-Cilantro Dressing (page 109).

BARBECUED DUCK BREASTS

A bed of crisp-cooked bean sprouts, leeks, and red peppers provides an ideal foil for thin slices of tender hoisin-baked duck. The high-temperature baking renders the fat, leaving the meat juicy and the skin dark and crisp. This dish can be served as an appetizer or, with rice or steamed bread, as an entrée. ● Serves 6

3 whole boneless duck breasts (about 10 ounces each)

Barbecue Sauce

½ cup hoisin sauce

2 tablespoons soy sauce

2 tablespoons rice wine or sake

2 tablespoons minced garlic

1½ tablespoons sugar

1½ teaspoons sesame oil

1½ tablespoons sesame oil

1½ tablespoons minced fresh ginger

2 cups leeks cut into very thin julienne shreds

1 cup red bell pepper cut into thin julienne slices

2 tablespoons rice wine or sake

4 cups bean sprouts, rinsed and drained

2½ tablespoons soy sauce

1 teaspoon sugar

Trim any fat or excess skin from the duck breasts and place them in a bowl. Using a small sharp paring knife or a carving knife, prick the skin all over rather deeply. Combine the Barbecue Sauce ingredients, add to the duck breasts, and toss to coat. Cover with plastic wrap and let marinate at room temperature for at least 1 hour, or up to 2 hours if possible.

Preheat the oven to 425°F. Arrange the duck breasts breast side up in a baking pan lined with aluminum foil. Pour the sauce on top. Bake for 55 minutes, or until the edges of the skin are very dark and crisp. Let cool, then cut crosswise into ⅙-inch-thick slices.

Heat a wok or a skillet, add the sesame oil and heat until hot. Add the ginger and leeks and stir-fry for about 1 minute over high heat. Add the red

(continued)

pepper and rice wine or sake and toss for 1 minute. Add the bean sprouts, soy sauce, and sugar and cook for about 45 seconds, until the bean sprouts are crisp-tender. Using a slotted spoon, transfer to a serving platter, making a slight indentation in the center. Arrange the slices of barbecued duck in the center of the vegetables. Serve warm or at room temperature.

BRAISED DUCK WITH BLACK MUSHROOMS

I can still recall my first taste of this dish some nineteen years ago at a humble noodle stand in Taiwan. The meat, saturated with the rich seasonings of the braising mixture, was tender, while the generous slices of black mushrooms were slightly chewy, providing a pleasant contrast. To this day, I enjoy it as much as ever, especially since it is easily prepared in a home kitchen. ● Serves 6

1 duck (about 5 to 6 pounds)

2 tablespoons soy sauce

Braising Mixture

½ cup soy sauce

3½ cups water

¼ cup rice wine or sake

1 tablespoon sugar

1 teaspoon aniseed

Zest of 1 orange, removed with a vegetable peeler, cut into thin strips about ½ inch wide, and blanched in boiling water for 1 minute

4 slices fresh ginger (about the size of a quarter), lightly smashed with the flat side of a knife or a cleaver

4 scallions, trimmed and lightly smashed with the flat edge of a knife or a cleaver

8 dried Chinese black mushrooms, softened in hot water for 20 minutes, stems removed, and caps cut in half

1 teaspoon cornstarch

1 tablespoon water

Preheat the oven to 475°F.

Remove any fat deposits from the neck and cavity of the duckling. Rinse, drain, and pat dry. Cut off the wing tips and trim away the large skin flap at the neck. Rub the soy sauce all over the duckling, inside and out. Place the duck breast side up on a rack in a shallow roasting pan. Pour 1 cup water in the roasting pan to prevent the drippings from smoking. Roast the duck, turning it once, for about 20 minutes, or until golden brown.

Meanwhile, combine the Braising Mixture ingredients in an ovenproof casserole or a Dutch oven and heat until boiling.

Reduce the oven temperature to 350°F. Place the duck breast side down in the braising liquid, add the black mushrooms, and bake for 1½ hours, or until the duck is very tender. Transfer the duck to a cutting board and let cool slightly.

Skim any fat from the braising mixture, and remove the zest, ginger, and scallions. Combine the cornstarch and water and blend well. Add to the braising liquid and cook over medium heat, stirring constantly to prevent lumps, until slightly thickened. Remove from the heat and cover to keep warm.

Using a sharp knife, cut away the duck legs from the carcass, and separate the legs and thighs at the joint. Split the carcass lengthwise in half, separating the back from the breast, and remove any meat from the back. Place the breast skin side up on the cutting board. Using the heel of your hand, press down on the breast to separate the bones from the meat. Remove the bones and cut the breast lengthwise in half, then cut each half crosswise into 1-inch-wide pieces. Arrange the duck on a serving platter and spoon some of the sauce over the top. Serve the remaining sauce on the side.

Serve with Stir-Fried Chinese Cabbage (page 297) and/or Spicy Cold-Tossed Broccoli (page 113).

SWEET-AND-SOUR DUCK WITH PINEAPPLE

The tart sweetness of pineapple is a fitting complement to duck meat. Here the duck is cooked in a subtly seasoned braising mixture until tender, then tossed with crunchy pineapple chunks, creating a pleasant textural contrast. ● Serves 6

1 duckling (5 to 6 pounds)

2 tablespoons soy sauce

Braising Mixture

1 cup Chinese Chicken Broth (page 367) or water

½ cup pineapple juice

2 tablespoons ketchup

2 tablespoons rice wine or sake

2 tablespoons sugar

¾ tablespoon soy sauce

1 teaspoon salt

2½ teaspoons cornstarch

1½ tablespoons water

1 tablespoon corn or safflower oil

Minced Seasonings

3 tablespoons minced scallions (white part only)

2 tablespoons minced fresh ginger

1½ tablespoons minced garlic

1 cup canned pineapple cubes in juice, drained

Remove any fat deposits from the duck. Rinse, drain, and pat dry. Cut off the wing tips and trim away the large skin flap at the neck. Using a sharp knife or a cleaver, cut the duck into serving pieces. Cut off the wings. Cut away the legs and thighs from the carcass, then separate the legs and thighs at the joint. Cut the carcass lengthwise in half, separating the back from the breast, and cut the back section crosswise into 4 pieces. Cut the breast section lengthwise in half, then cut each half crosswise into 2 pieces. Place the duck in a bowl, add the soy sauce, and toss to coat.

Combine the Braising Mixture ingredients and set aside. Combine the cornstarch and water and blend until smooth.

Preheat the oven to 375°F.

Heat a flameproof casserole or a Dutch oven until hot, add the oil, and heat until hot. Arrange as many of the duck pieces, skin side down, as will fit comfortably in the pan and sear the skin to a golden brown over high heat. Turn over and brown the other side. Remove with a slotted spoon and drain. Reheat the oil and fry the remaining duck. Drain off all but 1 tablespoon of the oil from the pan.

Reheat the oil, add the Minced Seasonings, and stir-fry for about 10 seconds, until fragrant. Add the braising mixture and heat until boiling. Add the duck pieces, cover, and reinforce the lid with aluminum foil, crimping the edges to prevent steam from escaping. Place on the middle shelf of the oven and bake for 1 hour, stirring once after 30 minutes and resealing the foil. Using a slotted spoon, remove the duck pieces.

Skim away any fat from the cooking liquid. Place the pan on a burner and heat until boiling. Add the cornstarch thickener and cook, stirring constantly to prevent lumps, until thickened. Add the pineapple cubes and toss to coat. Add the duck pieces and serve immediately.

Serve with Glazed Green Beans (page 301) and/or Roasted Black Bean Peppers (page 303).

SPICY TURKEY SALAD

As the shelves of the meat section at most supermarkets attest, turkey has become a popular alternative to beef and chicken. Breasts, thighs, wings, and drumettes, in addition to the whole bird, are uniformly available. Cooked turkey breast, combined with shredded carrots, celery, and cucumbers, makes a fine salad. Topped with a fresh cilantro dressing, this dish is excellent as an appetizer, or as a light meal when served with crusty French bread. ● Serves 6

3 cups cooked turkey breast cut into very thin julienne strips
    (about ⅛ inch thick and 3 inches long)
3 cups carrots cut into very thin julienne strips
2 cups cucumbers peeled and cut into very thin julienne strips
1 cup celery cut into very thin julienne strips

Dressing

½ cup soy sauce
¼ cup clear rice vinegar
3 tablespoons Chinese black vinegar or Worcestershire sauce
3 tablespoons sesame oil
1½ tablespoons sugar
1 tablespoon minced scallions (white part only)
2 tablespoons minced fresh ginger
3 tablespoons minced cilantro (fresh coriander)

Arrange the carrots, cucumbers, and celery in concentric circles on a serving platter, leaving a space in the center for the turkey. Arrange the turkey in the center, mounding it attractively.

Combine the Dressing ingredients and place in a serving bowl. Spoon the dressing over the salad, or pass it on the side.

Variation: Substitute cooked chicken breast or barbecued pork for the turkey.

STIR-FRIED TURKEY WITH ASPARAGUS

Turkey breasts, or cutlets, are ideal for stir-frying. Marinated in a little soy sauce, rice wine, and garlic, the lean meat is an agreeable partner for almost any vegetable, particularly broccoli, snow peas, bean sprouts, and asparagus. Bathed in oyster sauce, as in this recipe, the turkey is delicious served over a crisp bed of panfried noodles. Or serve with steamed rice for a simple but sumptuous meal. ● Serves 6

1½ pounds boneless turkey breast or turkey cutlets

Marinade

2 tablespoons soy sauce

1½ tablespoons rice wine or sake

1 teaspoon sesame oil

1 tablespoon cornstarch

1 tablespoon minced garlic

Sauce

¾ cup Chinese Chicken Broth (page 367) or water

5 tablespoons oyster sauce

1½ tablespoons rice wine or sake

1½ teaspoons sugar

1 teaspoon soy sauce

1 teaspoon sesame oil

1½ teaspoons cornstarch

2 pounds asparagus

4½ tablespoons corn or safflower oil

Minced Seasonings

3 tablespoons minced scallions (white part only)

1½ tablespoons minced fresh ginger

With a sharp knife or a cleaver, trim away any fat or sinew from the turkey. If using turkey breast, cut on an angle into wide, thin slices about ⅛ inch thick and 1½ inches long by 1½ inches wide. If using turkey cutlets, pound

(continued)

to flatten and then cut into 1½-inch squares. Place in a bowl, add the Marinade ingredients, and toss lightly to coat. Cover with plastic wrap and let marinate in the refrigerator for at least 1 hour or overnight.

Combine the Sauce ingredients and blend well.

Snap off the tough ends of the asparagus and peel if necessary. Cut on the diagonal into 1½-inch pieces. Heat a large pot of water until boiling, add the asparagus, and cook for about 3 minutes, or until crisp-tender. Drain and refresh immediately in cold water; drain again.

Heat a wok or a skillet, add 3½ tablespoons of the oil, and heat until very hot. Add the turkey slices and stir-fry over high heat, stirring continuously, until the meat loses its pink color and separates. Remove with a handled strainer or a slotted spoon and drain in a colander. Clean out the pan.

Reheat the pan, add the remaining 1 tablespoon oil, and heat until very hot. Add the Minced Seasonings and stir-fry over high heat until fragrant, about 10 seconds. Add the sauce mixture and cook, stirring constantly to prevent lumps, until thickened. Add the asparagus and cooked turkey, and toss lightly to coat. Transfer to a serving platter and serve immediately.

Variation: Substitute blanched broccoli spears or crisp-cooked snow peas for the asparagus.

STIR-FRIED TURKEY WITH PEPPERS AND SNOW PEAS

Few stir-fried dishes are easier to prepare, yet the combination of crisp snow peas, red bell peppers, and tender turkey slices tossed in a spicy hoisin sauce makes this recipe a memorable classic. ● Serves 6

1½ pounds boneless turkey breast or turkey cutlets

Marinade

2 tablespoons soy sauce
2 tablespoons rice wine or sake
1½ teaspoons sesame oil
1 tablespoon cornstarch

Sauce

⅓ cup hoisin sauce

2½ tablespoons soy sauce

2 teaspoons sugar

6 tablespoons water

5 tablespoons corn or safflower oil

1½ tablespoons minced fresh ginger

1 tablespoon minced garlic

1¼ teaspoons crushed dried red chile peppers or chile pepper flakes

2 medium red bell peppers, rinsed, cored, seeded, and cut into very
thin strips

1½ tablespoons rice wine or sake

¾ pound snow peas, ends trimmed and veiny strings removed

With a sharp knife or a cleaver, trim away any fat or sinew from the turkey. If using turkey breast, cut the meat on an angle into thin, wide slices about ⅛ inch thick and 1½ inches long by 1½ inches wide. If using turkey cutlets, pound to flatten and then cut into 1½-inch squares. Place in a bowl, add the Marinade ingredients, and toss lightly to coat. Cover with plastic wrap and let marinate for 30 minutes in the refrigerator. Combine the Sauce ingredients.

Heat a wok or a skillet, add 3½ tablespoons of the oil, and heat until very hot. Add the turkey slices and stir-fry over high heat, stirring continuously, until the meat loses its pink color and separates. Remove with a handled strainer or a slotted spoon and drain in a colander. Clean out the pan.

Reheat the pan, add the remaining 1½ tablespoons oil, and heat until very hot. Add the ginger, garlic, and dried peppers or pepper flakes and stir-fry for about 10 seconds over high heat. Add the bell peppers and stir-fry for about 1 minute, then add the rice wine or sake and toss briefly. Add the snow peas and stir-fry for about 30 seconds, until crisp-tender. Add the sauce mixture and heat until thickened, stirring constantly. Add the cooked turkey, toss lightly to coat, and transfer to a serving platter. Serve immediately.

TOASTED ALMOND
TURKEY CUTLETS

No one will be able to resist these thin cutlets lightly flavored with garlic and five-spice powder, coated with almonds, and panfried until golden brown. Crisp and fragrant, they are a delectable entrée. Or, served with soy sauce for dipping, they make addictive finger food. ● Serves 6

1½ pounds turkey cutlets

Marinade

3 tablespoons soy sauce

2 tablespoons rice wine or sake

1 tablespoon sugar

1 teaspoon five-spice powder (see page 5)

¼ teaspoon freshly ground black pepper

2 tablespoons minced fresh ginger

2 teaspoons minced garlic

2 tablespoons cornstarch

1 egg, lightly beaten

1 cup sliced almonds

¾ cup cornstarch

1 cup corn or safflower oil

Using a sharp knife or a cleaver, trim away any fat or sinew from the turkey. With a mallet or the side of a heavy knife, pound the meat until about ⅛ inch thick. Cut into pieces about 3 inches long and 2 inches wide and place in a bowl. Add the Marinade ingredients and toss lightly to coat. Cover with plastic wrap and let marinate for at least 3 hours, or overnight, in the refrigerator.

Add the egg to the turkey and toss lightly. Mix the almonds with the cornstarch and spread on a plate. Dip the turkey into the almond mixture and turn to coat, pressing lightly with your fingers to make the coating adhere. Arrange the turkey on a tray lightly dusted with cornstarch or flour, and let air-dry for 30 minutes, turning once.

Heat a skillet or a wok, add the corn or safflower oil, and heat to 375°F. Add only as many of the turkey pieces as will fit comfortably and fry, turning once, for about 3 to 4 minutes, or until the turkey is cooked through and the coating is a very deep golden brown. Remove with a slotted spoon and drain briefly in a colander, then transfer to paper towels to cool. Reheat the oil, skimming off any debris with a fine strainer, and fry the remaining turkey. Drain. Serve immediately.

Serve with Vegetarian Roll-Ups (page 306) and/or Sweet-and-Sour Chinese Pickles (page 106).

Variation: Substitute boneless skinless chicken breast for the turkey.

HOISIN TURKEY THIGHS
WITH SQUASH

Turkey, with its rich, slightly gamy, flavor, and sweet acorn or butter-nut squash have a natural affinity for each other. What makes the combination even more appealing in this dish is the spicy hoisin-based marinade used to coat the meat. The turkey thighs and squash are baked separately until tender, but before serving, the juicy meat is spooned over the squash, bathing the vegetable in the delicious juices. ● Serves 6

3 pounds turkey thighs

Marinade

½ cup hoisin sauce or sweet bean sauce

5 tablespoons soy sauce

3½ tablespoons rice wine or sake

1½ teaspoons sesame oil

2 tablespoons sugar

1¼ teaspoons crushed dried red chile peppers or chile pepper flakes, or to taste

3 tablespoons minced scallions (white part only)

2 tablespoons minced garlic

2 tablespoons minced fresh ginger

2 acorn or butternut squash (about 3 pounds total), cut in half and seeds removed

2 tablespoons minced scallion greens

Using a heavy knife or a cleaver, cut the turkey thighs through the bone into chunks about 1½ inches wide. Place in a bowl. Combine the Marinade ingredients, add to the turkey, and toss lightly to coat. Cover with plastic wrap and refrigerate for at least 2 hours, or overnight if possible.

Preheat the oven to 375°F.

Place the squash cut side up on a cookie sheet lined with aluminum foil. Spoon a few tablespoons of the turkey marinade over the squash. Arrange the turkey pieces in a shallow roasting pan lined with aluminum foil and pour the remaining marinade on top.

Bake the turkey for about 30 minutes, then turn the pieces and continue baking for another 30 minutes, or until tender and golden brown.

Meanwhile, bake the squash for about 45 minutes, or until the flesh is tender when pierced with a knife. Scoop out a little of the squash, and place the squash and flesh on a heatproof platter.

Arrange the turkey in and over the squash, and spoon the sauce on top. Return to the oven and bake for 10 minutes. Sprinkle the top with the minced scallion greens, and serve immediately.

SPICY TURKEY ROLL-UPS

A healthy dose of crushed dried red chile peppers, garlic, and ginger enlivens this turkey stir-fry. The cooked meat is spooned onto crisp lettuce leaves and rolled up tortilla-style to be eaten out of hand. Serve this for a refreshingly light lunch or dinner. ● Serves 6

1½ pounds ground turkey
2 tablespoons soy sauce
1½ tablespoons rice wine or sake

Sauce

½ cup Chinese Chicken Broth (page 367)
3½ tablespoons soy sauce
2½ tablespoons rice wine or sake
2 tablespoons Chinese black vinegar or Worcestershire sauce
2 teaspoons sugar
2 teaspoons sesame oil
¼ teaspoon freshly ground black pepper
1½ teaspoons cornstarch

2 heads Boston or Bibb lettuce, leaves separated, rinsed, and drained thoroughly
2½ tablespoons corn or safflower oil

Minced Seasonings

3 tablespoons minced scallions (white part only)
2½ tablespoons minced garlic
2 tablespoons minced fresh ginger

1¼ teaspoons crushed dried red chile peppers or 1½ teaspoons hot chili paste
3 cups thinly sliced water chestnuts, blanched in boiling water for 10 seconds, refreshed in cold water, and drained

Lightly chop the ground meat with a sharp knife until fluffy. Place in a bowl, add the soy sauce and rice wine or sake, and stir to mix.

Combine the Sauce ingredients and blend well. Separate the lettuce leaves, trimming the stem ends, and lightly flatten with the flat side of a knife or a cleaver. Arrange in a basket for serving.

Heat a wok or a skillet, add 1 tablespoon of the oil, and heat until hot. Add the ground meat and stir-fry over high heat, mashing and breaking up any lumps, until it loses its pink color. Remove with a handled strainer or a slotted spoon and drain.

Reheat the pan, add the remaining 1½ tablespoons oil, and heat until very hot. Add the Minced Seasonings and the dried chile peppers or chili paste and stir-fry for about 10 seconds, until fragrant. Add the water chestnuts and stir-fry for another 10 seconds, or until heated through. Add the sauce mixture and cook, stirring continuously to prevent lumps, until thickened. Add the cooked turkey and toss lightly to coat. Transfer to a serving platter, and serve warm or at room temperature. To serve, place some of the stir-fried mixture on a lettuce leaf, roll up, and eat.

TURKEY-CABBAGE CASSEROLE

This hearty casserole has all the elements of a great meal. The ground turkey balls are enticingly seasoned with bits of black mushroom and ginger, the rich chicken broth is soothing yet filling, and the cooked cabbage is sweet, tender, and juicy. Even better, the dish can be made in advance, as the flavors deepen upon reheating. ● **Serves 6**

1 head Chinese (Napa) cabbage (about 3 pounds)

1 pound ground turkey

Seasonings

¼ cup soy sauce

2 tablespoons rice wine or sake

2 tablespoons minced scallions (white part only)

2½ tablespoons minced fresh ginger

8 dried Chinese black mushrooms, softened in hot water for 20
      minutes, stems removed, and caps finely chopped

2 tablespoons cornstarch

1 tablespoon corn or safflower oil

8 cloves garlic, smashed with the flat side of a heavy knife or a
      cleaver and peeled

½ cup rice wine or sake

4 cups Rich Chinese Chicken Broth (recipe follows)

1 tablespoon soy sauce or salt to taste

Using a sharp knife, cut out the core of the cabbage. Reserve 4 of the outermost leaves. Cut the remaining leaves into 2-inch squares, trimming away the stems, and separate the tender leafy pieces from the firmer sections closer to the core.

Place the ground turkey in a bowl and add the Seasonings. Stir the mixture to mix well. Shape into 4 oval-shaped meatballs.

Preheat the oven to 350°F.

Heat the corn or safflower oil in a large flameproof casserole or a Dutch oven until very hot. Add the meatballs and fry over high heat until golden brown on the bottom. Carefully turn over and fry until golden brown. Remove with a slotted spoon and drain. Reheat the oil, add the garlic and the core sections of the cabbage, and stir-fry over high heat. Add 1 tablespoon of the rice wine or sake and cook for about 1 minute, until the cabbage begins to soften. Add the remaining cabbage pieces and 1 tablespoon rice wine or sake and cook for 1 minute. Add the chicken broth, cover, and heat until boiling. Reduce the heat to low and simmer for 10 minutes. Arrange the meatballs in the center of the layer of cabbage and cover with the reserved cabbage leaves. Cover, place on the middle oven shelf, and bake for 1 hour. Season with the soy sauce or salt, and serve.

Serve with Pickled Carrots (page 299) and/or Spicy Cucumber Spears (page 107).

Variation: Substitute ground chicken or pork for the turkey.

Rich Chinese Chicken Broth

● **Makes 8 cups**

2½ to 3 pounds chicken backs or necks and/or chicken wings
7 cups water
⅓ cup rice wine or sake
4 slices fresh ginger (about the size of a quarter), lightly smashed
   with the flat side of a heavy knife or a cleaver

Place the chicken backs or wings in a large stockpot, add cold water to cover, and bring to a boil. Drain in a colander, discarding the water. Rinse the backs lightly under cold running water and drain. Replace the backs in the pot, add the 7 cups water, the rice wine or sake, and ginger, and heat until boiling. Reduce the heat to low and simmer, uncovered, over low heat for 1½ hours. Strain.

Chicken broth will keep for up to a week in the refrigerator, but it's important to bring it to a full boil every 3 or 4 days. Or you can freeze it for up to a year.

PORK, BEEF, AND LAMB

When it comes to meat, the Chinese are ingeniously thrifty. First and foremost, they use each and every part of the animal, as a glance at any Asian meat counter will attest. But more important, unlike American entrées that feature whole slabs of meat presented on a plate, most Chinese meat dishes also include a selection of vegetables that complement and enhance the flavor of the meat. These are the dishes that are highlighted in this chapter.

For instance, Mu Shu Pork, the classic northern Chinese specialty, tosses shreds of marinated lean pork with stir-fried cabbage, scallions, and black mushrooms. Beef with Snow Peas offers tender slices of beef stir-fried with a generous amount of crispy water chestnuts and fresh snow peas. And Warm Lamb Salad features slivers of tender lamb atop a bed of fresh spinach garnished with shredded carrots and dressed with a refreshing cilantro vinaigrette. In these recipes, meat is used almost as a flavorful garnish, and most of the dishes are intended to be served with a staple such as rice or noodles. Others may be served in steamed pancakes. Despite the lesser role of meat in such meals, all these dishes nourish and satisfy.

Like many Americans, I have made a conscious effort to lower my consumption of red meat because of concerns about fat and cholesterol. With these dishes, I can enjoy meat and still feel comfortable about my health. This chapter emphasizes stir-fried dishes in which the leanest and most tender cuts of meat are used. For pork dishes, I recommend center-cut pork loin; for beef, flank steak or London broil is ideal; and for lamb dishes, I suggest the shank portion of the leg (I buy unmarinated pieces of shish kebab that are already trimmed and then cut them as the recipe directs). Any excess fat should be trimmed before cooking.

As these recipes illustrate, Chinese meat dishes, with their variety and their accompanying abundance of fresh vegetables, are perfectly suited to the contemporary American diet.

SAUCY
STIR-FRIED PORK

Just one bite of this homey northern-style specialty demonstrates all the robust and vibrant appeal of Peking cooking. Shreds of pork and leeks are tossed in a sweet bean sauce, then wrapped in Mandarin pancakes. For a slightly sweeter sauce, substitute hoisin for the bean sauce.

● Serves 6

2 pounds boneless center-cut pork loin

Marinade

2 tablespoons soy sauce

2 tablespoons rice wine or sake

1 tablespoon minced garlic

1 tablespoon minced fresh ginger

½ teaspoon crushed dried red chile peppers or chile pepper flakes

1 teaspoon sesame oil

1 tablespoon cornstarch

Sauce

5 tablespoons sweet bean sauce or hoisin sauce

2½ tablespoons soy sauce

1½ tablespoons rice wine or sake

1½ tablespoons sugar

7 tablespoons water

¼ cup corn or safflower oil

3 cups finely shredded leeks (white part only)

1 recipe Mandarin Pancakes (page 58) or 16 flour tortillas, steamed until hot

Using a sharp knife or a cleaver, trim away any fat or gristle from the pork. Cut the meat across the grain into slices about ⅛ inch thick. Then cut the slices, with the grain, into matchstick-size shreds about 1½ inches long, and place in a bowl. Add the Marinade ingredients and toss lightly to coat. Cover with plastic wrap and let marinate for at least 1 hour in the refrigerator, or overnight.

(continued)

Combine the Sauce ingredients and stir to dissolve the sugar.

Heat a wok or a skillet, add the oil, and heat until very hot. Add the pork shreds and stir-fry over high heat, stirring continuously, until the meat loses its raw color and separates. Remove with a handled strainer or a slotted spoon and drain in a colander. Clean out the pan.

Arrange the leeks in a mound on a platter, making a slight indentation in the center for the meat.

Reheat the pan, add the sauce mixture, and heat, stirring continuously, until thickened. Add the cooked meat, toss lightly to coat, and spoon over the leeks. Toss the leeks and pork lightly before spooning the mixture into the Mandarin pancakes or flour tortillas.

Serve with Pickled Carrots (page 299) and/or Wilted Cabbage Salad (page 105).

Variation: Substitute flank steak, boneless chicken breasts, or turkey cutlets for the pork.

SPICY TANGERINE PORK

In this Sichuanese classic, crunchy water chestnuts and tender pork slices are bathed in a fiery orange-garlic sauce. Serve with plenty of rice to soak up the hot-and-sour gravy. ● Serves 6

1½ pounds boneless center-cut pork loin

Marinade

3½ tablespoons soy sauce

2 tablespoons minced fresh ginger

2 tablespoons rice wine or sake

1½ teaspoons sesame oil

1 tablespoon cornstarch

2 tablespoons grated or finely shredded orange zest (removed with a vegetable peeler and cut into fine julienne shreds)

2 cups thinly sliced water chestnuts

Sauce

¾ cup Chinese Chicken Broth (page 367) or water

4½ tablespoons soy sauce

2½ tablespoons rice wine or sake

1½ teaspoons sesame oil

2 tablespoons Chinese black vinegar or Worcestershire sauce

2 teaspoons sugar

¼ teaspoon freshly ground black pepper

1¼ teaspoons cornstarch

5½ tablespoons corn or safflower oil

2 tablespoons minced garlic

1 teaspoon crushed dried red chile peppers or chile pepper flakes

With a sharp knife or a cleaver, trim away any fat or gristle from the pork loin. Cut the meat against the grain into thin slices about ⅛ inch thick. Cut the slices into pieces about 1½ inches long and 1 inch wide, and place in a bowl. Add the Marinade ingredients and toss lightly to coat. Cover with plastic wrap and let marinate for at least 1 hour in the refrigerator.

Heat a small pan of water until boiling, and blanch the orange zest or peel for 15 seconds. Remove with a fine-meshed strainer and squeeze dry in a paper towel. Reheat the water until boiling, add the water chestnuts, and blanch for 15 seconds. Drain thoroughly in a colander. Combine the Sauce ingredients and blend well.

Heat a wok or a skillet, add ¼ cup of the oil, and heat until very hot. Add the pork slices and stir-fry over high heat, stirring continuously, until the meat loses its raw color and separates. Remove with a handled strainer or a slotted spoon and drain in a colander. Clean out the pan.

Reheat the pan, add the remaining 1½ tablespoons oil, and heat until very hot. Add the orange zest or peel, minced garlic, and chile peppers or flakes and stir-fry over high heat for about 10 seconds, until fragrant. Add the water chestnuts and toss lightly for about 15 seconds. Add the sauce mixture and cook, stirring constantly to prevent lumps, until thickened. Add the cooked meat, toss lightly to coat, and transfer to a serving platter. Serve immediately.

Serve with Garlic Broccoli (page 296) and/or Sweet-and-Sour Chinese Pickles (page 106).

Variation: Substitute boneless chicken breasts or turkey cutlets for the pork.

DOUBLE-COOKED
BARBECUED PORK SLICES

Double-cooked pork has long been heralded as one of the signature dishes of the spicy Sichuanese school. In my version, which varies slightly from the traditional recipe, the pork is first baked in a garlicky barbecue sauce, then sliced paper-thin and stir-fried with red bell peppers and scallion greens. Sliced bean curd, which is barbecued along with the pork, tastes as delicious as the meat. Serve with plenty of steamed rice.

● Serves 6

1½ pounds boneless center-cut pork loin
1 1-pound cake firm bean curd, pressed under a heavy weight for 1 hour (see Note)

Marinade

¾ cup hoisin sauce

3 tablespoons ketchup

2 tablespoons soy sauce

1 teaspoon sesame oil

Sauce

3 tablespoons soy sauce

2½ tablespoons rice wine or sake

1 teaspoon sugar

1 teaspoon sesame oil

1½ tablespoons corn or safflower oil

1½ tablespoons minced garlic

1 teaspoon crushed dried red chile peppers or chile pepper flakes

2 red bell peppers, rinsed, cored, seeded, and cut into ½-inch squares

2 cups 1-inch pieces scallion greens

Preheat the oven to 375°F. Using a sharp knife, trim any excess fat or gristle from the pork. Place the pork in a bowl. Cut the bean curd into slices about ¼ inch thick and place in a bowl.

Combine the Marinade ingredients, and add half to the pork loin. Toss lightly to coat. Dip the bean curd slices one side at a time in the remaining marinade and arrange on a cookie sheet lined with aluminum foil. Place the pork loin on the baking pan and bake for 30 minutes, turning the meat and the bean curd slices once. Let cool.

Cut the pork across the grain into thin, wide slices that are about ⅙ inch thick, 1½ inches long, and 1 inch wide. Holding the knife or cleaver at an angle, cut the bean curd into very thin slices, about ⅛ inch thick. Combine the Sauce ingredients.

Heat a wok or a skillet, add the oil, and heat until very hot. Add the minced garlic, chile peppers or flakes, and bell peppers and stir-fry for about 1 minute over high heat. Add the sauce mixture, toss lightly, and stir-fry until the sauce begins to thicken. Add the scallions, pork, and bean curd slices and toss lightly to coat. Transfer to a serving platter and serve immediately.

Note: To press bean curd, wrap it in a kitchen towel or paper towels and place on a flat surface or a cutting board. Place a heavy pan or a weight on the bean curd and let sit for 30 minutes. Drain off any liquid, and press for another 30 minutes.

Variation: Substitute boneless chicken breasts for the pork and bake for just 25 minutes, then proceed as directed.

MU SHU PORK

I have resisted giving out a mu shu pork recipe for years since it is a dish too often bastardized in Chinese restaurants. My version of this venerable classic is chock-full of smoky black mushrooms and heady with fresh ginger and garlic. ● Serves 6

1½ pounds boneless center-cut pork loin

Marinade

2½ tablespoons soy sauce

1½ tablespoons rice wine or sake

1 teaspoon sesame oil

1 tablespoon cornstarch

Sauce

3 tablespoons Chinese Chicken Broth (page 367)

3 tablespoons soy sauce

2 tablespoons rice wine or sake

½ teaspoon sugar

¼ teaspoon freshly ground black pepper

½ teaspoon cornstarch

6 tablespoons corn or safflower oil

2 eggs, lightly beaten

1 tablespoon sesame oil

Minced Seasonings

2 tablespoons minced garlic

1½ tablespoons minced fresh ginger

10 dried Chinese black mushrooms, softened in hot water for 20 minutes, stems removed, and caps shredded

3½ cups green cabbage cut into thin julienne shreds

1½ cups 1-inch pieces scallion greens

½ cup sweet bean sauce or hoisin sauce

16 Mandarin Pancakes (page 58) or flour tortillas, steamed until hot and brushed with a little sesame oil

Using a sharp knife or a cleaver, trim any fat or gristle from the pork loin. Cut the meat across the grain into ⅛-inch-thick slices. Cut the slices, with the grain, into thin matchstick-size shreds about 1½ inches long, and place in a bowl. Add the Marinade ingredients and toss lightly to coat. Cover with plastic wrap and let marinate in the refrigerator for 30 minutes.

Combine the Sauce ingredients and blend well.

Heat a wok or a skillet, add ¼ cup of the corn or safflower oil, and heat until very hot. Add the pork shreds and stir-fry over high heat, stirring continuously, until the meat loses its raw color and separates. Remove with a handled strainer or a slotted spoon and drain in a colander. Clean out the pan.

Reheat the pan, add 1 tablespoon of the oil, and heat until very hot. Add the eggs and stir-fry over high heat to scramble, until thoroughly cooked. Remove and set aside.

Reheat the pan, add the remaining 1 tablespoon corn or safflower oil and the sesame oil, and heat until hot. Add the Minced Seasonings and stir-fry over high heat until fragrant, about 10 seconds. Add the cabbage and stir-fry until tender, about 1½ minutes. Add the scallions, pork, sauce mixture, and cooked eggs and toss lightly until the mixture thickens. Transfer to a serving platter. Spread a tablespoon of the bean or hoisin sauce on each pancake or tortilla, spoon some of the stir-fried mixture on top, and roll up and eat.

Variation: Substitute boneless chicken breasts or turkey cutlets for the pork. Or, for a vegetarian dish, omit the meat entirely and substitute water for the chicken broth in the sauce.

CANTONESE-STYLE SPARERIBS

Cantonese restaurants are renowned for their spareribs bathed in a pungent black bean sauce. I find that braising the ribs leaves them especially succulent, and I use country-style ribs so that each bone is heavy with tender meat. ● Serves 6

3 pounds country-style spareribs

Marinade

2 tablespoons soy sauce

8 cloves garlic, lightly smashed with the flat side of a knife or a cleaver and peeled

1½ tablespoons rice wine or sake

1 teaspoon sesame oil

Sauce

2½ cups Chinese Chicken Broth (page 367) or water

2½ tablespoons soy sauce

2 tablespoons rice wine or sake

2 teaspoons sugar

1 teaspoon cornstarch

2 tablespoons water

1 tablespoon corn or safflower oil

Minced Seasonings

2 tablespoons fermented black beans, rinsed and drained

1½ tablespoons minced garlic

1 tablespoon minced fresh ginger

2 tablespoons minced scallion greens

½ teaspoon minced hot red chile pepper (optional)

With a heavy knife or a cleaver, trim away any excess fat from the ribs and cut them into 1½-inch lengths, cutting through the bones. (If you prefer, have the butcher do this.) Place the ribs in a bowl, add the Marinade ingredients, and toss lightly to coat. Cover with plastic wrap and let marinate for 30 minutes in the refrigerator.

Preheat the oven to 450°F. Remove the ribs from the refrigerator.

Combine the Sauce ingredients and set aside. Combine the cornstarch and water and blend well. Arrange the ribs on a baking sheet lined with aluminum foil, discarding the garlic cloves, and bake for 7 to 8 minutes on each side, or until golden brown.

While the ribs are baking, heat a large flameproof casserole or a Dutch oven until hot, add the oil, and heat until hot. Add the Minced Seasonings and stir-fry over high heat until fragrant, about 10 seconds. Add the sauce mixture and heat until boiling.

Add the spareribs to the casserole, and bring back to a boil. Reduce the heat to low, cover, and simmer for 45 minutes. Uncover, increase the heat, and cook vigorously for about 5 minutes to reduce the sauce slightly. Add the cornstarch thickener and cook, stirring continuously to prevent lumps, until thickened. Add the scallion greens and chile pepper (if using), toss lightly, and serve immediately.

Serve with Vegetarian Roll-Ups (page 306) and/or Spicy Cucumber Spears (page 107).

SICHUAN
SWEET-AND-SOUR SPARERIBS

Chinese sweet-and-sour sauces can tend to be cloying, but the addition of Chinese black vinegar and sliced onions gives this rendition an especially appealing flavor. Serve with a steamed or stir-fried vegetable and rice for a filling and satisfying meal. ● Serves 6

3 pounds country-style spareribs

Marinade

2 tablespoons soy sauce

1½ tablespoons rice wine or sake

1 tablespoon minced garlic

1 teaspoon sesame oil

1 tablespoon cornstarch

Sweet-and-Sour Sauce

2½ cups Chinese Chicken Broth (page 367) or water

3 tablespoons soy sauce

3 tablespoons ketchup

1½ tablespoons Chinese black vinegar or Worcestershire sauce

1½ tablespoons sugar

¼ teaspoon freshly ground black pepper

1 tablespoon corn or safflower oil

1 tablespoon minced fresh ginger

2 medium onions, peeled and thinly sliced (about 2 cups)

2 tablespoons rice wine or sake

With a heavy knife or a cleaver, trim away any excess fat from the ribs and cut them into 1½-inch lengths, cutting through the bones. (If you prefer, have the butcher do this.) Place the ribs in a bowl, add the Marinade ingredients, and toss lightly to coat. Cover with plastic wrap and let marinate in the refrigerator for at least 30 minutes.

Preheat the oven to 450°F. Remove the ribs from the refrigerator and bring to room temperature.

Combine the Sauce ingredients and stir to dissolve the sugar.

Arrange the ribs on a baking sheet lined with aluminum foil, and bake for 7 to 8 minutes on each side, or until golden brown.

While the ribs are baking, heat a large flameproof casserole or a Dutch oven, add the oil, and heat until hot. Add the minced ginger and sliced onions and stir-fry over high heat for about 30 seconds. Reduce the heat to medium, add the rice wine or sake, and stir-fry until the onions turn transparent. Add the sauce mixture and heat until boiling.

Add the ribs to the casserole and bring back to a boil. Reduce the heat to low, cover partially, and simmer for 30 minutes, turning the ribs in the sauce occasionally. Skim away any fat from the sauce, turn up the heat to high, and cook uncovered, turning the ribs occasionally, until the sauce has reduced to a syrupy glaze. Serve the ribs directly from the pot.

Serve with Tossed Bean Sprouts (page 294) and/or Rainbow Corn Salad (page 110).

WARM GARLIC
BEEF WITH FENNEL

Although Chinese chefs are masters of the stir-fry, their appetizer platters of cooked meats and vegetables are also legendary. Drawing inspiration from both traditions, I created this dish of thinly sliced grilled or broiled steak served over a bed of crisp-cooked fennel or celery slices and topped with a garlic–chile pepper sauce. Serve as an appetizer or a light main course. ● Serves 6

2 pounds London broil or flank steak

Marinade

¼ cup soy sauce

3 tablespoons rice wine or sake

2 tablespoons sugar

10 cloves garlic, lightly smashed with the flat side of a knife or a
    cleaver and peeled

6 slices fresh ginger (about the size of a quarter), lightly smashed
    with the flat side of a knife or a cleaver

6 scallions, trimmed and lightly smashed with the flat side of a knife
    or a cleaver

1½ pounds fennel bulbs with stalks or 1 pound celery, rinsed and
    trimmed

1 teaspoon sesame oil

Garlic Sauce

3 tablespoons sesame oil

1 teaspoon crushed dried red chile peppers or chile pepper flakes

¼ cup soy sauce

2 tablespoons finely minced garlic

1 tablespoon sugar

2 tablespoons Chinese Chicken Broth (page 367) or water

2 tablespoons minced scallion greens

Using a sharp knife or a cleaver, trim any fat or gristle from the beef. Holding the knife at a 45° angle to the meat, score the steak lengthwise and crosswise at 1-inch intervals, making cuts about ½ inch deep. Place the steak in a shallow dish, add the Marinade ingredients, and toss lightly to coat. Cover with plastic wrap and let sit for 1 hour at room temperature, or for 3 hours or longer in the refrigerator.

Cut each fennel bulb lengthwise in half and then cut the fennel into thin slices; if using celery, cut into thin slices. Heat a large pot of water until boiling, add the fennel slices, and cook for about 3 minutes, or until tender; if using celery, blanch for about 1 minute. Drain in a colander, refresh in cold water, and drain thoroughly. Add the sesame oil and toss to coat. Arrange on a serving platter, making a slight indentation in the center.

Prepare a fire in a charcoal grill or preheat the broiler. Place the steak about 3 inches from the source of heat and grill or broil for about 5 to 7 minutes, until medium rare. Let rest for 10 minutes, then cut across the grain into very thin slices about ⅙ inch thick. Arrange the beef slices over the fennel.

To prepare the Garlic Sauce, heat the sesame oil in a saucepan or a wok until very hot. Add the crushed chile peppers or chile flakes and stir-fry for about 5 seconds. Cover, remove from the heat, and let sit for about 1 minute. Add the remaining sauce ingredients and stir to dissolve the sugar. Pour over the beef slices and sprinkle the minced scallions on top. Serve warm or at room temperature.

Variation: Substitute boneless pork chops or boneless chicken breasts for the beef and revise the cooking time accordingly.

BEEF WITH SNOW PEAS

When I was a child, instead of craving peanut butter and jelly sandwiches, I loved leftover Chinese take-out for lunch and afternoon snacks. Beef with Snow Peas was always one of my favorites, even if it did come from a mediocre Polynesian restaurant. Years later, I learned how to prepare the authentic version in the Far East. Here is my rendition of this time-honored dish. ● Serves 6

1½ pounds London broil or flank steak

Marinade

3½ tablespoons soy sauce

1½ tablespoons rice wine or sake

1 teaspoon sesame oil

1½ tablespoons minced garlic

1 tablespoon cornstarch

Sauce

½ cup Chinese Chicken Broth (page 367) or water

6 tablespoons oyster sauce

1½ tablespoons rice wine or sake

1 teaspoon soy sauce

1 teaspoon sesame oil

1½ teaspoons cornstarch

5½ tablespoons corn or safflower oil

Minced Seasonings

1 tablespoon minced garlic

3 tablespoons minced scallions (white part only)

1½ tablespoons minced fresh ginger

1 cup thinly sliced water chestnuts, blanched in boiling water for
    15 seconds, refreshed in cold water, and drained

¾ pound snow peas, ends trimmed and veiny strings removed

1 cup 1-inch pieces scallion greens

With a sharp knife or a cleaver, trim away any fat or gristle from the beef. Cut the meat, with the grain, into strips about 1½ inches wide. Then cut the strips across the grain into very thin slices about ⅙ inch thick. Place in a bowl, add the Marinade ingredients, and toss lightly to coat. Cover with plastic wrap and let marinate for 30 minutes at room temperature.

Combine the Sauce ingredients and blend well.

Heat a wok or a skillet, add ¼ cup of the corn or safflower oil, and heat until almost smoking hot. Add the beef slices and stir-fry over high heat, stirring continuously until the meat loses its raw color and separates. Remove with a handled strainer or a slotted spoon and drain in a colander. Clean out the pan.

Reheat the pan, add the remaining 1½ tablespoons oil, and heat until very hot. Add the Minced Seasonings and stir-fry for about 10 seconds, until fragrant. Add the water chestnuts and stir-fry for about 30 seconds, until heated through. Add the snow peas and the sauce mixture and heat until thickened, stirring continuously. Add the scallions and the cooked beef, toss lightly to coat, and transfer to a serving platter. Serve immediately.

Variation: Substitute boneless chicken breasts or boneless pork loin for the beef.

SICHUAN BEEF WITH CELERY

In the original recipe for this dish, tough Chinese beef is "tenderized" by deep-frying it until dry and crisp. Since American beef is superior, I simply quickly stir-fry the marinated meat in almost no oil so that it remains tender and juicy. Then I toss it in a spicy sauce along with crunchy sliced celery and carrots. ● Serves 6

1½ pounds London broil or flank steak

Marinade

3½ tablespoons soy sauce

1½ tablespoons rice wine or sake

1 tablespoon minced garlic

1 tablespoon minced fresh ginger

1 tablespoon sugar

1 teaspoon sesame oil

1 tablespoon cornstarch

Sauce

½ cup Chinese Chicken Broth (page 367)

¼ cup soy sauce

2½ tablespoons rice wine or sake

1 tablespoon sugar

2 teaspoons Chinese black vinegar or Worcestershire sauce

¼ teaspoon freshly ground black pepper

1½ teaspoons cornstarch

5 tablespoons corn or safflower oil

2 teaspoons sesame oil

Minced Seasonings

2 tablespoons minced garlic

2 tablespoons minced scallions (white part only)

1 tablespoon minced fresh ginger

1½ teaspoons hot chili paste or crushed dried red chile peppers

2 cups celery cut into thin slices about 1½ inches long and ⅙ inch thick

1 cup finely shredded carrots

With a sharp knife or a cleaver, trim away any fat or gristle from the beef. Cut the meat, with the grain, into strips about 1½ inches wide. Then cut the strips across the grain into very thin slices about ⅙ inch thick. Place the slices in a bowl, add the Marinade ingredients, and toss lightly to coat. Cover with plastic wrap and let marinate for 30 minutes at room temperature.

Combine the Sauce ingredients and blend well.

Heat a wok or a skillet, add ¼ cup of the corn or safflower oil, and heat until very hot. Add the beef slices and stir-fry over high heat, stirring continuously, until the meat loses its raw color and separates. Remove with a handled strainer or a slotted spoon and drain in a colander. Clean out the pan.

Reheat the pan, add the remaining 1 tablespoon corn or safflower oil and the sesame oil, and heat until very hot. Add the Minced Seasonings and stir-fry for about 10 seconds, until fragrant. Add the celery and carrots and stir-fry for about 1 minute over high heat. Add the cooked beef and the sauce mixture and cook until thickened, stirring continuously to prevent any lumps. Toss lightly to coat and transfer to a serving platter. Serve immediately.

CHILE PEPPER BEEF

The traditional recipe for pepper beef might be considered tame com-pared to this spicy rendition. I like to use a combination of sweet and hot peppers (such as red bell, Italian, and jalapeño), but my selection varies with the season. For a delicious rainbow effect, try a combination of red, green, yellow, orange, and purple peppers. ● Serves 6

1½ pounds London broil or flank steak

Marinade

2½ tablespoons soy sauce

1½ tablespoons rice wine or sake

1½ tablespoons minced garlic

1 teaspoon sesame oil

1 tablespoon cornstarch

Sauce

½ cup Chinese Chicken Broth (page 367)

2½ tablespoons soy sauce

2 teaspoons sugar

1½ teaspoons sesame oil

1½ teaspoons cornstarch

5½ tablespoons corn or safflower oil

Minced Seasonings

3 tablespoons minced scallions (white part only)

2½ tablespoons fermented black beans, rinsed lightly and drained

2 tablespoons minced fresh ginger

1 tablespoon minced garlic

1 teaspoon minced jalapeño pepper

6 sweet Italian peppers, rinsed, cored, seeded, and cut into thin julienne shreds

2 red bell peppers, rinsed, cored, seeded, and cut into thin julienne shreds

2½ tablespoons rice wine or sake

Using a sharp knife or a cleaver, trim away any fat or gristle from the beef. Cut the meat, with the grain, into strips 1½ inches wide. Then cut the strips across the grain into very thin slices about ⅙ inch thick. Place the slices in a bowl, add the Marinade ingredients, and toss lightly to coat. Cover with plastic wrap and let marinate for 30 minutes at room temperature.

Combine the Sauce ingredients and blend well.

Heat a wok or a skillet, add ¼ cup of the oil, and heat until very hot. Add the beef slices and stir-fry over high heat, stirring continuously, until the meat loses its raw color and separates. Remove with a handled strainer or a slotted spoon and drain in a colander. Clean out the pan.

Reheat the pan, add the remaining 1½ tablespoons oil, and heat until very hot. Add the Minced Seasonings and stir-fry for about 10 seconds, until fragrant. Add the julienned peppers and stir-fry for about 30 seconds over high heat. Add the rice wine or sake and stir-fry for 30 seconds. Add the sauce mixture and cook until thickened, stirring continuously to prevent lumps. Add the cooked meat, toss lightly to coat, and transfer to a serving platter. Serve immediately.

Variation: Substitute 1 pound peeled and deveined medium shrimp or thinly sliced scallops for the beef. Stir-fry the shrimp until pink, or the scallops until opaque.

STIR-FRIED BEEF WITH LEEKS AND BEAN SPROUTS

Marinated beef slices contrast beautifully with quick-cooked leeks and crunchy bean sprouts. This versatile stir-fry is excellent served with steamed rice. Or, like mu shu pork, it can be rolled up in Mandarin pancakes that have been spread with a sweet bean or hoisin sauce. ● Serves 6

1½ pounds London broil or flank steak

Marinade

3½ tablespoons soy sauce

2 tablespoons rice wine or sake

1 tablespoon sugar

1½ tablespoons minced garlic

1 tablespoon minced fresh ginger

1 teaspoon sesame oil

1 tablespoon cornstarch

Sauce

3 tablespoons soy sauce

2½ tablespoons rice wine or sake

2 teaspoons sugar

1 teaspoon sesame oil

3 tablespoons Chinese Chicken Broth (page 367)

1 teaspoon cornstarch

5 tablespoons corn or safflower oil

2 tablespoons minced garlic

1½ tablespoons minced fresh ginger

4 cups finely shredded leeks (white part only), rinsed and drained

1 tablespoon rice wine or sake

4 cups bean sprouts, rinsed and drained

Using a sharp knife or a cleaver, remove any fat or gristle from the beef. Cut the beef, with the grain, into strips about 1½ inches wide. Then cut the strips across the grain into very thin slices about ⅙ inch thick. Place the slices in a bowl, add the Marinade ingredients, and toss lightly to coat. Cover with plastic wrap and let marinate for 30 minutes at room temperature.

Combine the Sauce ingredients and blend well.

Heat a wok or a skillet, add ¼ cup of the corn or safflower oil, and heat until very hot. Add the beef slices and stir-fry over high heat, stirring continuously, until the meat loses its raw color and separates. Remove with a handled strainer or a slotted spoon and drain in a colander. Clean out the pan.

Reheat the pan, add the remaining 1 tablespoon oil, and heat until very hot. Add the garlic, ginger, and leeks and stir-fry for about 1 minute over high heat. Add the rice wine or sake, then add the bean sprouts and the sauce mixture and toss lightly over high heat until the sauce thickens. Add the cooked beef, toss lightly to coat, and transfer to a serving platter. Serve immediately.

Variation: Substitute boneless pork loin or boneless chicken breasts for the beef.

CHINESE BEEF STEW

When I lived in Taipei, on raw winter evenings we often feasted on spicy beef stew served over noodles. In remembrance of those meals, I decided to experiment and created this dish, which blends Chinese and Western influences. You can serve it over noodles or rice, but slices of crusty bread are excellent for soaking up the rich gravy. ● Serves 6

 2 pounds stewing beef, such as rump or bottom round roast
 2 tablespoons soy sauce
 ½ cup all-purpose flour
 ¼ cup corn or safflower oil
10 cloves garlic, lightly smashed with the flat side of a knife or a
     cleaver and peeled
 4 slices fresh ginger (about the size of a quarter), lightly smashed
     with the flat side of a knife or a cleaver
 2 cups beef stock, heated until boiling
 1 cup water
1½ cups red wine
2½ teaspoons soy sauce
 2 star anise, lightly smashed with the flat side of a knife or a cleaver
12 small carrots, trimmed and scraped
12 small white onions, trimmed and peeled

(continued)

With a sharp knife or a cleaver, trim away any fat or gristle from the beef. Cut the meat into 1½-inch cubes, and place in a bowl. Add the soy sauce and toss lightly to coat. Place the flour in a plastic bag and add the beef cubes to the bag, tossing to coat. Transfer the beef to a plate, shaking off the excess flour.

Heat a flameproof casserole or a Dutch oven, add 2 tablespoons of the oil, and heat until hot. Add as many of the beef cubes as will fit comfortably in the pan and fry on all sides until golden brown. Remove with a slotted spoon and drain. Reheat the oil and fry the remaining beef, adding the remaining oil as necessary.

Reheat the oil, add the smashed garlic and ginger, and stir-fry for about 10 seconds, until fragrant. Add the boiling broth, the water, red wine, soy sauce, and star anise and heat until boiling. Return the meat to the pan and bring back to a boil. Reduce the heat, cover, and simmer for 45 minutes.

Add the carrots and onions and cook for 45 minutes longer, or until the meat is tender when pierced with the tip of a knife. Skim any fat off the surface of the stew, and serve.

SEARED STEAK SMOTHERED WITH GARLIC AND SHIITAKES

After a long, hard day contending with four children, my mother would often reward herself with a broiled steak smothered with mushrooms and garlic. We were given small tastes as a treat, and although I've never been a big meat lover, the flavor is firmly etched in my memory. This is my contemporary version of that luscious dish, which I like to serve with good crusty bread to mop up the fragrant juices. ● Serves 6

1½ pounds sirloin or porterhouse steak

Marinade

2½ tablespoons soy sauce

1½ tablespoons rice wine or sake

1 tablespoon sugar

1 tablespoon corn or safflower oil

Seasonings

12 cloves garlic, smashed with the flat side of a heavy knife or a
   cleaver, peeled, and very finely sliced

1 pound shiitake mushrooms, stems trimmed and finely sliced

1½ tablespoons rice wine or sake

1 tablespoon soy sauce

With a sharp knife or a cleaver, trim away any fat or gristle from the meat.
Place the meat in a bowl, add the Marinade ingredients, and toss lightly to
coat. Cover with plastic wrap and let marinate for 30 minutes at room
temperature.

Preheat the broiler or prepare a charcoal fire. If using the broiler, line a broiler
pan with aluminum foil and place the meat on the pan.

Broil or grill the steak about 3 inches from the heat source for 4 minutes on
each side. Let sit for 5 minutes before slicing, then cut the steak across the
grain into ¼-inch-thick slices and arrange on a serving platter.

While the steak is resting, heat a wok or a skillet, add the corn or safflower
oil, and heat until very hot. Add the Seasonings and stir-fry for about 30
seconds. Add the rice wine or sake and stir-fry for about 30 seconds longer.
Add the soy sauce and toss lightly. Spoon the mushrooms and juices over the
steak slices, and serve.

*Serve with Roasted Black Bean Peppers (page 303) and/or Spicy Cold-Tossed
Broccoli (page 113).*

FLASH-COOKED LAMB WITH LEEKS

A dish for those who love lamb, but especially for those who don't. In this recipe, the meat is shredded, marinated, and then stir-fried with generous amounts of leeks and garlic. The dish is also delicious prepared with boneless pork loin or flank steak. Serve the meat with a vegetable and rice, or wrap the mixture in steamed Mandarin pancakes or flour tortillas.

● Serves 6

2 pounds boneless leg of lamb (shank portion)

Marinade

2½ tablespoons soy sauce

2 tablespoons rice wine or sake

1½ teaspoons sugar

2 teaspoons minced fresh ginger

1 tablespoon cornstarch

Sauce

3 tablespoons soy sauce

2 tablespoons rice wine or sake

1 tablespoon Chinese black vinegar or Worcestershire sauce

5 tablespoons corn or safflower oil

2½ tablespoons sesame oil

8 cloves garlic, peeled and very thinly sliced

4 cups leeks (white part only) cut into fine julienne shreds

Using a sharp knife or a cleaver, trim the lamb of any fat or gristle and remove any tendons. Separate the muscles of the meat and remove any filmy skin. Cut the meat across the grain into thin slices about ⅙ inch wide and 1½ inches long. Place the slices in a bowl, add the Marinade ingredients, and toss lightly to coat. Cover with plastic wrap and let marinate for 30 minutes in the refrigerator.

Combine the Sauce ingredients and set aside.

Heat a wok or a skillet, add ¼ cup of the corn or safflower oil, and heat until very hot. (The oil must be very hot, about 400°F, to tenderize the meat.) Add the lamb slices and stir-fry over high heat, stirring continuously, until the meat loses its raw color and separates. Remove with a handled strainer or a slotted spoon and drain in a colander. Clean out the pan.

Reheat the pan, add the remaining 1 tablespoon corn or safflower oil and the sesame oil, and heat until very hot. Add the garlic and leeks and stir-fry over high heat for about 1½ minutes, until the leeks are just tender. Add the cooked lamb slices and the sauce mixture and toss lightly to coat. Transfer to a serving platter and serve immediately.

Serve with Hot-and-Sour Bok Choy (page 298) and/or Zucchini and Squash in Lemon-Cilantro Dressing (page 109).

SPICY ORANGE-GINGER LAMB

Although this is a simple stir-fry, the sauce offers a complexity of flavors and taste sensations. The palate is immediately bombarded by the hot peppers, but then the ginger and orange zest prevail, with a background of tart vinegar. Sliced water chestnuts offer a pleasing crunch and textural contrast. ● Serves 6

2 pounds boneless leg of lamb (shank portion)

Marinade

2 tablespoons soy sauce

1½ tablespoons rice wine or sake

2 tablespoons minced garlic

1 teaspoon sesame oil

1 tablespoon cornstarch

Sauce

½ cup Chinese Chicken Broth (page 367) or water

3½ tablespoons soy sauce

2 tablespoons rice wine or sake

1½ tablespoons sugar

2 teaspoons Chinese black vinegar or Worcestershire sauce

1½ teaspoons cornstarch

5 tablespoons corn or safflower oil

2 tablespoons sesame oil

3½ tablespoons very finely shredded fresh ginger

1 tablespoon grated or minced orange zest

1 teaspoon crushed dried red chile peppers or chile pepper flakes

2 cups finely sliced water chestnuts, blanched in boiling water for 15
    seconds, refreshed in cold water, and drained

2½ cups 1-inch pieces scallion greens

Using a sharp knife or a cleaver, trim the lamb of any fat or gristle and remove any tendons. Separate the muscles of the meat and remove the filmy skin. Cut the meat across the grain into thin slices about ⅛ inch wide and 1½ inches long. Place the slices in a bowl, add the Marinade ingredients, and toss lightly to coat. Cover with plastic wrap and let marinate for 30 minutes in the refrigerator.

Combine the Sauce ingredients and blend well.

Heat a wok or a skillet, add ¼ cup of the corn or safflower oil, and heat until almost smoking hot. Add the lamb slices and stir-fry over high heat, stirring continuously, until the meat loses its raw color and separates. Remove with a handled strainer or a slotted spoon and drain in a colander. Clean out the pan.

Reheat the pan, add the remaining 1 tablespoon corn or safflower oil and the sesame oil, and heat until very hot. Add the ginger, orange zest, and red peppers or pepper flakes and stir-fry for about 15 seconds, until fragrant. Add the water chestnuts and stir-fry for about 15 seconds, until heated through. Add the scallions and the sauce mixture and heat until thickened, stirring continuously. Add the cooked lamb, toss lightly to coat, and transfer to a serving platter. Serve immediately.

Serve with Glazed Green Beans (page 301) and/or "New" Potato Salad with Scallion-Oil Dressing (page 112).

Variation: Substitute boneless pork loin, boneless chicken breasts, or flank steak for the lamb.

WARM LAMB SALAD

Tender slices of marinated lamb are tossed with leafy spinach in a warm sesame-cilantro vinaigrette. This dish is excellent as an appetizer or, served with steamed or crusty bread, as a light but filling entrée. For a change of pace, try making the salad with pork or beef. ● Serves 6

1¾ pounds boneless leg of lamb (shank portion)

Marinade

2 tablespoons soy sauce

1 tablespoon rice wine or sake

1 tablespoon minced fresh ginger

1 tablespoon minced garlic

1 teaspoon sesame oil

1 tablespoon cornstarch

Vinaigrette

⅓ cup soy sauce

3 tablespoons clear rice vinegar

2 tablespoons sesame oil

1 tablespoon sugar

5 tablespoons corn or safflower oil

1 pound (or 2 ten-ounce packages) fresh spinach, stems trimmed, rinsed, and drained

1 teaspoon minced garlic

2 tablespoons rice wine or sake

¼ teaspoon salt

1½ cups finely shredded carrots

3 tablespoons minced cilantro (or fresh coriander)

Using a sharp knife or a cleaver, trim the lamb of any fat or gristle and remove any tendons. Separate the muscles of the meat and remove any filmy skin. Cut the meat across the grain into thin slices about ⅛ inch wide and 1½ inches long. Place the slices in a bowl, add the Marinade ingredients, and toss lightly to coat. Cover with plastic wrap and let marinate for 30 minutes in the refrigerator. Combine the Vinaigrette ingredients.

Heat a wok or a skillet, add ¼ cup of the oil, and heat until very hot. Add the lamb slices and stir-fry over high heat, stirring continuously, until the meat loses its raw color and separates. Remove with a handled strainer or a slotted spoon and drain in a colander. Clean out the pan.

Reheat the pan, add the remaining 1 tablespoon oil, and heat until nearly smoking. Add the spinach, garlic, rice wine or sake, and salt and toss lightly over high heat until the spinach is slightly wilted. Remove with a handled strainer or a slotted spoon and place on a serving platter, making a slight indentation in the center. Sprinkle the shredded carrots over the spinach, leaving a green border around the outside, and arrange the cooked lamb in the center.

Reheat the pan, add the vinaigrette mixture, and heat until boiling. Add the cilantro and toss lightly. Pour the hot dressing over the salad, and serve warm.

LEG OF LAMB WITH GARLIC AND SWEET BEAN SAUCE

Sweet bean sauce and garlic perfectly complement the flavor of lamb. Here a mixture of the two is used as a marinade for a boned leg so the meat becomes infused with the seasonings. Then while the lamb cooks, the flavors mingle further, resulting in a delicious, natural gravy. Serve this hot or cold, with a spicy vegetable dish. The sliced lamb is also delicious stuffed into Mandarin pancakes or flour tortillas. ● Serves 6

1 3½- to 4-pound boned and rolled leg of lamb (shank portion)

Seasonings

2 tablespoons minced garlic

1½ tablespoons minced fresh ginger

3 tablespoons sweet bean sauce (see Note)

Basting Mixture

¾ cup rice wine or sake

⅓ cup water

1 tablespoon soy sauce

Using a sharp knife, make slits all over the surface of the lamb. Place in a bowl. Combine the Seasonings and rub the mixture all over the lamb and into the slits. Cover with plastic wrap and let marinate for 1 hour at room temperature. (Or refrigerate and marinate for up to 3 hours, but bring the lamb to room temperature before roasting.)

Preheat the oven to 400°F.

Combine the Basting Mixture ingredients. Place the lamb in a roasting pan and roast for 10 minutes. Pour the basting mixture over the lamb, baste generously, and roast for 30 minutes. Baste generously again and roast for 30 minutes longer for medium rare (145°F), or 45 minutes longer for well done (160°F). Let stand for 15 minutes before carving.

Carve the lamb into thin slices and serve.

Serve with Potato Pancakes (page 302) and/or Hot-and-Sour Cabbage Slaw (page 108).

Note: If sweet bean sauce is unavailable, you can substitute hoisin sauce.

CHINESE
BARBECUE

Most Americans are surprised to learn that grilling is popular in China. After all, Chinese cooking is usually defined in terms of stir-frying and steaming, but as a trip to the Far East will confirm, the Chinese relish a variety of grilled meats and vegetables.

On the streets of Beijing, *shashlik* (skewered grilled lamb), seasoned with a fine dusting of five-spice powder, is a staple snack. Mongolian barbecue, a specialty enjoyed in the north, is a combination of thinly sliced meats and vegetables grilled quickly over a charcoal brazier. And in Taipei, street vendors carry portable grills strapped onto pushcarts and sell roasted corn on the cob cooked over coals.

According to legend, a Chinese man by the name of Sui Ren invented grilling in prehistoric times. As the story goes, he noticed that his friends were suffering from intestinal problems, which he attributed to the consumption of raw meat. To prove his theory, he built a fire and roasted some meat over the coals. Everyone enjoyed the food—and from then on, their health markedly improved.

Chinese barbecue dishes are not unlike their Western counterparts. Marinades and spice pastes are regularly used to tenderize food and provide flavor and color. A rice wine–based mixture with ginger and sesame oil is often used to remove any excessively fishy flavor from seafood. And with meats, soy sauce with a touch of sugar gives the cooked food an attractive glaze.

The majority of the grilled dishes in this chapter are cooked over a medium-hot fire. The surest way to gauge the temperature of a charcoal fire is by looking at the color of the coals: A hot fire has a deep red color and a dusting of white ash. A medium fire has a more orange color and a solid coating of gray ash. A low fire has a very low glow and is mostly reduced to gray ash.

The same rules that apply to stir-frying can be used when barbecuing: Organization is the key to success. Have all the ingredients at hand and the accompanying sauces or relishes ready to be served before you start cooking.

GRILLED PEPPERS
IN GARLIC DRESSING

Smoky grilled peppers are delicious on their own, but a garlicky sesame oil dressing spiked with a bit of hot chili paste accentuates their sweet flavor. Serve these as an appetizer or a relish for any grilled meat or seafood, or, for a nontraditional treat, spread on slices of grilled or toasted Italian bread. ● Serves 6

3 red bell peppers, rinsed, cored, seeded, and halved lengthwise

3 yellow bell peppers, rinsed, cored, seeded, and halved lengthwise

3 green bell peppers, rinsed, cored, seeded, and halved lengthwise

2 tablespoons sesame oil

Garlic Dressing

6 tablespoons soy sauce

2½ tablespoons rice wine or sake

1½ tablespoons puréed garlic (chopped to a smooth paste with a sharp knife or a cleaver)

2 teaspoons sugar

1 tablespoon sesame oil

1 teaspoon hot chili paste (optional)

Prepare a medium-hot fire for grilling, and place the grill about 3 inches above the coals.

Brush the inside of the peppers with the sesame oil. Arrange the peppers, oiled side down, on the grill and cook for about 6 to 7 minutes, or until tender and charred at the edges. Then turn the peppers over and cook for about 1 minute longer, or until slightly browned. Place in a paper bag, close securely, and allow to cool. The peppers will steam in their own juices, making it easy to peel them. Pull the skins off the red and yellow peppers, but leave the skin on the green.

Combine the Garlic Dressing ingredients, stirring to dissolve the sugar. Cut the peppers into thin julienne strips about ¼ inch wide and place in a bowl. Add the dressing and toss lightly to coat. Let marinate for about 30 minutes before serving.

GRILLED ZUCCHINI AND SQUASH WITH PEANUT DIP

Spicy peanut sauce is an incredibly versatile mixture that can be used for dressing noodles, seafood, or chicken. Made with less broth than usual, the same sauce becomes an all-purpose dip for cooked and raw vegetables such as peppers, carrots, snow peas, celery, or grilled zucchini and squash. ● Serves 6

3 medium zucchini (about 1¼ pounds), rinsed and ends trimmed

3 medium summer squash (about 1¼ pounds), rinsed and ends trimmed

2 tablespoons sesame oil

Peanut Dip

1 cup smooth peanut butter, plus more if necessary

2½ tablespoons soy sauce

2 tablespoons rice wine or sake

2 tablespoons sugar

2 tablespoons Chinese black vinegar or Worcestershire sauce

2 tablespoons sesame oil

1 tablespoon minced garlic

1 tablespoon minced fresh ginger

1½ teaspoons hot chili paste, or to taste

7 tablespoons Chinese Chicken Broth (page 367) or water, plus more if necessary

2 tablespoons minced scallion greens

Prepare a medium-low fire for grilling, and place the grill about 3 inches above the coals.

Cut the zucchini and squash lengthwise into quarters, then cut each quarter crosswise into "finger-size" pieces about 3 inches long. Brush with the sesame oil. Place skin side down on the grill and cook for about 3 to 4 minutes, or until golden brown. Turn over and cook for 3 to 4 minutes longer. Arrange on a serving platter in separate piles, alternating piles of zucchini and summer squash.

To prepare the Peanut Dip, combine the peanut butter, soy sauce, and rice wine or sake in a blender or a food processor fitted with a steel blade and blend until smooth. Add the remaining ingredients one at a time, blending well after each addition. If the sauce seems too thick, add a little more chicken broth or water; if it seems too thin, add more peanut butter. Transfer to a bowl, sprinkle with the minced scallion greens, and serve as a dipping sauce for the grilled vegetables.

Note: The sauce can be prepared 2 to 3 days in advance, covered, and refrigerated. If it separates slightly, stir until smooth. Sprinkle with the scallions just before serving.

HOT-AND-SOUR EGGPLANT SALAD

Oriental and Western influences converge in this recipe, as diced grilled eggplant is tossed with red pepper bits, scallion greens, and a traditional Sichuanese sesame oil dressing. The "hot" comes from the crushed chile peppers that season the oil and the "sour" from the Chinese black vinegar. All combine to make an unusual and delectable salad. Serve this as a side dish, or stuff into pita bread and serve as an appetizer or a light entrée.

● Serves 6

> 2 medium eggplant (about 2½ pounds), ends trimmed and cut
>   lengthwise into ½-inch-thick slices
>
> 2 teaspoons salt
>
> **Hot-and-Sour Dressing**
>
> ¼ cup sesame oil
>
> 1 teaspoon crushed dried red chile peppers or chile pepper flakes
>
> 6 tablespoons soy sauce
>
> 3½ tablespoons rice wine or sake
>
> 1½ tablespoons Chinese black vinegar or Worcestershire sauce
>
> 1½ tablespoons sugar
>
> 2 tablespoons minced fresh ginger
>
> 2 tablespoons minced garlic
>
> 1 tablespoon sesame oil
>
> ½ cup diced red bell pepper
>
> 1 cup ¼-inch-slices scallion greens

Sprinkle the eggplant slices lightly with the salt and let drain on paper towels for 30 minutes. Pat dry and brush off any remaining salt.

Meanwhile, prepare the Hot-and-Sour Dressing: Heat the sesame oil in a saucepan until very hot. Add the crushed red peppers or pepper flakes, cover, and remove from the heat. Let sit for 10 minutes, then add the remaining ingredients and stir to dissolve the sugar.

Prepare a medium-low fire for grilling, place the grill about 3 inches above the coals.

Brush the eggplant slices with the sesame oil. Arrange the eggplant slices on the grill and cook for about 3 to 4 minutes on each side, until tender and deep golden brown. Let cool.

Cut the eggplant into ¼-inch dice and place in a bowl. Add the red pepper, scallions, and dressing and toss lightly to coat. Let marinate for about 20 minutes. Serve at room temperature or chilled.

BARBECUED TOFU
WITH PEPPERS AND SCALLIONS

Tofu naturally absorbs the flavors of other foods. If pressed to remove its own liquid, it becomes even more of a sponge. In this recipe, tofu acquires extraordinary flavor when marinated in a spicy soy-based mixture and then grilled with scallions and bell peppers, until golden on all sides. Serve these kabobs hot off the fire or at room temperature, with stir-fried rice or noodles. ● Serves 6

1½ pounds firm or extra-firm tofu

Marinade

2 tablespoons sesame oil

¼ cup soy sauce

3 tablespoons rice wine or sake

2 tablespoons minced scallions

1 tablespoon minced garlic

1 tablespoon minced fresh ginger

1½ red bell peppers, rinsed, cored, and seeded

3 scallions (white part only), cut into 1½-inch lengths

3 tablespoons hoisin sauce

1 tablespoon ketchup

2 tablespoons water

6 eight-inch bamboo skewers, soaked in water for 1 hour

2 tablespoons corn or safflower oil

(continued)

Wrap the tofu in paper towels or a dishcloth and place a heavy weight (such as a skillet) on top. Let drain for 1 hour.

Cut the tofu lengthwise into thirds and crosswise in half. Place in a bowl. Combine the Marinade ingredients and add to the tofu. Let marinate for at least 1 hour, turning occasionally.

Cut the red peppers into 12 squares. Thread a scallion length, a piece of bell pepper, tofu cube, and then another pepper piece and scallion section onto each skewer. Brush generously with the marinade and set aside.

Prepare a medium-low fire for grilling, and place the grill about 3 inches above the coals. Thoroughly oil the grill to prevent the tofu from sticking. Arrange the skewered tofu and vegetables on the grill and cook for about 5 to 6 minutes on each side, or until the tofu is golden brown, turning once. Meanwhile, combine the hoisin sauce, ketchup, and water in a saucepan and heat slightly.

Brush the tofu skewers liberally on all sides with the hoisin mixture, and serve hot or at room temperature.

TERIYAKI MUSHROOMS

Fresh shiitake mushrooms are meaty enough to hold a nice smoky flavor, which contrasts beautifully with a ginger dipping sauce. If shiitakes are unavailable, substitute large white or cremini mushrooms. The teriyaki sauce is also delicious with other grilled vegetables, such as bell peppers, summer squash, zucchini, leeks, onions, and eggplant. ● Serves 6

24 medium to large shiitake mushrooms (about 1½ pounds)
12 scallions, trimmed and cut into 1½-inch lengths
2 tablespoons sesame oil

Teriyaki Sauce

6 tablespoons soy sauce
¼ cup rice wine or sake
2 tablespoons sugar
1½ tablespoons minced fresh ginger

About 16 to 20 ten-inch bamboo skewers, soaked in water for 1 hour

Trim the stem ends of the mushrooms, rinse lightly, and drain thoroughly. If the mushroom caps are large, cut in half or into quarters. Thread 2 mushroom pieces and 3 scallion pieces alternately onto each skewer, starting and ending with scallions. Arrange the skewered vegetables on a cookie sheet and brush with the sesame oil.

Prepare a medium-low fire for grilling, and place the grill 3 to 4 inches from the heat. Arrange the skewered mushrooms and scallions on the grill and cook, turning frequently, for about 4 to 5 minutes, or until golden brown and crisp at the edges. Arrange on a serving platter.

Meanwhile, combine the Teriyaki Sauce ingredients in a saucepan and heat until boiling. Stir to dissolve the sugar and transfer to a serving bowl.

Drizzle a little sauce over the skewers, and serve the rest on the side for dipping.

GRILLED SHRIMP SALAD

In this unusual recipe, the shrimp is first marinated in a feisty teriyaki-type sauce, then grilled and arranged on a crisp bed of vegetables. The tart vinaigrette ties all of the components together. This dish makes a superb appetizer or a main-dish entrée. ● Serves 6

1¾ pounds medium (16 to 20) shelled shrimp, peeled, deveined, rinsed, and drained

Marinade

¼ cup water

¼ cup soy sauce

¼ cup rice wine or sake

3 tablespoons sugar

2 tablespoons minced fresh ginger

1 tablespoon sesame oil

1½ teaspoons crushed red pepper flakes, or to taste

1 tablespoon cornstarch

2 tablespoons water

Vinaigrette

2 tablespoons soy sauce

1½ tablespoons clear rice vinegar

1 tablespoon sesame oil

½ tablespoon sugar

10 ten-inch bamboo skewers, soaked in water for 1 hour

1½ teaspoons corn or safflower oil

1 cup finely sliced leeks

1 cup diced red bell peppers

¾ pound snow peas, ends trimmed and stringy veins removed

3 tablespoons finely chopped or crushed dry-roasted peanuts (optional)

Place the shrimp in a bowl and set aside. Combine the Marinade ingredients and stir to dissolve the sugar. Combine the cornstarch and water and stir to blend.

Place the marinade in a saucepan and heat until boiling. Add the cornstarch thickener and boil for 1 to 2 minutes, stirring to prevent any lumps from forming. Let cool to room temperature and add to the shrimp. Toss lightly to coat.

Combine the Vinaigrette ingredients and stir to dissolve the sugar. Thread the shrimp onto the bamboo skewers and brush with the marinade.

Prepare a medium-hot fire for grilling. Place the grill about 3 inches over the coals, brush generously with corn or safflower oil, and heat.

Arrange the skewered shrimp on the grill and grill for about 2½ minutes on each side, or until cooked through. Remove and let cool slightly.

Meanwhile, heat a wok or a skillet, add the corn or safflower oil, and heat until very hot. Add the leeks and stir-fry over high heat for 30 seconds. Add the red peppers and toss lightly for about 1 minute. Add the snow peas and stir-fry for 1 minute. Add the vinaigrette and stir-fry for 30 seconds. Remove and mound onto a platter, forming a slight well in the center. Remove the shrimp from the skewers and arrange over the vegetables. Sprinkle the peanuts on top (if using). Serve immediately.

GRILLED SHRIMP WITH SPICY SALSA

This fresh sauce of scallions, garlic, tomatoes, and cilantro is a delicious accompaniment to either grilled shrimp or squid. It is at its most flavorful during peak tomato season; in the cooler months, I use plum tomatoes. Serve this dish on its own as an appetizer, or, with a vegetable and rice or noodles, as a light main course. ● Serves 6

1½ pounds medium (16/20 count) shrimp, peeled, deveined, rinsed, and drained

Marinade

2 tablespoons rice wine or sake

1 teaspoon sesame oil

1 tablespoon minced fresh ginger

¼ teaspoon salt

Spicy Salsa

1 to 2 jalapeño peppers (to taste), cored and seeded

1 tablespoon minced garlic

1 cup minced scallions

1 pound ripe tomatoes, rinsed, drained, cored, and cut into chunks

Juice of 1 lemon

½ cup cilantro (fresh coriander), stems removed and coarsely chopped

½ teaspoon salt, or more to taste

6 ten-inch bamboo skewers, soaked in water for 1 hour

1½ cups shredded leaf lettuce (optional)

Place the shrimp in a bowl. Combine the Marinade ingredients, add to the shrimp, and toss lightly to coat. Cover with plastic wrap and refrigerate for 30 minutes.

Meanwhile, prepare the Salsa: Combine the jalapeño peppers and garlic in a food processor fitted with a steel blade or in a blender and chop to a fine paste. Add the minced scallions and pulse to blend. Add the tomatoes and pulse until finely chopped. Transfer to a serving bowl and stir in the lemon juice, chopped cilantro, and salt. Taste for seasoning, and add more salt if necessary. Cover with plastic wrap and let sit for 30 minutes at room temperature, then refrigerate until ready to serve.

Thread the shrimp lengthwise onto the skewers, being careful not to push them too close together.

Prepare a medium-hot fire for grilling, and place the grill about 3 inches above the coals. Arrange the skewered shrimp on the grill and cook for about 3 to 4 minutes on each side, until cooked through.

Arrange the lettuce (if using) on a platter or individual serving plates. Place the skewers of shrimp on top and spoon the salsa over. Serve hot, at room temperature, or chilled.

Serve with Garlic Broccoli (page 296) and/or Rainbow Corn Salad (page 110).

SWEET-AND-SOUR SCALLOPS

On a recent trip to Beijing, I tasted tiny scallops that had been lightly stir-fried in a sweet-and-sour sauce. The pungent seasonings accentuated their natural sweetness. This is my version of that memorable dish. I serve these either as an entrée or, on their own, as an unusual appetizer.

● Serves 6

1½ pounds sea scallops, rinsed lightly and drained (see Note)

Marinade

3 tablespoons rice wine or sake

2 teaspoons minced fresh ginger

½ teaspoon sesame oil

½ teaspoon salt

9 to 10 eight-inch bamboo skewers, soaked in water for 1 hour

1½ tablespoons sesame oil

Sweet-and-Sour Glaze

¼ cup ketchup

¼ cup brown sugar

2 tablespoons clear rice vinegar

1 tablespoon soy sauce

1 tablespoon sesame oil

1 tablespoon minced garlic

1 teaspoon minced fresh ginger

Place the scallops in a bowl. Combine the Marinade ingredients, add to the scallops, and toss to coat. Cover with plastic wrap and refrigerate for 30 minutes.

Pour 2 cups water into a medium saucepan and heat until boiling. Add the scallops, with the marinade, bring back to a boil, and cook for 30 seconds. Drain. Thread the scallops onto the bamboo skewers, and brush with the sesame oil. Combine the Glaze ingredients in a saucepan and set aside.

Prepare a medium-hot fire for grilling, place the grill about 3 inches above the coals. Arrange the skewered scallops on the grill and cook for about 2 to 3 minutes per side, until cooked through. Meanwhile, heat the glaze mixture until warm.

Brush the scallops liberally with the glaze. Remove from the skewers and serve hot or at room temperature.

Serve with Vegetarian Roll-Ups (page 306) and/or Black Bean Tofu with Vegetables (page 316).

Note: You may substitute bay scallops. If so, reduce the grilling time to 1½ minutes per side.

GRILLED
BLACK BEAN HALIBUT

Halibut is a firm, meaty fish that takes nicely to the grill. In this recipe, the ginger-scallion marinade adds a delicate taste to the fish, and the pungent black bean and garlic sauce further accentuates its inherent sweetness. ● Serves 6

6 halibut steaks, about 1 inch thick and about 6 ounces each, rinsed and drained

Marinade

⅓ cup rice wine or sake
1 tablespoon minced fresh ginger
1 tablespoon minced scallions
½ teaspoon salt
2 tablespoons sesame oil

Sauce

1 cup Chinese Chicken Broth (page 367)
2 tablespoons soy sauce
2 tablespoons rice wine or sake
1½ teaspoons sugar
2 teaspoons cornstarch

1 tablespoon corn or safflower oil

Seasonings

3 tablespoons fermented black beans, rinsed and drained
1½ tablespoons minced garlic

3 tablespoons minced scallion greens

Place the fish steaks in a bowl. Combine the Marinade ingredients, add to the fish, and toss to coat. Cover with plastic wrap and marinate for 20 minutes at room temperature, turning several times in the marinade.

Combine the Sauce ingredients and blend well.

Prepare a medium-hot fire for grilling, and place the grill about 3 inches above the coals. Arrange the fish steaks on the grill and cook for about 5 to 6 minutes on each side, or until the flesh is opaque all the way through. Transfer to individual serving dishes.

While the fish is cooking, heat the oil in a wok or a skillet until very hot. Add the Seasonings and stir-fry over high heat until fragrant, about 10 seconds. Add the sauce mixture and cook, stirring continuously, until thickened. Transfer to a serving bowl.

Spoon some of the sauce over each fish steak. Sprinkle with the minced scallions and serve immediately.

Serve with Stir-Fried Spinach (page 308) and/or Tossed Bean Sprouts (page 294).

Variation: Substitute any firm-fleshed fish, such as swordfish steaks or cusk or cod fillets, for the halibut.

GRILLED SALMON WITH SWEET-AND-SOUR CUCUMBER RELISH

In this unusual dish, the crisp sweet-and-sour cucumbers are a superb contrast—both in flavor and texture—to the grilled salmon steaks. The cucumber relish is also excellent with other grilled seafood or meats.

● Serves 6

> 6 Kirby or pickling cucumbers or 1 seedless cucumber, rinsed and drained
> ½ cup sugar
> ½ cup clear rice vinegar
> 1½ teaspoons minced fresh ginger
> ½ teaspoon salt
> 6 salmon steaks, about 1 inch thick and about 6 ounces each, rinsed and drained

> **Marinade**
> ¼ cup rice wine or sake
> 1 tablespoon minced fresh ginger
> 1 tablespoon minced scallions
> 1 teaspoon salt
> 2 tablespoons sesame oil

Trim the ends of the cucumbers, slice them lengthwise in half, remove the seeds, and cut crosswise into paper-thin slices. Place in a bowl. Combine the sugar, rice vinegar, ginger, and salt and stir until the sugar dissolves. Add to the cucumbers, toss lightly, and cover with plastic wrap. Let marinate for at least 30 minutes, or longer if possible, in the refrigerator, tossing occasionally.

Place the fish steaks in a bowl. Combine the Marinade ingredients, add to the fish, and toss to coat. Cover with plastic wrap and let marinate for 30 minutes at room temperature, turning several times.

Prepare a very hot fire for grilling, and place the grill about 3 inches above the coals. Arrange the fish steaks on the grill and cook for about 4 to 5 minutes on each side, basting occasionally with the marinade, until the fish is opaque all the way through. Transfer to serving dishes. Serve the cucumber relish on the side or spoon it over the fish.

Variation: Substitute halibut steaks or cusk fillets for the salmon.

SPICY CUSK

This dish was inspired by my friend and colleague Chris Schlesinger, chef and coauthor of *The Thrill of the Grill* (William Morrow, 1990), who routinely seasons his grilled meats and seafood with a spice paste. The seasonings vary depending on the food and the dish. I like to use a combination of ground ginger, ground coriander, five-spice powder, and chili paste with firm, meaty cusk. If it is unavailable, substitute cod or another firm whitefish, such as halibut or swordfish. ● **Serves 6**

2 pounds cusk fillets, about 1 inch thick, cut into 6 portions, rinsed, and drained

Spice Rub

1 teaspoon ground ginger

1 teaspoon ground coriander

1 teaspoon five-spice powder (see page 5)

½ teaspoon hot chili paste

½ tablespoon sugar

1 tablespoon rice wine or sake

1 tablespoon sesame oil

Sauce

¼ cup soy sauce

1 tablespoon sugar

2 tablespoons freshly squeezed lemon juice

1 tablespoon sesame oil

Place the fillets in a nonreactive baking dish. Combine the Spice Rub ingredients and rub the mixture all over the fillets. Cover with plastic wrap and let marinate at room temperature for 30 minutes.

Combine the Sauce ingredients and set aside.

Prepare a medium-hot fire for grilling, and place the grill about 3 inches above the coals. Arrange the fillets on the grill and cook for about 4 to 5 minutes on each side, or until the fish is opaque all the way through but not dry. Pour the sauce over the grilled fish and serve.

Serve with Saucy Eggplant (page 300) and/or Spicy Cucumber Spears (page 107).

BARBECUED SWORDFISH WITH CILANTRO DRESSING

In this dish, meaty swordfish is drenched in a delicate cilantro dressing while still hot from the grill. For those who are not fond of cilantro's musky flavor, you can substitute scallion greens for the pungent herb.

● Serves 6

2½ pounds swordfish, cut into 6 steaks about 1 inch thick, rinsed, and drained

Marinade

¼ cup rice wine or sake

1 tablespoon minced fresh ginger

2 tablespoons soy sauce

1 teaspoon sesame oil

Cilantro Dressing

3 tablespoons Chinese Chicken Broth (page 367) or water

3 tablespoons soy sauce

1 tablespoon sugar

2 tablespoons sesame oil

1½ tablespoons rice wine or sake

3½ tablespoons chopped cilantro (fresh coriander)

Place the fish steaks in a bowl. Combine the Marinade ingredients, add to the fish, and toss to coat. Cover with plastic wrap and marinate for 20 minutes at room temperature, turning several times in the marinade.

Combine the Cilantro Dressing ingredients and set aside.

Prepare a medium-hot fire for grilling, and place the grill about 3 inches above the coals. Arrange the fish fillets on the grill and cook for about 4 to 5 minutes on each side, or until the flesh is opaque all the way through. Transfer to serving dishes, spoon the dressing over the fish, and serve immediately.

Serve with Hot-and-Sour Bok Choy (page 298) and/or Cold-Tossed Garlicky Green Beans (page 114).

GRILLED TURKEY
IN LETTUCE PACKAGES

Turkey cutlets are a natural choice for grilling. The lean meat readily absorbs spicy marinades, and the cutlets cook quickly over hot coals. In this recipe the grilled meat is wrapped inside lettuce leaves seasoned with hoisin sauce. You can also use steamed Mandarin pancakes or flour tortillas, adding a sprinkling of shredded scallion greens for flavor. I serve this as an appetizer or as an entrée, with a vegetable and noodles or rice.

● Serves 6

1½ pounds boneless turkey cutlets, about ¼ inch thick

Marinade

3 tablespoons soy sauce

2½ tablespoons rice wine or sake

2 teaspoons sugar

1½ tablespoons minced fresh ginger

2 teaspoons minced garlic

½ teaspoon crushed dried red chile peppers or chile pepper flakes

3 tablespoons sesame oil

¾ cup hoisin sauce

2 teaspoons soy sauce

3 tablespoons water

2 heads Boston lettuce, separated into leaves, rinsed, and drained

12 to 14 ten-inch bamboo skewers, soaked in water for 1 hour

Using a sharp knife or a cleaver, trim away any fat or sinew from the turkey. Place in a bowl. Combine the Marinade ingredients, add to the turkey, and toss to coat. Cover with plastic wrap and let marinate for 1 hour at room temperature, or longer in the refrigerator.

Combine the hoisin sauce, soy sauce, and water in a saucepan and heat until reduced and thickened. Transfer to a serving bowl and set aside. With a large knife or a cleaver, trim away the stems from the lettuce leaves and lightly press each leaf with the flat side of the knife or cleaver to flatten it. Arrange in a basket or a serving dish. Loosely thread the cutlets onto the skewers, making sure the meat lies flat.

(continued)

Prepare a medium-hot fire for grilling, and place the grill about 3 inches above the coals. Arrange the turkey cutlets on the grill and cook for about 2 to 3 minutes on each side, or until the meat is opaque all the way through. Carefully take the meat off the skewers, and cut crosswise into pieces about 3 inches long. Arrange on a platter.

To serve, spread a dollop of the hoisin sauce mixture over a lettuce leaf and arrange a turkey piece on top. Roll up and eat.

Serve with Broccoli in Oyster Sauce (page 295) and/or Pickled Carrots (page 299).

Variation: Substitute boneless chicken breasts for the turkey.

FOUR-SPICE
CHICKEN DRUMSTICKS

My son, a very fussy eater, usually shuns meat, but even he relents when he smells the aroma of these delectable drumsticks. For optimum flavor, marinate them overnight so that the chicken has time to absorb all the piquant seasonings. ● Serves 6

Four-Spice Rub

1½ teaspoons ground ginger

1½ teaspoons ground coriander

1½ teaspoons ground allspice

1 teaspoon ground cinnamon

1 teaspoon crushed dried red chile peppers or chile pepper flakes

½ teaspoon salt

¼ cup rice wine or sake

3 tablespoons soy sauce

3 tablespoons sesame oil

1½ tablespoons sugar

1 tablespoon minced garlic

1 tablespoon minced fresh ginger

18 chicken drumsticks, rinsed and drained

To prepare the Spice Rub, combine the ginger, coriander, allspice, cinnamon, crushed red peppers or pepper flakes, and salt in a dry skillet or a wok and stir-fry over medium heat until fragrant, about 2 to 3 minutes. Let cool. Add the remaining ingredients and mix to a paste. Place the drumsticks in a bowl and rub all over with the spice paste. Cover with plastic wrap and refrigerate for at least 3 hours, or preferably overnight.

Prepare a medium-hot fire for grilling, and place the grill about 3 inches above the coals. Arrange the drumsticks on the grill, cover, and cook for about 10 to 12 minutes, turning several times so that they cook evenly. To test for doneness, pierce the thickest part of a drumstick with a sharp knife; the juice should run clear and the meat should be opaque all the way through. Serve immediately.

Serve with Spicy Snow Peas and Water Chestnuts (page 304) and/or Hot-and-Sour Cabbage Slaw (page 108).

GINGER CHICKEN

I often use an all-purpose marinade of soy sauce, rice wine, and brown sugar, enlivening the flavor by adding different flavorings such as ginger, garlic, or five-spice powder. It is as delicious with turkey, shrimp, and fish fillets as with chicken. ● Serves 6

1½ pounds boneless skinless chicken breasts

Marinade

½ cup soy sauce

⅓ cup rice wine or sake

3 tablespoons light brown sugar

1 tablespoon sesame oil

3 tablespoons minced fresh ginger

¼ teaspoon freshly ground black pepper

24 1½-inch-long pieces scallions (white part only)

12 eight-inch bamboo skewers, soaked in water for 1 hour

Using a sharp knife, trim away any fat or sinew from the chicken. Cut into 1-inch cubes and place in a bowl. Combine the Marinade ingredients, add to the chicken, and toss lightly to coat. Cover with plastic wrap and refrigerate for at least 1 hour, turning occasionally.

Thread the chicken and scallion pieces onto the skewers, starting and ending each skewer with a scallion section.

Prepare a medium-hot fire for grilling, and place the grill about 3 inches above the coals. Arrange the skewered chicken on the grill and cook for about 4 to 5 minutes on each side, basting with the marinade, until cooked through and golden at the edges. Arrange on a serving plate, and serve immediately.

Serve with Potato Pancakes (page 302) and/or Wilted Cabbage Salad (page 105).

BEEF AND
VEGETABLE KABOBS

A simple mixture of soy sauce, sugar, and minced garlic truly enhances the flavor of grilled beef or lamb. When the meat is cooked over coals, the marinade forms a light glaze, sealing in all the juices. ● Serves 6

1½ pounds boneless sirloin steak

Marinade

⅓ cup soy sauce

¼ cup rice wine or sake

2 tablespoons sugar

1 teaspoon sesame oil

1½ tablespoons minced garlic

12 small white boiling onions

12 large white mushrooms, trimmed and cleaned

3 large red and/or yellow bell peppers, rinsed, cored, seeded, and cut into 1-inch squares

12 ten-inch bamboo skewers, soaked in water for 1 hour

Using a sharp knife or a cleaver, trim away any fat or gristle from the meat. Cut the beef into twenty-four 1- to 1½-inch cubes and place in a bowl. Combine the Marinade ingredients, add to the meat, and toss lightly to coat. Cover with plastic wrap and refrigerate for at least 1 hour.

Meanwhile, heat 2 quarts of water until boiling. Add the onions and cook for about 3 minutes, or until barely tender. Drain in a colander and refresh under cold running water. Remove the skins.

Thread the meat, onions, mushrooms, and peppers alternately onto the skewers, starting and ending with peppers. Reserve the marinade.

Prepare a medium-hot fire for grilling, and place the grill about 3 inches above the coals. Arrange the skewered meat and vegetables on the grill and cook for 3 to 4 minutes on each side, or until medium-rare, basting occasionally with the reserved marinade. Arrange on a serving platter and serve immediately.

Serve with Spicy Bean Sprouts (page 292) and/or "New" Potato Salad with Scallion-Oil Dressing (page 112).

SEARED SIRLOIN
WITH OYSTER SAUCE

At Carl's Pagoda, a famous Cantonese-American restaurant in Boston's Chinatown, the house specialty is a fried steak topped with oyster sauce and surrounded by stir-fried vegetables. Inspired by that classic, I developed this recipe for thinly sliced sirloin served on a bed of crisp stir-fried snow peas. My friends agree that this version rivals Carl's original. Serve with crusty bread to mop up the succulent juices. ● Serves 6

1½ pounds boneless sirloin steak, about 1¼ inches thick

Marinade

¼ cup soy sauce

2 tablespoons sugar

1½ tablespoons minced garlic

2 teaspoons sesame oil

Sauce

1 cup Chinese Chicken Broth (page 367)

3½ tablespoons oyster sauce

1½ tablespoons rice wine or sake

1½ teaspoons sugar

1 teaspoon soy sauce

1 teaspoon sesame oil

1½ teaspoons cornstarch

1 tablespoon corn or safflower oil

1 pound snow peas, ends trimmed and veiny strings removed

1½ tablespoons rice wine or sake

¼ teaspoon salt

Minced Seasonings

1½ tablespoons minced scallions (white part only)

1 tablespoon minced fresh ginger

Using a sharp knife or a cleaver, trim any fat or gristle from the meat. Place the steak in a baking pan. Combine the Marinade ingredients and rub the mixture all over the steak. Cover with plastic wrap and let sit for 1 hour at room temperature.

Combine the Sauce ingredients and blend well.

Prepare a medium-hot fire for grilling, and place the grill about 3 inches above the coals. Place the steak on the grill and cook for about 6 to 7 minutes per side, or until well browned and crusty. Remove and let sit for 5 minutes.

Meanwhile, heat a wok or a skillet, add ½ tablespoon of the oil, and heat until very hot. Add the snow peas, rice wine or sake, and salt and stir-fry over high heat for about 2 minutes, until the peas are crisp-tender. Transfer to a serving plate, making an indentation in the center.

Reheat the wok or skillet, add the remaining ½ tablespoon oil, and heat until very hot. Add the Minced Seasonings and stir-fry for about 15 seconds, until fragrant. Add the sauce mixture and cook, stirring continuously, until thickened. Remove from the heat.

Cut the steak across the grain into thin slices, and arrange over the snow peas. Pour the sauce over the steak and serve immediately.

Variation: Substitute a butterflied boneless leg of lamb for the beef, and grill it for 5 minutes on each side over a hot fire, then for 15 to 20 minutes longer, or until cooked but still pink on each side over a low fire.

BARBECUED PORK STRIPS

Barbecued pork, with its burnished skin and honeylike flavor, is the quintessential Chinese appetizer. When accompanied by a vegetable side dish and rice or good crusty bread, it becomes a filling meal. Try this delectable hoisin-based marinade with center-cut pork loin or spareribs, as well as with boneless chops. ● Serves 6

1½ to 2 pounds boneless pork chops

Marinade

¾ cup hoisin sauce

3 tablespoons ketchup

2 tablespoons soy sauce

2 tablespoons sesame oil

1 teaspoon five-spice powder (see page 5; optional)

1½ tablespoons minced garlic

2 teaspoons minced fresh ginger

½ teaspoon crushed dried red chile peppers or chile pepper flakes (optional)

Using a sharp knife or a cleaver, trim any fat or gristle from the meat. Place in a bowl. Combine the Marinade ingredients, add to the meat, and turn to coat on all sides. Cover with plastic wrap and refrigerate for at least 3 hours or overnight.

Prepare a medium-hot fire for grilling, and place the grill about 3 inches from the coals. Arrange the meat on the grill, cover, and cook, turning several times, for about 8 to 10 minutes, or until cooked through. Remove and let sit for about 5 minutes. Slice the pork across the grain into thin slices, and serve immediately.

Serve with Stir-Fried Asparagus with Crabmeat (page 291) and/or Vegetarian Roll-Ups (page 306).

VEGETABLES
AND TOFU

Fresh Chinese vegetables used to be a rarity in American supermarkets. Bean sprouts always came in cans and snow peas were only available in the frozen food section. Today, most well-stocked markets offer a range of Chinese produce. Heads of leafy Napa cabbage are flanked by ivory stalks of bok choy. Fresh snow peas are heaped high next to mounds of knobby ginger, fresh bean sprouts glisten, and a diverse selection of fresh Chinese mushrooms, such as shiitake, enokitake, and oyster, is displayed next to more familiar varieties.

But most vegetables, not just the Chinese varieties, are prime candidates for Chinese cooking. Tender asparagus spears are delectable when steamed or stir-fried and seasoned with sesame oil and shreds of fresh ginger. Broccoli is superb stir-fried until just tender and dressed with oyster sauce, and roasted bell peppers are succulent bathed in pungent black bean sauce.

The recipes in this chapter aptly illustrate the sophistication and brilliance of Chinese cooking. Stir-frying and steaming, two of the most popular techniques, are ideal for preserving and accentuating the vibrant colors, crunchy textures, and fresh flavors of produce. Simplicity is usually stressed in order to highlight the natural flavors of the foods. But seasonings like ginger, garlic, fermented black beans, and oyster sauce are often used in subtle sauces to complement or underscore the pure taste of the vegetable.

Along with Chinese vegetables, tofu is another Asian product that is now widely available in American markets. Supermarket produce sections routinely offer a selection of grades of bean curd, from soft to firm. Americans, who have become savvy to the bean curd's nutritional value, are finally experimenting and discovering its versatility. It can be stir-fried, braised, stuffed, deep-fried, steamed, and cooked in soups and casseroles. Because tofu has a very mild flavor, it tends to take on the tastes of the seasonings and other ingredients it is cooked with.

Tofu is made from soybean milk in a process similar to cheese making. Generally, tofu squares are sold in different grades according to their firmness and density. Silken or soft tofu, with its delicate creamy flavor and custardy consistency, is most often used in sweet and savory soups, dressings, and desserts. Firm and extra-firm tofu can be stuffed with meat or seafood, and it is used in stir-fried dishes, stews, and casseroles. Since the curd is dense, it retains its shape when tossed in a pan. Deep-frying, panfrying, broiling, and freezing all alter the density of tofu, making it more compact and easier to cook without falling apart. In fact, many cooks prefer to precook tofu before stir-frying it.

The recipes here should convince any cook that when cooked properly, tofu is delicious.

STIR-FRIED ASPARAGUS WITH CRABMEAT

With its delicate sauce and lovely presentation, this dish embodies the refined sophistication of classic Chinese cooking. The subtle seasonings of ginger and scallions bring out the fresh flavor of the asparagus. Top-quality ingredients are crucial to the success of this stir-fry. Serve it as a side dish or, with steamed rice, as an entrée. ● Serves 6

2 pounds asparagus

Sauce

½ cup Chinese Chicken Broth (page 367)

¾ teaspoon salt

1 teaspoon sesame oil

1½ teaspoons cornstarch

½ pound lump crabmeat, picked through to remove any shells and cartilage

2 tablespoons rice wine or sake

1 tablespoon corn or safflower oil

Minced Seasonings

3 tablespoons minced scallions (white part only)

1 tablespoon minced fresh ginger

Snap off the tough ends of the asparagus. If the stalks are very large, peel away the tough skin with a vegetable peeler. Combine the Sauce ingredients and blend well.

Fill a wok or a large pot with an inch or so of water for steaming and heat until boiling. Place the asparagus directly in the pot or on a steamer tray (see page 7) over the boiling water and cook for 4 to 5 minutes, or until just tender. Refresh under cold running water and drain thoroughly. Cut into 2-inch lengths.

Heat a wok or a well-seasoned skillet, add the crabmeat and rice wine or sake, and toss lightly over high heat for 30 seconds. Remove and set aside. Reheat the pan, add the corn or safflower oil, and heat until very hot. Add the Minced Seasonings and stir-fry for about 15 seconds, until fragrant. Add

(continued)

the sauce mixture and cook, stirring continuously to prevent lumps, until thickened. Add the cooked asparagus and crabmeat, toss lightly to coat, and transfer to a serving platter.

Variation: Substitute blanched broccoli, snow peas, or hearts of baby Chinese cabbage for the steamed asparagus.

Note: Stir-frying the crabmeat with rice wine or sake before combining it with the asparagus both adds flavor and removes any "fishy" taste.

SPICY BEAN SPROUTS

This dish reminds me of a light, spicy, more sophisticated version of egg fu yung, modified for the contemporary diet. Leeks, bean sprouts, and slivers of egg sheets are stir-fried briefly in a piquant hot-and-sour sauce that highlights the texture of the crisp vegetables. Served hot or cold, this dish will please even the most discriminating palate. ● Serves 6

2 tablespoons corn or safflower oil

2 eggs, lightly beaten

Sauce

¼ cup Chinese Chicken Broth (page 367) or water

1½ tablespoons soy sauce

1 tablespoon rice wine or sake

2 teaspoons sugar

1½ teaspoons Chinese black vinegar or Worcestershire sauce

1 teaspoon sesame oil

1 teaspoon cornstarch

Minced Seasonings

1 tablespoon minced garlic

1 tablespoon minced fresh ginger

1 teaspoon hot chili paste

2 cups leeks cut into fine julienne shreds

6 cups bean sprouts, rinsed and drained

Heat a well-seasoned 10-inch frying pan and wipe with a little of the corn or safflower oil. Add one quarter of the beaten eggs to the pan, tilting the pan to evenly coat the bottom, and cook over medium-high heat just until set. Flip over and cook for about 15 seconds. Transfer to a plate, and cook the remaining eggs in 3 batches, to make 4 egg sheets. Stack the sheets one on top of the other and cut into thin julienne shreds. Set aside.

Combine the Sauce ingredients and blend well.

Heat a wok or a well-seasoned skillet, add the remaining corn or safflower oil, and heat until hot. Add the Minced Seasonings and stir-fry for about 10 seconds, until fragrant. Add the leeks and cook over high heat, tossing lightly, for about 1 minute. Add the bean sprouts and cook for about 30 seconds, then add the sauce mixture and cook, stirring constantly to prevent lumps, until thickened. Add the shredded eggs and toss lightly to coat. Transfer to a serving platter. Serve hot or at room temperature.

Variation: Add 1½ cups of cooked shredded chicken or pork to the stir-fry and serve as an entrée; add the meat to the pan along with the bean sprouts.

TOSSED BEAN SPROUTS

Simple yet subtle, this lively salad of fresh bean sprouts and slivers of red bell peppers is tossed with a light cilantro dressing. The preparation takes only minutes, and the dish complements almost any entrée.

● Serves 6

Dressing

3½ tablespoons soy sauce

1 tablespoon sugar

1 tablespoon sesame oil

1½ tablespoons clear rice vinegar

1½ tablespoons chopped cilantro (fresh coriander)

1 tablespoon sesame oil

1½ tablespoons minced fresh ginger

1 cup red bell peppers cut into fine julienne shreds

6 cups bean sprouts, rinsed and drained thoroughly

1 cup 1-inch pieces scallion greens

Combine the Dressing ingredients and blend well.

Heat a wok or a skillet, add the sesame oil, and heat until very hot. Add the ginger and stir-fry for about 10 seconds until fragrant. Add the red peppers and stir-fry for about 30 seconds over high heat. Add the bean sprouts and scallion greens and stir-fry for about 30 seconds. Remove to a serving bowl and toss with the dressing while still warm. Serve warm, at room temperature, or chilled.

Variation: Substitute minced scallion greens for the cilantro.

Note: For a more refined presentation, pinch off the ends of the bean sprouts.

BROCCOLI IN OYSTER SAUCE

The marriage of broccoli and oyster sauce is a time-honored classic, for good reason: The fresh, vibrant taste of the vegetable is perfectly complemented by the rich, unctuous oyster sauce. But snow peas could be substituted for the broccoli in this dish and the result would be just as good. Briefly blanching the broccoli and immediately refreshing it in cold water preserves its vivid color and crisp texture. ● Serves 6

1½ pounds broccoli

Sauce

½ cup Chinese Chicken Broth (page 367) or water

3½ tablespoons oyster sauce

1½ tablespoons rice wine or sake

1½ teaspoons sugar

1 teaspoon soy sauce

1 teaspoon sesame oil

1¼ teaspoons cornstarch

1 tablespoon corn or safflower oil

Minced Seasonings

1½ tablespoons minced garlic

1 tablespoon minced fresh ginger

Using a sharp knife, peel away the tough skin from the broccoli stems and cut away the stem ends. Cut off the florets and cut the stems on the diagonal into 1½-inch sections. Separate the larger florets so that they all are approximately the same size as the stem pieces.

Combine the Sauce ingredients and blend well.

Heat a large pot of 3 quarts water until boiling, add the broccoli, and bring back to a boil. Cook for about 3 minutes, or just until the broccoli is crisp-tender. Immediately drain in a colander and refresh under cold running water; drain thoroughly.

Heat a wok or a skillet, add the corn or safflower oil, and heat until hot. Add the Minced Seasonings and stir-fry for about 15 seconds, until fragrant. Add the sauce mixture and cook, stirring continuously to prevent lumps, until thickened. Add the broccoli, toss lightly to coat, and transfer to a serving dish. Serve hot.

GARLIC BROCCOLI

Inspired by the Italian technique of tossing cooked broccoli in olive oil and garlic, I developed an Asian version, using sesame oil flavored with crushed red peppers and combined with minced garlic, soy sauce, and fresh lemon juice. The spicy dressing is excellent tossed with almost any cooked vegetable, including cauliflower, zucchini, or snow peas.

● Serves 6

1½ pounds broccoli

Spicy Sesame Dressing

2 tablespoons sesame oil

1½ tablespoons corn or safflower oil

½ teaspoon crushed dried red chile peppers or chile pepper flakes

1½ tablespoons minced garlic

¼ cup soy sauce

1 tablespoon sugar

1 tablespoon freshly squeezed lemon juice

Using a sharp knife, peel away the tough skin near the broccoli stems and cut away the stem ends. Cut off the florets and cut the stems on the diagonal into 1½-inch sections. Separate the larger florets so that they all are approximately the same size as the stem pieces.

To prepare the Dressing, combine the sesame oil and corn or safflower oil in a heavy saucepan, heat until very hot but not smoking, and add the crushed red peppers or pepper flakes. Remove from the heat, cover, and let stand for 10 minutes, then add the garlic, soy sauce, sugar, and lemon juice and stir to dissolve the sugar.

Heat a large pot of water until boiling, add the broccoli, and bring back to a boil. Cook for about 3 minutes, or just until the broccoli is crisp-tender. Immediately drain in a colander and refresh under cold running water; drain thoroughly. Transfer to a bowl, add the spicy dressing, and toss to coat. Serve at room temperature or chilled.

STIR-FRIED CHINESE CABBAGE

Of all the Chinese cabbages, Napa, with its full, juicy leaves, is one of my favorites. I like to use it as a base for hearty soups and casseroles or prepare it as a simple side dish. In this recipe, minced garlic and rice wine accentuate the delicate, sweet taste of the cabbage. ● Serves 6

1½ pounds Chinese (Napa) cabbage
1 tablespoon corn or safflower oil
2 tablespoons water
1 tablespoon minced garlic
2 tablespoons rice wine or sake
½ teaspoon salt

Trim the leafy tips and ends of the cabbage stalks, removing any tough or damaged sections. Cut the leaves into 2-inch pieces, separating the leafy sections and the harder core sections.

Heat a wok or a skillet until very hot, add the oil, and heat until smoking. Add the firmer core sections of the cabbage and toss over high heat for about 30 seconds. Add the water, cover, and cook for about 1 minute, or until crisp-tender. Add the remaining cabbage sections, the garlic, rice wine or sake, and salt, and toss over high heat for about 45 seconds, or until the leafy pieces are wilted. Transfer to a serving platter, and serve immediately or at room temperature.

Variation: Substitute flowering bok choy or Chinese broccoli for the Napa cabbage. If using broccoli, trim away any yellowed leaves, trim the ends, and cut into 2-inch lengths. Increase the water to 3 to 4 tablespoons of water and cook for about 2 to 3 minutes, or until crisp-tender, before proceeding with the recipe.

HOT-AND-SOUR
BOK CHOY

Bok choy, the stalkier version of Chinese cabbage, is now available in almost every supermarket. It's extremely versatile and can be used in soups, casseroles, or stir-fries, as in this dish. Cooked over high heat and seasoned with ginger, crushed red peppers, and black vinegar, the bok choy is transformed into a spicy "pickle" that is delicious served hot, at room temperature, or cold. ● Serves 6

1½ pounds bok choy, outer leaves removed (see Note)

Hot-and-Sour Sauce

1½ tablespoons soy sauce

¾ teaspoon salt

1 tablespoon sugar

2½ teaspoons Chinese black vinegar or Worcestershire sauce

½ teaspoon cornstarch

1 tablespoon corn or safflower oil

¾ teaspoon crushed dried red chile peppers or chile pepper flakes

2 tablespoons finely shredded fresh ginger

2 tablespoons rice wine or sake

2 tablespoons water

Separate the cabbage stalks from the cabbage, and trim the stem ends and the leafy tips. Rinse thoroughly and drain. Slice each stalk on the diagonal into 2-inch-long pieces, separating the stem sections and the leafy sections. Combine the Sauce ingredients and blend well.

Heat a wok or a skillet, add the oil, and heat until very hot. Add the crushed peppers or pepper flakes and the ginger and stir-fry over high heat for about 15 seconds. Add the stem sections of the cabbage and the rice wine or sake and stir-fry for about 30 seconds. Add the water, cover, and cook for about 1 minute, or until the cabbage is crisp-tender. Add the leafy sections and stir-fry for about 45 seconds. Add the sauce mixture and cook, stirring continuously to prevent lumps, until thickened. Transfer to a serving platter and serve hot, at room temperature, or chilled.

Note: If bok choy is unavailable, you can use Chinese (Napa) cabbage. Cut the cabbage into 1½-inch-long pieces, keeping the leafy sections and the firmer stalky sections separate. Omit the water from the recipe. Cook the stalky cabbage sections with the seasonings for 1 minute, then add the leafy sections and proceed as directed.

PICKLED CARROTS

Cantonese cooks have devised a master marinade for "quick-pickling" such vegetables as carrots, cucumbers, and radishes, using equal parts of sugar and clear rice vinegar and a generous amount of minced fresh ginger. I like to prepare large batches of this recipe since the crisp, tart pickles are great for munching on at mealtimes and in between as snacks.

● **Serves 6**

 1 pound carrots, peeled and trimmed (see Note)
 1½ tablespoons minced fresh ginger
 ¾ cup clear rice vinegar
 ¾ cup sugar

With a sharp knife, cut the carrots on the diagonal, or roll-cut them, into 1-inch pieces. Place in a nonreactive bowl.

Combine the ginger, rice vinegar, and sugar and stir until the sugar dissolves. Add to the carrots and toss lightly to coat. Cover with plastic wrap and refrigerate overnight, tossing occasionally. Serve chilled. (These will keep for at least 1 week in the refrigerator.)

Note: If the carrots are very large, blanch in boiling water for 2 minutes and refresh under cold running water before proceeding with the recipe.

SAUCY EGGPLANT

When salted to remove the bitter juices, eggplant becomes a sponge that soaks up the flavors of any sauces. I especially like to cook it in a broth generously seasoned with garlic, ginger, scallions, and hot chili paste. Bowls of steamed rice are the perfect accompaniment to this heady dish.

● Serves 6

> 2 pounds eggplant, rinsed, trimmed, and cut lengthwise into ½-inch-thick slices
> 1 teaspoon salt
> 1½ tablespoons plus 1 teaspoon sesame oil

Sauce

> 1½ cups Chinese Chicken Broth (page 367)
> 3 tablespoons soy sauce
> 1½ tablespoons rice wine or sake
> 1 tablespoon sugar
> 1 tablespoon Chinese black vinegar or Worcestershire sauce
> 1 teaspoon sesame oil
> 1 teaspoon cornstarch

Minced Seasonings

> 2 tablespoons minced scallions
> 1½ tablespoons minced fresh ginger
> 1½ tablespoons minced garlic
> 1½ teaspoons hot chili paste
>
> 2 tablespoons minced scallion greens

Arrange the eggplant slices on a cookie sheet lined with paper towels and sprinkle on both sides with the salt. Let sit for 1 hour.

Preheat the broiler. Brush off the salt from the eggplant, and brush lightly with 1½ tablespoons of the sesame oil on both sides. Place the eggplant about 3 inches from the heat source and broil for about 8 to 10 minutes, or until golden. Turn over and broil for 8 to 10 minutes longer, or until golden on both sides. Let cool slightly, then cut into finger-size pieces about 3 inches long and 1 inch wide.

Combine the Sauce ingredients and blend well.

Heat a large flameproof casserole, add the remaining 1 teaspoon oil, and heat until hot. Add the Minced Seasonings and stir-fry for about 15 seconds, until fragrant. Add the sauce mixture and heat until boiling. Add the eggplant fingers, cover, and cook over medium heat for about 10 minutes, or until tender. Uncover, increase the heat to high, and cook until the sauce is reduced to a glaze. Transfer to a serving platter and sprinkle with the minced scallions.

GLAZED GREEN BEANS

When I lived in the Far East, we always cooked green beans very simply, in a combination of soy sauce and rice wine, seasoned with scallions and sugar. Reduced to a light glaze, the sauce highlights the texture and flavor of the beans. I still cherish this home-style recipe, and the dish is equally irresistible served hot from the pan at dinnertime or cold the next day.

● Serves 6

> 2 pounds green beans
>
> **Sauce**
>
> ¼ cup soy sauce
>
> 3 tablespoons rice wine or sake
>
> 1½ tablespoons sugar
>
> ½ cup water
>
> 1½ tablespoons corn or safflower oil
>
> ½ cup minced scallions (white part only)

Cutting on the diagonal, trim off the ends of the beans and then cut the beans into 3-inch lengths. Combine the Sauce ingredients and stir to dissolve the sugar.

Heat a wok or a skillet until hot, add the oil, and heat until very hot. Add the scallions and stir-fry over high heat for about 15 seconds, until fragrant. Add the green beans and stir-fry over high heat for about 1 minute. Add the sauce mixture and heat until boiling. Cover, reduce the heat to medium, and cook for about 12 minutes, or until the beans are tender. Uncover, increase the heat to high, and cook, stirring occasionally, until the sauce has reduced to a glaze. Toss lightly and transfer to a serving platter.

POTATO PANCAKES

I grew up relishing my mother's crisp potato pancakes, and when I lived in the Far East, I was inspired one evening to prepare them for my "surrogate" Chinese family. On a whim, I added some scallions and Chinese ham for additional flavor, and the dish became an instant hit. Today when my family makes potato pancakes, we prepare lots of both the traditional and the revised versions. ● Serves 6

6 medium red potatoes (about 2 pounds)

¾ cup minced scallion greens

¼ pound prosciutto or Chinese ham, minced (optional)

2 large eggs, lightly beaten

6 to 8 tablespoons flour

½ teaspoon freshly ground black pepper

¾ cup corn or safflower oil

Preheat the oven to 200°F. Line one cookie sheet with paper towels and another with aluminum foil.

Peel the potatoes and grate them with a grater or the shredding blade of a food processor. Place in a bowl and add the scallion greens, prosciutto or ham (if using), eggs, 6 tablespoons of the flour, and the pepper. Mix to blend, adding up to 2 tablespoons more flour if the mixture seems too loose.

Add enough of the oil to a deep skillet or a frying pan to reach a depth of about ¼ inch, and heat to about 350°F. Drop the potato mixture by full tablespoons into the hot oil, flattening each mound with a spatula. Fry for about 1 minute on each side, or until golden brown and crisp. Remove with a slotted spoon and drain on the paper towel–lined cookie sheet. Then place on the aluminum foil–lined sheet and keep warm in the oven while you fry the remaining pancakes, adding more oil as necessary. (Replace the paper towels as they absorb the oil.) Serve hot or at room temperature.

Variation: Zucchini Pancakes: Substitute 2 pounds zucchini for the potatoes. Squeeze the grated zucchini dry before proceeding with the recipe.

ROASTED
BLACK BEAN PEPPERS

Beef with peppers in a black bean sauce is a Cantonese classic. For a vegetarian alternative, I omit the meat and toss roasted red, yellow, and orange peppers in a garlicky black bean sauce. Serve as a side dish or a light entrée with plenty of steamed rice. ● Serves 6

2 red bell peppers, rinsed, cored, seeded, and cut lengthwise in half

2 yellow bell peppers, rinsed, cored, seeded, and cut lengthwise in half (see Note)

1 orange bell pepper, rinsed, cored, seeded, and cut lengthwise in half (see Note)

Sauce

½ cup Chinese Chicken Broth (page 367)

1½ tablespoons soy sauce

1½ tablespoons rice wine or sake

2 teaspoons sugar

1 teaspoon sesame oil

1½ teaspoons cornstarch

1 tablespoon corn or safflower oil

Seasonings

2 tablespoons fermented black beans, drained and minced

1½ tablespoons minced garlic

2 tablespoons minced scallions (white part only)

1 tablespoon minced fresh ginger

⅓ pound snow peas, ends trimmed and veiny strings removed

1½ tablespoons rice wine or sake

Prepare a fire for grilling or preheat a broiler. Arrange the pepper halves skin side down about 3 inches from the heat source and roast, turning occasionally, for 15 to 20 minutes, or until blackened. Place in a paper bag, close the bag securely, and let steam for 15 minutes.

(continued)

Using a sharp knife, remove the skin from the peppers and cut them lengthwise into ¼-inch-wide julienne strips. Combine the Sauce ingredients and blend well.

Heat a wok or a skillet, add the oil, and heat until very hot. Add the Seasonings and stir-fry for about 15 seconds, until fragrant. Add the snow peas and stir-fry over high heat for about 1 minute. Add the rice wine or sake and stir-fry for about 30 seconds. Add the sauce mixture and cook, stirring continuously to prevent lumps, until thickened. Add the roasted pepper strips and toss lightly to coat. Transfer to a serving platter and serve hot or at room temperature.

Note: If yellow and/or orange peppers are unavailable, substitute red bell peppers.

SPICY SNOW PEAS AND WATER CHESTNUTS

All too often, Chinese-American restaurants concoct "mixed vegetable" combinations from bland sauces and unappetizing canned vegetables. My standard mixed vegetable recipe is just the opposite: I like to stir-fry fresh snow peas with sliced water chestnuts and toss them in a tart, fiery sauce, using generous amounts of ginger, garlic, and chili paste. The sauce, even with its strong seasonings, accentuates the appealing texture and flavor of the fresh products. ● Serves 6

Sauce

⅓ cup Chinese Chicken Broth (page 367)

3 tablespoons soy sauce

1½ tablespoons sugar

2 teaspoons Chinese black vinegar or Worcestershire sauce

1 teaspoon sesame oil

1 teaspoon cornstarch

⅛ teaspoon freshly ground black pepper

1 tablespoon corn or safflower oil

Minced Seasonings

3 tablespoons minced scallions (white part only)

1½ tablespoons minced fresh ginger

1½ tablespoons minced garlic

1 teaspoon hot chili paste or crushed dried red chile peppers

¾ pound snow peas, ends trimmed and veiny strings removed

2 tablespoons rice wine or sake

1 cup thinly sliced water chestnuts, blanched in boiling water for
      15 seconds, refreshed in cold water, and drained

Combine the Sauce ingredients and blend well.

Heat a wok or a skillet, add the oil, and heat until very hot. Add the Minced Seasonings and stir-fry over high heat for about 15 seconds, or until fragrant. Add the snow peas and toss lightly over high heat for 1 minute. Add the rice wine or sake, then add the water chestnuts and stir-fry until heated through. Add the sauce mixture and cook, stirring continuously to prevent lumps, until thickened. Transfer to a serving platter and serve hot or at room temperature.

Note: Unlike vegetables such as broccoli and asparagus, snow peas should not be blanched before being added to a stir-fry; if cooked briefly over very high heat with little liquid, they will retain their vibrant green color and crisp texture even after they have cooled.

VEGETARIAN ROLL-UPS

This dish is a fine example of the robust flavors that characterize Chinese vegetarian cooking. Shredded leeks, carrots, smoky black mushrooms, and cabbage are stir-fried with garlic, ginger, and a fragrant sauce, then rolled up in steamed pancakes that have been generously smeared with hoisin sauce. The unique combination of textures and flavors makes this dish truly memorable.　●　Serves 6

Sauce

⅓ cup reserved mushroom soaking liquid (see below)

2½ tablespoons soy sauce

2 tablespoons rice wine or sake

1½ teaspoons sesame oil

1½ teaspoons cornstarch

½ cup hoisin sauce

2 tablespoons water

1 teaspoon soy sauce

½ cup dry-roasted peanuts, coarsely chopped

1½ tablespoons sugar

16 Shanghai spring roll wrappers, lumpia wrappers, or flour tortillas

2 tablespoons corn or safflower oil

Minced Seasonings

2 tablespoons minced garlic

1½ tablespoons minced fresh ginger

8 dried Chinese black mushrooms, softened in hot water for 20
　　minutes, drained (reserve ⅓ cup of the soaking liquid), stems
　　removed, and caps shredded

3 cups shredded leeks

1½ cups grated carrots

4 cups finely shredded Chinese (Napa) cabbage

1½ tablespoons rice wine or sake

4 cups bean sprouts, rinsed and drained

Combine the Sauce ingredients and blend well. Set aside. Combine the hoisin sauce, water, and soy sauce in a small saucepan and heat until boiling. Transfer to a serving bowl and set aside. Combine the peanuts and sugar in another serving bowl.

Fill a wok or a large pot with water for steaming and heat until boiling. Separate the spring roll wrappers or tortillas and wrap in a linen or cotton towel. Place in a steamer tray (see page 7) over the boiling water, cover, and steam for 10 minutes, or until heated through. Turn off the heat and let sit covered until ready to serve.

Heat a wok or a skillet, add the oil, and heat until hot. Add the Minced Seasonings and stir-fry for about 15 seconds, until fragrant. Add the black mushrooms and leeks and stir-fry over high heat for about 1 minute. Add the carrots, cabbage, and rice wine or sake and toss lightly for 1½ minutes, or until the vegetables are tender. Add the bean sprouts and toss for 30 seconds, then add the sauce mixture and cook, stirring continuously to prevent lumps, until thickened. Transfer to a serving platter and serve hot or at room temperature.

To serve, spread a wrapper or a tortilla with the hoisin sauce mixture and sprinkle some of the chopped peanuts on top. Place a heaping teaspoonful of the stir-fried mixture on top, roll up, and eat.

Variation: Add ½ pound of shredded cooked chicken, beef, or pork to the stir-fried mixture along with the bean sprouts.

STIR-FRIED SPINACH

Watercress, lettuce, or any leafy Chinese vegetable can be substituted for spinach in this quick stir-fry. To preserve the vivid color of the vegetable and prevent overcooking, heat the pan and oil until smoking hot before adding the spinach to the pan. ● Serves 6

½ tablespoon corn or safflower oil

½ tablespoon sesame oil

1 pound (or 2 ten-ounce packages) fresh spinach, stemmed, rinsed, and thoroughly drained

1 tablespoon minced garlic

1½ tablespoons rice wine or sake

½ teaspoon salt

Heat a wok or a large skillet, add both the oils, and heat until smoking. Add the spinach, garlic, rice wine or sake, and salt and toss lightly over high heat for about 1 minute, until slightly wilted but still bright green. Transfer to a serving platter. Serve hot or at room temperature.

SWEET-AND-SOUR TOFU

In this dish, golden-fried tofu slices, stir-fried with a colorful mélange of red and yellow peppers, are bathed in a classic sweet-and-sour sauce. The fried tofu is crisp and firm, a delicious contrast to the crunchy peppers and tart sauce. Serve with steamed rice. ● Serves 6

1½ pounds firm tofu or bean curd

Sauce

¼ cup ketchup

⅔ cup water

3 tablespoons clear rice vinegar

3 tablespoons sugar

2 teaspoons soy sauce

½ teaspoon sesame oil

2 teaspoons cornstarch

3½ tablespoons corn or safflower oil

Minced Seasonings

2 tablespoons minced scallions (white part only)
1½ tablespoons minced garlic
1 tablespoon minced fresh ginger
¾ teaspoon crushed dried red chile peppers or chile pepper flakes

1 red bell pepper, rinsed, seeded, cored, and thinly sliced
1 yellow bell pepper, rinsed, seeded, cored, and thinly sliced

Wrap the tofu in paper towels or a cotton towel and place a heavy weight, such as a skillet, on top. Let stand for 30 minutes to press out the excess water, then cut into slices about ¼ inch thick. Trim to 2-inch squares.

Combine the Sauce ingredients and blend well.

Heat a nonstick frying pan, add 3 tablespoons of the oil, and heat until very hot. Fry the tofu slices in batches until golden brown on both sides. Remove with a slotted spoon and drain on paper towels. Be sure to reheat the oil between each batch. Drain and wipe out the pan with paper towels.

Reheat the pan, add the remaining ½ tablespoon oil, and heat until very hot. Add the Minced Seasonings and stir-fry for about 15 seconds, until fragrant. Add the peppers and stir-fry over high heat for about 1 minute. Add the sauce mixture and cook, stirring continuously, until thickened. Add the tofu slices, toss lightly to coat, and transfer to a serving platter.

Note: Pressing the tofu to remove the excess water makes it firm enough to withstand stir-frying.

TOFU-NOODLE SALAD WITH SPICY PEANUT SAUCE

With its mild flavor, tofu serves as a perfect foil for piquant peanut sauce. In this filling noodle salad, carrots, cucumbers, and red bell peppers are used as garnishes, but many different shredded vegetables can be substituted for a contrast of colors, flavors, and textures. ● Serves 6

¾ pound firm tofu or bean curd

½ pound spinach or egg vermicelli

1 teaspoon sesame oil

3 cups grated carrots

2½ cups grated, peeled, and seeded cucumbers

2 red bell peppers, rinsed, cored, seeded, and cut into thin julienne strips

Peanut Dressing

1 tablespoon minced garlic

1 tablespoon minced fresh ginger

¼ cup smooth peanut butter, plus more if necessary

2½ tablespoons soy sauce

1 tablespoon sesame oil

1½ tablespoons rice wine or sake

2 tablespoons Chinese black vinegar or Worcestershire sauce

1½ tablespoons sugar

1 teaspoon hot chili paste, or to taste

3 tablespoons Chinese Chicken Broth (page 367) or water, plus more if necessary

1 tablespoon minced scallion greens

Wrap the tofu in paper towels or a cotton towel and place a heavy weight, such as a skillet, on top. Let stand for 30 minutes to press out the excess water, then cut into slices about ½ inch thick and then into julienne shreds.

Heat 4 quarts of water in a large pot until boiling. Add the noodles and cook until just tender. Drain in a colander and refresh under cold running water. Drain thoroughly and toss with the sesame oil. Arrange the noodles in a deep dish or on a platter.

Arrange the tofu shreds, grated carrot and cucumber, and red peppers in concentric circles or in mounds on top of the noodles.

To prepare the Dressing, finely mince the garlic and ginger in a food processor fitted with a steel blade or in a blender. Add the remaining ingredients one at a time, blending well after each addition. If the dressing seems too thick, add about 1 tablespoon additional broth or water; if it seems thin, add more peanut butter. Transfer to a serving container and sprinkle with the minced scallion greens. To serve, drizzle some of the dressing over the noodle salad and pass the remaining dressing on the side.

Note: If you like, prepare a large batch of the peanut dressing to have on hand. It will keep for up to a month in the refrigerator.

SPICY TOFU
WITH SHRIMP

Seasoned Chinese cooks will recognize the name *Ma po tofu,* a **spicy** classic made with ground pork and cubes of tofu cooked in a rich sauce. I like to make the dish substituting shrimp and other seafood for the meat. The flavor is as delicious as the original. Serve with rice for a light meal. ● Serves 6

1 pound firm tofu or bean curd
½ pound medium shrimp, peeled
1½ tablespoons rice wine or sake
½ teaspoon sesame oil
1 teaspoon minced fresh ginger

Sauce

2½ cups Chinese Chicken Broth (page 367)
1½ tablespoons soy sauce
1 tablespoon rice wine or sake

1 tablespoon cornstarch
1½ tablespoons water
2 tablespoons corn or safflower oil

Minced Seasonings

3½ tablespoons minced scallions (white part only)
1½ tablespoons minced garlic
1 tablespoon minced fresh ginger
1 teaspoon hot chili paste, or to taste

Wrap the tofu in paper towels or a cotton towel and place a heavy weight, such as a skillet, on top. Let stand for 30 minutes to press out the excess water, then cut into ½-inch cubes.

Meanwhile, using a sharp knife, cut the shrimp down the back to butterfly and remove the dark vein. Rinse and drain. Place in a bowl, add the rice wine or sake, sesame oil, and minced ginger and toss lightly to coat. Cover with plastic wrap and refrigerate for 20 minutes. Combine the Sauce ingredients and set aside. Combine the cornstarch and water and blend until smooth.

Drain the shrimp.

Heat a wok or a skillet, add 1 tablespoon of the oil, and heat until hot. Add the shrimp and stir-fry over high heat for about 1 minute, until the shrimp turn pink. Drain and wipe out the pan.

Reheat the pan, add the remaining 1 tablespoon oil, and heat until hot. Add the Minced Seasonings and stir-fry for about 15 seconds, until fragrant. Add the sauce mixture and heat until boiling. Add the tofu cubes, reduce the heat to low, and simmer for about 20 minutes, or until the sauce is reduced by one quarter. Increase the heat to high, add the cornstarch thickener, and cook, stirring continuously to prevent lumps, until thickened. Add the shrimp, toss lightly to coat, and transfer to a serving dish.

Variation: Substitute ½ pound ground pork or ground chicken or turkey for the shrimp and add 1 tablespoon soy sauce to the marinade mixture.

BRAISED TOFU WITH MUSHROOMS

In this dish, smoky dried mushrooms and chicken broth flavor tofu cubes and provide a rich base for the sumptuous sauce. Served with bowls of steaming rice, this dish makes a delicious and filling meal.
● Serves 6

1½ pounds firm tofu or bean curd

Braising Mixture

2 cups Chinese Chicken Broth (page 367)

1 cup reserved mushroom soaking liquid (see below)

2½ tablespoons oyster sauce

1½ tablespoons soy sauce

1 tablespoon rice wine or sake

1 teaspoon sugar

1 tablespoon cornstarch

2 tablespoons water

2 teaspoons corn or safflower oil

1 medium leek (white part only), cleaned and cut into 1-inch lengths

1 tablespoon minced garlic

10 dried Chinese black mushrooms, soaked in 1½ cups hot water for 20 minutes, drained (reserve 1 cup of the soaking liquid), stems discarded, and caps cut in half or in thirds if very large

¼ pound shiitake mushrooms, stems removed and caps halved (optional)

Wrap the tofu in paper towels or a cotton towel and place a heavy weight, such as a skillet, on top. Let stand for 30 minutes to press out the excess water, then cut into ½-inch cubes.

Combine the Braising mixture ingredients and set aside. Combine the cornstarch and water and blend well.

Heat a flameproof casserole or a Dutch oven, add the corn or safflower oil, and heat until hot. Add the leek, garlic, and softened black mushrooms and stir-fry for about 10 seconds, until fragrant. Add the braising mixture and heat until boiling. Add the tofu and the shiitake mushrooms (if using) and bring back to a boil. Reduce the heat to medium low, cover, and simmer for 20 minutes. Uncover, increase the heat to medium, and cook until the sauce is reduced by half. Add the cornstarch thickener and cook, stirring continuously to prevent lumps, until thickened. Transfer to a serving bowl or serve directly from the pot.

BLACK BEAN
TOFU WITH VEGETABLES

Redolent with five-spice powder, crisp-broiled tofu slices are stir-fried in a pungent black bean sauce with a rainbow of peppers and snow peas. The flavor of this dish is so outstanding that even dedicated meat eaters will be satisfied. ● Serves 6

1½ pounds firm tofu or bean curd

Marinade

2 tablespoons rice wine or sake

1 tablespoon soy sauce

1 teaspoon five-spice powder (see page 5)

½ teaspoon sesame oil

Sauce

½ cup Chinese Chicken Broth (page 367) or water

1½ tablespoons soy sauce

1½ tablespoons rice wine or sake

2 teaspoons sugar

¼ teaspoon freshly ground black pepper

1 tablespoon cornstarch

1½ tablespoons corn or safflower oil

Seasonings

2 tablespoons fermented black beans, rinsed, drained, and minced

2 tablespoons minced garlic

1½ tablespoons minced fresh ginger

1 teaspoon hot chili paste

1 medium red bell pepper, rinsed, cored, seeded, and cut into thin julienne strips

1 medium yellow bell pepper, rinsed, cored, seeded, and cut into thin julienne strips

¼ pound snow peas, ends snapped and veiny strings removed

1 tablespoon rice wine or sake

Wrap the tofu in paper towels or a cotton towel and place a heavy weight, such as a skillet, on top. Let stand for 30 minutes to press out the excess water, then cut lengthwise into ½-inch slabs. Cut into 2-inch squares and place in a bowl. Combine the Marinade ingredients, add to the tofu, and carefully toss to coat. Cover with plastic wrap and let stand at room temperature for 25 minutes.

Combine the Sauce ingredients and blend well.

Preheat the broiler. Line a baking sheet with aluminum foil and arrange the tofu slices on it. Place the tofu 4 inches from the heat source and broil for 8 to 10 minutes on each side, or until lightly browned and crisp. Set aside.

Heat a wok or a skillet, add the oil, and heat until very hot. Add the Seasonings and stir-fry for 10 to 15 seconds, or until fragrant. Add the bell peppers and toss lightly over high heat for 1 minute. Add the snow peas and the rice wine or sake and stir-fry for 30 seconds. Add the sauce mixture and cook, stirring constantly, for about 45 seconds, or until thickened. Add the tofu slices, toss to coat, and transfer to a serving platter. Serve immediately.

TURKEY-STUFFED TOFU

In this hearty casserole, ground turkey is seasoned liberally with ginger, scallions, and sesame oil, stuffed into tofu squares, and braised in a rich broth. Serve with generous helpings of steamed rice for a filling meal.

● Serves 6

¾ pound firm tofu or bean curd

¾ pound ground turkey

Seasonings

2 tablespoons minced scallions (white part only)

1½ tablespoons minced fresh ginger

2 tablespoons soy sauce

1 tablespoon rice wine or sake

1½ teaspoons sesame oil

¼ teaspoon freshly ground black pepper

1½ teaspoons cornstarch

Braising Mixture

2 cups Chinese Chicken Broth (page 367)

2½ tablespoons soy sauce

1½ tablespoons rice wine or sake

4 slices fresh ginger (about the size of a quarter), lightly smashed with the flat side of a knife or a cleaver

4 scallions, trimmed and lightly smashed with the flat side of a knife or a cleaver

1½ teaspoons cornstarch

2 tablespoons water

1 tablespoon corn or safflower oil

Wrap the tofu squares in paper towels or a cotton towel and place a heavy weight, such as a skillet, on top. Let stand for 30 minutes to drain out the excess water, then cut the tofu lengthwise into 1½-inch-thick slabs. Cut each slab into rectangles about 1½ inches wide by 2 inches long. Using a spoon and a knife, scoop out an oval pocket about 1 inch deep in about 10–12 squares on one side of each tofu rectangle. (Reserve the scooped-out tofu for another use.)

Using a sharp knife or a cleaver, lightly chop the ground turkey until fluffy. Place in a mixing bowl. Add the Seasonings in the order listed and stir vigorously in one direction to combine evenly. Stuff the pockets of the tofu squares with the turkey mixture and smooth the surface with the back of a spoon dipped in water. Roll any remaining turkey mixture into small balls about 1 inch in diameter.

Combine the Braising Mixture ingredients and set aside. Combine the cornstarch and water and blend until smooth.

Heat a wok or a large skillet until hot, add the oil, and heat until very hot. Place 3 or 4 of the stuffed tofu pieces meat side down in the pan and fry over high heat until golden. Remove with a slotted spoon and drain. Reheat the oil and fry the remaining tofu squares. Fry the turkey meatballs (if any) over high heat until browned on all sides. Drain the oil from the pan and wipe clean.

Add the braising mixture to the pan and heat until boiling. Add the stuffed tofu squares meat side up and bring back to a boil. Reduce the heat to medium low, cover, and cook for 20 minutes. Transfer the cooked tofu squares to a platter. Remove and discard the ginger slices and scallions from the braising liquid and raise the heat to high. Bring to a boil, add the cornstarch thickener, and cook, stirring continuously, until the sauce thickens. Pour the sauce over the tofu and serve.

Variation: Substitute ground pork or chicken for the turkey.

NORTHERN-STYLE TOFU

In northern China, cooks like to simmer panfried tofu until plump and juicy in a rich chicken broth seasoned with fresh ginger and scallions. The dish has become popular here at home with my friends and students, who implored me to include this recipe in the book. The tender tofu literally melts in your mouth. ● Serves 6

1½ pounds soft tofu or bean curd

Braising Mixture

2 cups Chinese Chicken Broth (page 367)

2½ tablespoons rice wine or sake

1½ tablespoons soy sauce

½ teaspoon salt

½ teaspoon sugar

2 eggs, lightly beaten

½ cup cornstarch

¼ cup corn or safflower oil

Seasonings

1½ tablespoons minced fresh ginger

1½ tablespoons minced scallions (white part only)

2 teaspoons sesame oil

2 tablespoons minced scallion greens

Wrap the tofu in paper towels or a cotton towel and place a heavy weight, such as a skillet, on top. Let stand for 30 minutes to press out the excess water. Cut the tofu lengthwise into ½-inch slabs, then cut into 2-inch squares.

Combine the Braising Mixture ingredients. Place the eggs in a shallow bowl, and spread the cornstarch on a plate. Dredge the tofu slices in the cornstarch to coat both sides and set aside.

Heat a nonstick frying pan or a wok, add the corn or safflower oil, and heat until very hot. Dip 4 or 5 of the tofu slices in the beaten eggs to coat on both sides, add to the pan, and fry over medium heat until golden brown on both sides. Remove with a handled strainer and drain. Reheat the oil and fry the remaining tofu in batches. Drain off all but 1 teaspoon of the oil from the pan. Prick the fried tofu slices with a fork so that they will absorb the braising liquid.

Reheat the pan and oil until hot. Add the Seasonings and stir-fry for about 10 seconds, until fragrant. Add the braising mixture and heat until boiling. Add the fried tofu and bring back to a boil. Cook uncovered over medium heat until all the liquid is absorbed, about 20 minutes. Add the sesame oil, toss lightly, and transfer the tofu slices to a platter. Sprinkle the minced scallions on top, and serve.

TOSSED ANISE-FLAVORED TOFU

Most Chinese supermarkets carry red-cooked tofu, which has been simmered in a fragrant braising liquid, but it is easily prepared at home. Soy sauce tints the tofu a deep copper brown, and aniseed, cinnamon, and orange peel impart a pungent flavor. In this recipe, the cooked tofu is dressed with sesame oil mixed with some of the braising liquid and tossed with crunchy celery slices. A delightful appetizer, this can also be served as an unusual salad. ● Serves 6

1 pound firm tofu or bean curd

Braising Mixture

4 cups water

½ cup soy sauce

2 tablespoons sugar

1 teaspoon aniseed

1 cinnamon stick

Zest of 1 orange, removed in thin strips with a vegetable peeler

4 slices fresh ginger (about the size of a quarter), smashed with the flat side of a knife or a cleaver

4 scallions, trimmed and smashed with the flat side of a knife or a cleaver

2 cups thinly sliced celery (3 inches long and about ⅛ inch wide)

1½ tablespoons sesame oil

Wrap the tofu in paper towels or a cotton towel and place a heavy weight, such as a skillet, on top. Let stand for 30 minutes to press out the excess water, then cut lengthwise in half.

Combine the Braising Mixture ingredients in a heavy pot and heat until boiling. Simmer uncovered over low heat for 20 minutes to combine the flavorings. Add the tofu, bring just to a simmer, and cook uncovered for 30 minutes. Remove from the heat and let the tofu cool in the liquid.

Reserve 3 tablespoons of the braising mixture. Cut the tofu into ¼-inch slices about 3 inches long by 1 inch wide. Place in a large bowl.

Heat a medium pot of water until boiling. Add the celery slices, bring back to a boil, and cook for 1½ minutes. Drain and refresh under cold running water. Drain thoroughly, and add to the tofu. Add the sesame oil and the reserved braising mixture and carefully toss to coat. Arrange on a serving dish and serve at room temperature or chilled.

Variation: Substitute blanched snow peas (ends trimmed and veiny strings removed) for the celery.

SPICY TOFU KABOBS

Marinated tofu squares become a delectable meat substitute, which can be skewered along with peppers, onions, and mushrooms and baked, broiled, or grilled. While the marinade can be as basic as simply soy sauce and garlic, in this dish I've made it slightly more complex with the addition of hoisin sauce, ginger, sesame oil, and ketchup. ● Serves 6

1½ pounds firm tofu or bean curd

Barbecue Sauce

¼ cup hoisin sauce

¼ cup rice wine or sake

2½ tablespoons soy sauce

1½ tablespoons sugar

1½ tablespoons ketchup

1 tablespoon minced garlic

½ tablespoon minced fresh ginger

½ teaspoon sesame oil

1 teaspoon corn or safflower oil

2 red bell peppers, rinsed, cored, seeded, and cut into 1-inch squares

12 button mushrooms, rinsed, drained, and stems trimmed

12 small white boiling onions, peeled

12 ten-inch bamboo skewers, soaked in water for 1 hour

Wrap the tofu in paper towels or a cotton towel and place a heavy weight, such as a skillet, on top. Let stand for 30 minutes to press out the excess water, then cut into 1½-inch cubes.

Combine the Barbecue Sauce ingredients in a bowl, add the tofu cubes, and toss lightly to coat. Cover with plastic wrap and let marinate at room temperature for 1 hour.

Preheat the oven to 450°F. Lightly oil a baking sheet with the corn or safflower oil.

Place the peppers, mushrooms, and onions in a bowl and drain the marinade from the tofu into the bowl. Toss to coat. Thread the tofu squares and vegetables alternately onto the bamboo skewers, distributing them evenly. Arrange them on the oiled baking sheet and brush with some of the remaining marinade. Place in the oven, bake for 10 minutes, and baste with the remaining marinade. Bake for 10 to 15 minutes longer, or until the vegetables are tender. Transfer to a platter and serve.

NOODLES
AND RICE

Perhaps no other category of foods figures as prominently in the Chinese repertoire as rice and noodle dishes. Every region of China has its favorite specialty: The Cantonese crave panfried brown noodles garnished with beef, snow peas, and oyster sauce, as well as shrimp-fried rice. Easterners adore delicate rice noodles floating in a rich chicken broth and Yangchow fried rice studded with bits of barbecued pork, shrimp, and black mushrooms. In steamy western China, the Sichuanese relish cold and room-temperature noodle salads drenched in spicy peanut and sesame dressings. And northerners lust after saucy noodles tossed with cool shredded vegetables, seasoned with sweet bean sauce. Of course, there is also the grand family of stir-fried meat and vegetable dishes served over steaming hot rice, universally enjoyed as snacks or satisfying meals.

These hearty, delectable foods have long played an important role in the Chinese diet for several reasons: They are easy to prepare; they lend themselves to infinite variation; and they are wholesome, reasonably priced dishes that can conveniently be served as meals in themselves.

Today, a love of rice and noodle dishes is no longer confined to the Far East. In recent years, Americans have developed a passion for pasta and rice. And the revised dietary guidelines recommended by the USDA confirm the wisdom behind the passion.

Over the years, Chinese agriculturalists have developed hundreds of different strains of rice that vary in size, color, and starch content, but only about four or five varieties are used in everyday cooking.

Long-grain rice is probably the most popular, since its cooked texture is the fluffiest. Many Asian markets now offer jasmine rice, a long-grain cousin to Indian basmati rice that has the same delightfully nutty flavor.

Short-grain or Japanese rice, which is stickier than long-grain, is the ideal choice for making sushi. Glutinous or sweet rice is even stickier than short-grain, and it is primarily used for stuffings, sweet and savory pastries, and coatings. When glutinous rice is unavailable, Italian Arborio rice can be substituted.

Noodle varieties are another vast category, as a visit to any Oriental market will confirm. They may be thin or thick, flat or round. In addition to the basic flour and water, with or without egg, they are made from rice powder, mung bean starch, buckwheat flour, and sweet potato starch.

Wheat flour noodles, made with just flour and water, are used primarily for soups and casseroles. Thin egg, flour, and water noodles are ideal for panfried noodle cakes with meat, seafood, or vegetable toppings, or stir-fried dishes in which meat, seafood, and vegetables are tossed together.

Rice noodles vary in thickness, and their delicate flavor complements the foods they are cooked with. Chinese cooks prefer thin rice sticks or vermicelli for soups and for stir-fried dishes with meat and vegetables. On occasion, they will also fry thin rice noodles in hot oil until they puff, perfect as a crunchy bed for stir-fried dishes. The broadest rice noodles, which in general are preferred by Thai and Vietnamese cooks, are primarily reserved for hearty stews and soups.

Bean threads, or cellophane noodles, are made from the starch of the protein-rich mung bean. Bean threads absorb the flavors of foods they are cooked with and so are good in soups and stir-fries. Like thin rice noodles, they can be deep-fried and used as a crisp bed for stir-fries.

Noodles play a vital role in China's culture as well as its cuisine. Noodles, whatever the shape or size, but especially the lengthy variety, symbolize longevity, and so consuming them is believed to guarantee a long and healthy life.

CHINESE NOODLES: USES AND SUBSTITUTES

Description	Use	Substitute
Thin flour and water noodles	soups	spaghettini, vermicelli, capellini
Flat flour and water noodles	soups	linguine or fettucine
Thin, straight egg noodles (flour, egg, and water)	panfrying, stir-fries, lo mein, saucy noodle dishes	linguine, fettucine
Thin egg noodle clusters	panfrying	spaghettini, vermicelli
Rice stick noodles (rice powder and water)	stir-fries, soups	no substitute
Cellophane noodles (mung bean starch and water)	stir-fries, soups, salads	no substitute

SAUCY NOODLES

This delicious dish is relished in northern China. The smooth noodles, crunchy vegetables, and tender shredded meat, all coated in a rich sweet bean sauce, create a memorable contrast of flavors and textures. The original calls for pork, but I like to make a leaner dish using turkey cutlets.

● Serves 6

1 pound turkey cutlets

Marinade

1 tablespoon soy sauce

1 tablespoon rice wine or sake

1 teaspoon sesame oil

2 teaspoons cornstarch

Sauce

¾ cup sweet bean sauce or paste or hoisin sauce

3 tablespoons rice wine or sake

2 tablespoons soy sauce

2½ tablespoons sugar

½ pound flat noodles, such as linguine

1 teaspoon sesame oil

3 tablespoons corn or safflower oil

3 tablespoons minced scallions

1½ tablespoons fresh ginger

1 tablespoon minced garlic

2 cups grated carrots

1 cup red bell peppers cut into fine julienne strips

With a sharp knife or a cleaver, trim any fat or sinew from the turkey. Cut the turkey cutlets into thin julienne strips about 1½ inches long. Place in a bowl, add the Marinade ingredients, and toss lightly. Let marinate for 20 minutes.

Combine the Sauce ingredients and stir to dissolve the sugar.

Heat 4 quarts of water in a large pot until boiling. Add the noodles and cook until just tender, about 5 minutes. Drain and briefly rinse under cold running water to remove the starch. Toss with the sesame oil and arrange on a deep serving dish.

Heat a wok or a deep skillet, add 2 tablespoons of the corn or safflower oil, and heat until very hot. Add the turkey and stir-fry until the meat loses its raw color and separates. Remove with a slotted spoon or a handled strainer and drain.

Add the remaining 1 tablespoon oil to the pan and heat until very hot. Add the scallions, ginger, and garlic and stir-fry for about 15 seconds, until fragrant. Add the sauce mixture and stir-fry until the sauce has reduced and thickened. Add the cooked turkey and toss lightly to coat. Spoon the mixture over the center of the noodles. Arrange the carrots and red peppers in separate mounds, or in concentric circles, around the turkey. Serve warm or at room temperature. Just before serving, toss lightly to coat the noodles and vegetables with the sauce.

Variation: Substitute boneless pork loin or chicken breasts for the turkey.

CRISP-FRIED VEGETARIAN NOODLES

[A] panfried noodle cake is an ideal foil for all types of toppings. In this unusual variation on the classic presentation, strips of Chinese black mushrooms, leeks, carrots, and bean sprouts, tossed in a delicate sauce, are served atop a bed of crisp, golden brown noodles. Serve as a light meal or as a delectable alternative to a rice dish. ● Serves 6

½ pound thin noodles, such as spaghettini or vermicelli
1 teaspoon sesame oil

Sauce

1½ cups Chinese Chicken Broth (page 367)
3½ tablespoons soy sauce
2 tablespoons rice wine or sake
1½ teaspoons sugar
1 teaspoon sesame oil
2 tablespoons cornstarch

3 tablespoons corn or safflower oil

Minced Seasonings

1½ tablespoons minced garlic
1½ tablespoons minced fresh ginger

10 dried Chinese black mushrooms, softened in water for 20 minutes, stems discarded, and caps cut into fine julienne strips
3 cups finely julienned leeks
2 cups grated carrots
1½ tablespoons rice wine or sake
4 cups bean sprouts, rinsed and drained

Heat 4 quarts of water in a large pot until boiling. Add the noodles and cook until just tender, about 5 minutes. Drain, toss with the sesame oil, and immediately transfer the noodles into a round cake pan or pie plate. Press them evenly into the pan and let cool.

Combine the Sauce ingredients and blend well.

Preheat the oven to 200°F.

Heat a well-seasoned wok or a skillet until very hot, add 1½ tablespoons of the oil, and heat until nearly smoking. Invert the noodle cake into the pan and cook to a deep, golden brown, swirling the pan from time to time to keep the cake from sticking. Flip the noodle cake over and brown on the other side. Transfer to a heatproof serving platter and keep warm in the oven.

Reheat the pan, add the remaining 1½ tablespoons oil, and heat until very hot. Add the Minced Seasonings and stir-fry for about 10 seconds, until fragrant. Add the mushrooms, leeks, and carrots and stir-fry over high heat for about 1 minute. Add the rice wine or sake and cook for 1 minute, then add the sauce mixture. Heat until boiling, add the bean sprouts, and cook until thickened, stirring continuously to prevent lumps. Spoon over the fried noodle cake and serve immediately.

Note: If you prefer, brown the noodle cake on both sides under a broiler instead of frying it.

PANFRIED NOODLES
WITH BEEF AND SNOW PEAS

In this superb dish, beef and snow peas, coated in a rich oyster sauce, are mounded on a crown of crispy noodles. Serve this as a satisfying meal in itself. ● Serves 6

½ pound thin noodles, such as spaghettini or vermicelli

1½ pounds flank steak or London broil

Marinade

2 tablespoons soy sauce

1 tablespoon rice wine or sake

2 teaspoons minced garlic

1 teaspoon sesame oil

1 teaspoon cornstarch

Sauce

2 cups Chinese Chicken Broth (page 367)

¼ cup oyster sauce

1 teaspoon soy sauce

2 teaspoons sugar

1 teaspoon sesame oil

1⅓ tablespoons cornstarch

5½ tablespoons corn or safflower oil

Minced Seasonings

3 tablespoons minced scallions (white part only)

1 tablespoon minced fresh ginger

½ tablespoon minced garlic

⅔ pound snow peas, ends trimmed and veiny strings removed

Heat 4 quarts of water in a large pot until boiling. Add the noodles and cook until just tender, about 5 minutes. Drain and immediately transfer to a round cake pan or a pie pan. Press them evenly into the pan and let cool.

With a sharp knife, trim away any fat or gristle from the meat. Cut lengthwise, with the grain, into long strips about 2 inches wide. Cut the strips across the grain into thin slices about ⅙ inch wide. Place in a bowl, add the Marinade ingredients, and toss lightly to coat. Cover with plastic wrap, and let sit for 1 hour at room temperature, or refrigerate overnight.

Combine the Sauce ingredients and blend well.

Preheat the oven to 200°F.

Heat a well-seasoned wok or a skillet until very hot, add 2 tablespoons of the oil, and heat until almost smoking. Invert the noodle cake into the pan and cook to a deep golden brown, swirling the pan from time to time to keep the noodles from sticking. Flip the noodle cake over and brown on the other side. Transfer to a heatproof serving platter and keep warm in the oven.

Reheat the pan, add 2½ tablespoons of the oil, and heat until very hot. Add the beef and stir-fry over high heat until the meat loses its raw color and separates. Remove with a handled strainer or a slotted spoon and drain. Wipe out the pan.

Reheat the pan, add the remaining 1 tablespoon oil, and heat until very hot. Add the Minced Seasonings and stir-fry for about 10 seconds, until fragrant. Add the sauce mixture and snow peas and heat until the sauce is thickened, stirring continuously to prevent lumps. Add the cooked beef slices, toss to mix, and spoon over the fried noodle cake. Serve immediately.

Variation: Substitute boneless chicken breasts or turkey for the beef, and/or substitute blanched broccoli, cut into 1½-inch pieces, for the snow peas.

SEAFOOD
NOODLE SALAD

In this light salad, noodles flavored with sesame oil and ginger form a bed for poached scallops and shrimp, snow peas, and red bell peppers. The whole platter is dressed with a tangy cilantro vinaigrette. Try this with lobster and crab, for a more extravagant dish, or with other combinations of vegetables, such as carrots, celery, and green beans, to be inventive.

● Serves 6

1 pound medium shrimp, peeled

1 pound sea scallops

Marinade

¼ cup rice wine or sake

6 slices fresh ginger (about the size of a quarter), lightly smashed with the flat side of a knife or a cleaver

1 teaspoon sesame oil

½ pound flat noodles, such as linguine or fettucine

1 teaspoon sesame oil

2 teaspoons minced fresh ginger

1 tablespoon minced scallion greens

Dressing

¼ cup soy sauce

½ teaspoon salt

3 tablespoons clear rice vinegar

2 tablespoons sesame oil

1 tablespoon sugar

3 tablespoons chopped cilantro (fresh coriander)

½ pound snow peas, ends trimmed and veiny strings removed

1 red bell pepper, rinsed, cored, seeded, and thinly sliced

Using a sharp knife or a cleaver, score the shrimp down the back so they will butterfly when cooked, and remove the dark vein. Rinse, drain, and place in a bowl. If the scallops are very large, slice in half horizontally. Place in another bowl. To prepare the Marinade, combine the rice wine or sake and ginger, pinching the ginger to impart the flavor. Then stir in the sesame oil. Pour half the mixture over the scallops and half over the shrimp, and toss lightly to coat. Cover with plastic wrap and refrigerate for 20 minutes.

Heat 4 quarts of water in a large pot until boiling. Add the noodles and cook until just tender, about 5 minutes. Drain and rinse under cold running water. Add the sesame oil, minced ginger, and scallions and toss lightly to coat. Arrange on a platter or in a serving bowl.

Combine the Dressing ingredients.

Heat a medium pot of water until boiling, add the snow peas, and cook for ½ minute. Remove with a slotted strainer, refresh in cold water, then drain thoroughly and blot dry with paper towels. Reheat the water until boiling, add the scallops with their marinade, and cook for about 2 minutes, or until opaque. Remove with a slotted spoon or a handled strainer and drain; discard the seasonings. Reheat the water, add the shrimp, and cook for 3 minutes, or until they turn pink and become opaque. Drain in a colander and discard the seasonings.

Arrange the scallops, shrimp, snow peas, and red pepper strips over the noodles. Serve at room temperature or chilled. Just before serving, pour the dressing over the salad, and toss lightly if desired.

BARBECUED
PORK NOODLES

Scallion greens and crunchy bean sprouts provide an admirable foil to the barbecued pork in this stir-fry, but try crisp-cooked broccoli or snow peas for a delicious variation. ● Serves 6

1½ pounds boneless center-cut pork loin

Barbecue Sauce

⅓ cup hoisin sauce

3 tablespoons ketchup

2 tablespoons rice wine or sake

1 tablespoon minced garlic

1 tablespoon soy sauce

½ pound flat noodles, such as fettucine

1½ teaspoons sesame oil

Hoisin Sauce

1½ cups Chinese Chicken Broth (page 367)

3 tablespoons soy sauce

1½ tablespoons rice wine or sake

2 tablespoons hoisin sauce

1½ tablespoons ketchup

2 teaspoons sesame oil

1 tablespoon cornstarch

2 tablespoons corn or safflower oil

Seasonings

1½ tablespoons minced garlic

1 tablespoon minced fresh ginger

1 teaspoon hot chili paste

1½ cups 1-inch pieces scallion greens

3 cups bean sprouts, rinsed and drained

To prepare the barbecued pork, with a sharp knife or a cleaver, trim any fat or gristle from the pork. Combine the Barbecue Sauce ingredients in a bowl. Add the pork and toss to coat. Cover with plastic wrap and refrigerate for 1 hour.

Preheat the oven to 350°F.

Place the pork in a baking pan lined with aluminum foil, and bake for 30 to 45 minutes, until cooked through. Let cool. Cut the pork loin lengthwise in half, then cut across the grain into very thin slices, about ⅛ inch thick.

Heat 4 quarts of water in a large pot until boiling. Add the noodles and cook until just tender, about 5 minutes. Drain, rinse under cold running water, and drain thoroughly. Toss with the sesame oil.

Combine the Hoisin Sauce ingredients and blend well.

Heat a wok or a well-seasoned skillet, add the corn or safflower oil and heat until hot. Add the Seasonings and stir-fry over high heat until fragrant, about 10 seconds. Add the scallion greens and bean sprouts and toss for about 1 minute. Add the sauce mixture and cook, stirring continuously, until thickened. Add the sliced pork and noodles and toss to coat. Transfer to a serving platter and serve immediately.

CHICKEN NOODLE SOUP

There are few dishes as soothing as chicken soup. But in this recipe, I've bolstered the intoxicating broth with generous amounts of rice wine, ginger, and smoky black mushrooms. The delicate rice noodles, which are added at the last minute, lend substance to the fragrant soup. ● Serves 6

1 chicken (about 3½ to 4 pounds)
1 tablespoon corn or safflower oil
1 teaspoon sesame oil
1½ tablespoons finely shredded fresh ginger
10 dried Chinese black mushrooms, softened in hot water for 20 minutes, stems discarded, and caps cut in half
½ cup rice wine or sake
10 cups water
¼ pound thin rice noodles, softened in hot water to cover for 10 minutes and drained
1 teaspoon salt, or more to taste

Remove and discard the fat from the cavity and around the neck of the chicken. Using a sharp knife or a cleaver, cut the chicken into serving pieces. Cut off the wings. Cut away the legs and thighs and split them in half at the joint, then cut the thighs in half. Split the carcass lengthwise in half, and cut the breast in two. Cut the back in half.

Heat a heavy flameproof casserole or a large pot, add the corn or safflower oil, and heat until very hot. Add half the chicken pieces, skin side down, and fry over high heat until golden. Remove with a slotted spoon and drain. Reheat the oil and fry the remaining chicken. Clean out the pot.

Reheat the pot, add the sesame oil, and heat until very hot. Add the ginger and stir-fry for about 10 seconds, until fragrant. Add the black mushrooms and toss over high heat for about 10 seconds, then add the rice wine or sake, chicken, and the water. Cover and heat until boiling. Reduce the heat to low and simmer uncovered for 1½ hours, skimming any impurities from the surface.

Increase the heat slightly and add the rice noodles and salt. Cover, bring to a boil, and cook for 1 minute. Taste for seasoning, adding more salt if necessary, and transfer to serving bowls. Serve immediately.

Variation: Substitute vermicelli for the rice noodles.

SPICY BEEF NOODLES

On many a raw winter day, I've warmed myself with a bowlful of this hearty beef soup. The tender meat, infused with the flavorings of anise, cinnamon, orange zest, and soy sauce, is exceptionally good and provides a pungent contrast to the noodles. ● Serves 6

2 pounds chuck or beef stew meat

Cooking Broth

½ cup soy sauce

1½ tablespoons sweet bean sauce or hoisin sauce

1 teaspoon aniseed

1 cinnamon stick

Zest of 1 orange, removed in thin strips with a vegetable peeler

6 cups water

1 teaspoon corn or safflower oil

Seasonings

3 tablespoons minced scallions

1½ tablespoons minced garlic

1½ tablespoons minced fresh ginger

1 teaspoon crushed dried red chile peppers

½ pound thin noodles, such as vermicelli

4 cups Chinese Chicken Broth (page 367)

½ teaspoon salt

1½ teaspoons sesame oil

¾ pound (or 1 10-ounce bag) fresh spinach, stems removed, rinsed thoroughly, and drained

3 tablespoons minced scallions (green part only)

Using a sharp knife, cut the beef into 1½-inch cubes. Combine the Cooking Broth ingredients.

Heat a casserole or a heavy pot, add the corn or safflower oil, and heat until hot. Add the Seasonings and stir-fry for about 10 seconds, until fragrant. Add the cooking broth and heat until boiling. Add the meat and bring back to a boil. Reduce the heat to low, cover, and simmer, skimming the surface to

(continued)

remove any impurities and fat, for 1½ to 2 hours, or until the beef is very tender.

Meanwhile, heat 4 quarts water in a large pot until boiling. Add the noodles and cook until tender, about 4 minutes; drain. Combine the chicken broth, salt, and sesame oil in a large pot and heat until boiling. Add the spinach and scallions, and remove from the heat.

Portion the noodles into individual serving bowls. Ladle the spinach and broth over the noodles, and then spoon the beef and about ⅓ cup of the cooking liquid over each portion. Serve immediately.

HOME-STYLE PORK NOODLES

On weekends, my "surrogate" Chinese mother often made a variation of this dish for a hearty one-pot lunch or dinner. The bell peppers and tomatoes impart a full, mellow flavor while the cooked pork slices lend richness to the broth. ● Serves 6

1 pound boneless center-cut pork loin

Marinade

2 tablespoons soy sauce

1½ tablespoons rice wine or sake

1 tablespoon hoisin sauce

1 teaspoon sesame oil

1 teaspoon cornstarch

2½ tablespoons corn or safflower oil

Minced Seasonings

3 tablespoons minced scallions (white part only)

1½ tablespoons minced garlic

1½ tablespoons minced fresh ginger

2 red bell peppers, rinsed, cored, seeded, and cut into small dice

2 medium tomatoes, cored, seeded, and cut into small dice

¼ pound mushrooms, rinsed, drained, stems trimmed, and cut
lengthwise in half and then halved crosswise

1½ tablespoons soy sauce

1½ tablespoons rice wine or sake

Soup Base

4½ cups Chinese Chicken Broth (page 367)

1 teaspoon salt

1½ teaspoons sesame oil

¼ teaspoon freshly ground black pepper

½ pound flat Chinese flour and water noodles (or fettucine)

½ pound snow peas, ends trimmed and veiny strings removed

With a sharp knife, trim any fat or gristle from the pork. Cut the pork loin lengthwise into thirds, then cut across the grain into thin slices about ⅛ inch thick. Place in a bowl, add the Marinade ingredients, and toss lightly to coat. Cover with plastic wrap and let sit for 1 hour at room temperature, or refrigerate overnight.

Heat a wok or a large skillet, add 2 tablespoons of the oil, and heat until very hot. Add the pork and toss lightly over high heat until it loses its raw color and separates. Remove with a slotted spoon or a handled strainer and drain. Clean out the pan.

Reheat the pan, add the remaining ½ tablespoon of oil, and heat until hot. Add the Minced Seasonings and stir-fry over high heat until fragrant, about 10 seconds. Add the peppers, tomatoes, and mushrooms and toss for about 30 seconds. Add the soy sauce and rice wine or sake and cook for about 1 minute. Add the Soup Base ingredients and heat until boiling. Reduce the heat to low and simmer for about 15 minutes, skimming any impurities from the surface.

Meanwhile, heat 4 quarts water in a large pot until boiling. Add the noodles and cook until just tender, about 5 minutes; drain.

Portion the cooked noodles into large serving bowls. Add the cooked pork slices and the snow peas to the soup and heat until boiling. Ladle over the noodles, and serve immediately.

CHICKEN NOODLE PLATTER
WITH PEANUT SAUCE

T his is a staple in my noodle repertoire and it is one of my most re-
quested recipes. Few dishes are so easy yet so delicious. Shredded,
crisp vegetables and chicken arranged on a bed of noodles are bathed in a
spicy peanut dressing. Serve as an appetizer or as a light and satisfying meal.

● Serves 6

2 boneless skinless chicken breasts (about 2 pounds)

Poaching Liquid

4 cups water

⅓ cup rice wine or sake

4 slices fresh ginger (about the size of a quarter), smashed with the
flat side of a knife or a cleaver

4 scallions, trimmed and smashed with the flat side of a knife or a
cleaver

½ pound flat spinach or egg noodles, such as fettucine

1 teaspoon sesame oil

2 cups grated carrots

2 cups grated, peeled, and seeded cucumbers

1 red bell pepper, rinsed, cored, seeded, and sliced into thin julienne
strips

1½ cups bean sprouts, rinsed and drained

Peanut Sauce

1½ tablespoons minced garlic

1½ tablespoons minced fresh ginger

6 tablespoons smooth peanut butter

3½ tablespoons soy sauce

2 tablespoons rice wine or sake

1½ tablespoons sesame oil

3 tablespoons Chinese black vinegar or Worcestershire sauce

2½ tablespoons sugar

1½ teaspoons hot chili paste, or to taste

4 to 6 tablespoons reserved Poaching Liquid

With a sharp knife, trim any fat or sinew from the chicken. Combine the Poaching Liquid ingredients in a large saucepan and heat until boiling. Place the chicken breasts in the poaching liquid, partially cover, and simmer over low heat for 20 to 25 minutes, until cooked through. Remove and let cool, reserving 6 tablespoons of the poaching liquid. Cut the chicken into thin julienne shreds.

Heat 4 quarts water in a large pot until boiling. Add the noodles and cook until just tender, about 5 minutes. Drain and rinse under cold running water to remove the starch; drain thoroughly. Toss with the sesame oil, and arrange on a large serving platter.

Arrange the carrots, cucumbers, red pepper strips, and bean sprouts in separate mounds or in concentric circles over the noodles, leaving a slight well in the center for the chicken. Arrange the chicken in the center.

To prepare the Peanut Sauce, combine the garlic and ginger in a food processor fitted with a steel blade or in a blender and process to a paste. Add the remaining ingredients except the reserved poaching liquid, one at a time, and blend until smooth after each addition. Add 4 tablespoons of the poaching liquid and blend well; if the sauce seems too thick, add additional liquid and blend until smooth. Transfer the sauce to a serving container. Pass with the noodle salad, or pour over the salad just before serving.

Variation: For a vegetarian noodle platter, omit the chicken and substitute water for the poaching liquid in the peanut sauce.

FRIED SHRIMP
RICE NOODLES

Inspired by the memorable Thai classic *pad thai,* this rice noodle stir-fry is garnished with shrimp, bean sprouts, and chopped peanuts and bathed in a light tomato-based sauce. The delicate rice vermicelli are pleasantly spicy and filling. ● Serves 6

1 pound medium shrimp, peeled

Marinade

2 tablespoons rice wine or sake

3 slices fresh ginger (about the size of a quarter), lightly smashed
    with the flat side of a knife or a cleaver

½ teaspoon sesame oil

Sauce

½ cup soy sauce

⅓ cup homemade or prepared tomato sauce

1 cup water

3½ tablespoons sugar

1½ tablespoons rice wine or sake

3½ tablespoons corn or safflower oil

1 tablespoon minced garlic

2 large eggs, lightly beaten

¾ pound very thin rice stick noodles or rice vermicelli, softened in
    cold water to cover for 30 minutes and drained

Garnishes

2 cups bean sprouts, rinsed and drained

3 tablespoons chopped dry-roasted peanuts

2 tablespoons minced scallion greens

½ teaspoon crushed dried red chile peppers

2 tablespoons coarsely chopped cilantro (fresh coriander)

With a sharp knife, score the shrimp down the back so they will butterfly when cooked, and remove the dark vein. Rinse and drain. Place in a bowl, add the Marinade ingredients, and pinch the ginger in the rice wine or sake to impart the flavor. Toss lightly to coat, cover with plastic wrap, and refrigerate for 1 hour.

Combine the Sauce ingredients and stir to dissolve the sugar.

Heat a wok or a skillet, add 2 tablespoons of the oil, and heat until hot. Add the shrimp and stir-fry over high heat until they turn pink, about 2 minutes. Remove with a handled strainer or a slotted spoon and drain. Wipe out the pan.

Reheat the pan, add the remaining 1½ tablespoons oil, and heat until hot. Add the garlic and stir-fry for about 5 seconds, until fragrant. Add the eggs and stir-fry to scramble. Add the sauce mixture and heat until boiling. Add the noodles and cook for about 1½ minutes, stirring occasionally, over high heat. Transfer to a serving platter and sprinkle with the cooked shrimp and the Garnishes. Toss lightly and serve.

Variation: Substitute thinly sliced sea scallops for the shrimp.

SINGAPORE FRIED RICE NOODLES

Singapore is a melting pot, and its cuisine reflects that diversity, with its exotic dishes that combine ingredients from all over Asia and the West. Such is the case with this noodle platter, in which delicate rice noodles are garnished with barbecued pork, shrimp, bean sprouts, and leeks and seasoned with a dusting of curry powder. ● Serves 6

1½ pounds Barbecued Pork (see Barbecued Pork Noodles, page 338)

½ pound medium shrimp, peeled

2 tablespoons rice wine or sake

1 teaspoon minced fresh ginger

½ teaspoon sesame oil

Sauce

3 tablespoons Chinese Chicken Broth (page 367)

1 tablespoon soy sauce

1 teaspoon salt

½ teaspoon sugar

2½ tablespoons corn or safflower oil

1½ tablespoons curry powder

2 cups finely shredded leeks

3 cups bean sprouts, rinsed and drained

7 ounces very thin dried rice stick noodles or rice vermicelli,
softened in cold water to cover for 30 minutes and drained

With a sharp knife or a cleaver, cut the pork into thin slices about ⅛ inch thick, then cut into julienne shreds about 2 inches long.

Slice the shrimp in half down the back, removing the dark vein. Rinse and drain. Place in a bowl, add the rice wine or sake, ginger, and sesame oil, and toss to coat. Cover with plastic wrap and let stand at room temperature for 20 minutes. Combine the Sauce ingredients and set aside.

Heat a wok or a skillet, add 1 tablespoon of the oil, and heat until hot. Add the shrimp and stir-fry over high heat until they turn pink, about 2 minutes. Remove with a handled strainer or a slotted spoon and drain. Wipe out the pan.

Reheat the pan, add the remaining 1½ tablespoons oil, and heat until very hot. Add the curry powder and stir-fry for about 10 seconds, until fragrant. Add the leeks and stir-fry over high heat for about 1½ minutes. Add the bean sprouts and toss lightly for 20 seconds. Add the pork, shrimp, rice noodles, and sauce mixture and carefully toss for 15 to 20 seconds, until the noodles are heated through. Transfer to a serving dish and serve immediately.

Variation: For a simplified version, omit the barbecued pork and increase the shrimp to ¾ pound.

SPICY CELLOPHANE NOODLES

Cellophane noodles, or bean threads, have a smooth, slippery texture. While they have little flavor of their own, they absorb the flavors of the ingredients they are cooked with. In this spicy dish, they become plump in a savory sauce seasoned generously with ginger, garlic, and hot chili paste.

● **Serves 6**

¾ pound ground turkey

Marinade

1 tablespoon soy sauce

2 teaspoons rice wine or sake

1 teaspoon sesame oil

Sauce

2 cups Chinese Chicken Broth (page 367)

2 tablespoons soy sauce

1½ tablespoons rice wine or sake

1 teaspoon sugar

1 teaspoon sesame oil

1 tablespoon corn or safflower oil

Minced Seasonings

3 tablespoons minced scallions

1½ tablespoons minced fresh ginger

1 tablespoon minced garlic

1 teaspoon hot chili paste or crushed dried red chile peppers

4 ounces cellophane noodles (or bean threads), softened in hot water to cover for 20 minutes and drained

2 tablespoons minced scallion greens

With a sharp knife or a cleaver, lightly chop the ground meat until fluffy. Place in a bowl, add the Marinade ingredients, and stir to mix. Cover with plastic wrap and let stand at room temperature for 20 minutes.

Combine the Sauce ingredients and set aside.

Heat a wok or a skillet, add ½ tablespoon of the oil, and heat until hot. Add the ground meat and cook, mashing and breaking it up, until it loses its raw color. Remove with a handled strainer or a slotted spoon and drain. Clean out the pan.

Reheat the pan, add the remaining ½ tablespoon oil, and heat until hot. Add the Minced Seasonings and stir-fry for 10 seconds, until fragrant. Add the sauce mixture, the cellophane noodles, and the cooked meat, and heat, stirring, until boiling. Reduce the heat to medium low and cook until almost all the liquid has evaporated. Transfer to a serving bowl and sprinkle with the minced scallions. Serve immediately.

Variation: Substitute ground pork or beef for the turkey.

BOILED OR STEAMED WHITE RICE

Many American cooks marvel at the fluffy, light consistency of the rice in Chinese restaurants. The secret is to rinse the rice thoroughly before cooking, removing any talc and excess starch, and to cook the rice just until tender. Follow the simple steps outlined here and your rice should be worthy of any Chinese feast. Steamed rice has a slightly fluffier texture than boiled rice; try both methods to see which one you prefer. ● Serves 6

3 cups long-grain white rice

Using your fingers as a rake, rinse the rice under cold running water until the water runs clear. Drain in a colander.

To boil the rice: Combine the rice and 6 cups water in a saucepan with a tight-fitting lid. Heat, uncovered, until boiling. Reduce the heat to low, cover, and simmer for 20 minutes, or until all the water has evaporated and craters appear on the surface of the rice. Remove from the heat and let sit, covered, for 10 minutes. Fluff the rice with a fork or chopsticks and serve.

To steam the rice: Fill a wok or a pot with water for steaming and heat until boiling. Spread the rice in a steamer tray lined with damp cheesecloth or parchment paper (see page 7). Place over the boiling water, cover, and steam for 35 to 40 minutes over high heat. Turn off the heat and let the rice sit, covered, for 10 minutes. Fluff the rice with a fork or chopsticks and serve.

SHRIMP FRIED RICE

Fried rice is one of the most versatile dishes in the Chinese repertoire, lending itself to creativity using all sorts of combinations of ingredients. Chinese-American restaurants tend to be heavy-handed with the soy sauce, but in the Far East only a bit of the sauce is added to the dish. Here the pearly white rice contrasts beautifully with the pink shrimp, scrambled eggs, and bright green baby peas. ● **Serves 6**

½ pound medium shrimp, peeled

Marinade

1½ tablespoons rice wine or sake

1 teaspoon minced fresh ginger

½ teaspoon sesame oil

Sauce

2 tablespoons Chinese Chicken Broth (page 367)

1½ tablespoons rice wine or sake

1 tablespoon soy sauce

1 teaspoon salt

1 teaspoon sesame oil

3 tablespoons corn or safflower oil

2 large eggs, lightly beaten

¾ cup minced scallions

1½ cups frozen peas, thawed

5 cups cold cooked rice, separated with a fork

Using a sharp knife or a cleaver, slice the shrimp in half down the back, removing the dark vein. Rinse and drain. Place in a bowl, add the Marinade ingredients, and toss to coat. Cover with plastic wrap and let stand at room temperature for 20 minutes.

Combine the Sauce ingredients and set aside.

Heat a wok or a skillet, add 1 tablespoon of the oil, and heat until hot. Add the shrimp and stir-fry over high heat until they turn pink, about 2 minutes. Remove with a handled strainer or a slotted spoon and drain. Wipe out the pan.

Reheat the pan, add the 2 remaining tablespoons oil, and heat until hot. Add the eggs and stir-fry over high heat for about 30 seconds to scramble. Add the minced scallions and stir-fry for about 1 minute. Add the peas and stir-fry briefly to heat through. Add the rice, breaking it up with the spatula, and cook for 2 to 3 minutes, until heated through. Add the shrimp and the sauce mixture, toss to coat, and transfer to a serving dish. Serve immediately.

Variation: Substitute diced boneless chicken breasts or boneless pork loin for the shrimp. Add 1 tablespoon soy sauce to the marinade.

CURRIED FRIED RICE

One of the secrets to making perfect fried rice is to use cold cooked rice that has been separated with a fork before it is added to the pan. Then, when tossed in the delicate sauce, the grains retain their shape and don't clump together. This fried rice is sparingly seasoned with a hint of curry powder, giving it an appealing color and flavor. Ground turkey, marinated in soy sauce, rice wine, and sesame oil, adds even more flavor.

● Serves 6

½ pound ground turkey

Marinade

1½ tablespoons soy sauce

1 tablespoon rice wine or sake

½ teaspoon sesame oil

Sauce

2½ tablespoons Chinese Chicken Broth (page 367)

1 tablespoon soy sauce

1 teaspoon salt

2 tablespoons corn or safflower oil

1 cup finely diced onions

1½ tablespoons curry powder

1½ cups finely diced carrots, blanched in boiling water for
     1½ minutes and refreshed in cold water

1½ cups frozen peas, thawed

5 cups cold cooked rice, separated with a fork   *(continued)*

Lightly chop the ground turkey with a knife or a cleaver until fluffy. Place in a bowl, add the Marinade ingredients, and toss to mix. Cover with plastic wrap and refrigerate for 30 minutes.

Combine the Sauce ingredients and set aside.

Heat a wok or a skillet, add ½ tablespoon of the oil, and heat until very hot. Add the turkey, mashing it lightly with a spatula to break up any lumps, and stir-fry over high heat until the meat loses its raw color, about 2 to 3 minutes. Remove with a handled strainer or a slotted spoon and drain. Wipe out the pan.

Reheat the pan, add the remaining 1½ tablespoons oil, and heat until hot. Add the diced onions and stir-fry over medium heat until softened and transparent, about 2 minutes. Add the curry powder and stir-fry for 10 seconds, until fragrant. Add the carrots and peas and stir-fry until heated through, about 1 minute. Add the rice, breaking it up with the spatula, then add the cooked turkey and the sauce mixture. Toss lightly to coat and transfer to a serving dish. Serve immediately.

Variation: Substitute diced boneless pork loin, flank steak, or boneless chicken breasts for the turkey.

YANGCHOW FRIED RICE

L ong a staple in Cantonese restaurants, Yangchow fried rice is a colorful, delicious dish loaded with shrimp, Chinese ham, peas, and Chinese black mushrooms. Pair it with a light soup for a filling lunch or dinner.
● Serves 6

⅓ pound medium shrimp, peeled, deveined, rinsed, drained, and cut into ¼-inch dice

Marinade

2 tablespoons rice wine or sake

1 teaspoon minced fresh ginger

½ teaspoon sesame oil

Sauce

2 tablespoons Chinese Chicken Broth (page 367)

1½ tablespoons rice wine or sake

1 tablespoon soy sauce

1 teaspoon salt

1 teaspoon sesame oil

3 tablespoons corn or safflower oil

2 large eggs, lightly beaten

1½ cups minced scallion greens

8 dried Chinese black mushrooms, softened in hot water for 20 minutes, stems removed, and caps cut into ¼-inch dice

1 cup frozen peas, thawed

2 ounces thinly sliced Chinese or Smithfield ham or prosciutto, cut into ¼-inch dice

5 cups cold cooked rice, separated with a fork

Place the shrimp in a bowl, add the Marinade ingredients, and toss to coat. Cover with plastic wrap and let stand at room temperature for 20 minutes.

Combine the Sauce ingredients and set aside.

Heat a wok or a skillet, add 1 tablespoon of the oil, and heat until hot. Add the shrimp and stir-fry over high heat until pink, about 1½ minutes. Remove with a handled strainer or a slotted spoon and drain. Wipe out the pan.

Reheat the pan, add the remaining 2 tablespoons oil, and heat until hot. Add the eggs and stir-fry over high heat for about 30 seconds to scramble. Add the minced scallions and black mushrooms and stir-fry for about 20 seconds until fragrant. Add the peas and stir-fry briefly to heat through. Add the ham or prosciutto and then the rice, breaking it up with the spatula, and cook for 2 to 3 minutes, until heated through. Add the shrimp and the sauce mixture and toss to coat. Transfer to a serving dish and serve immediately.

RAINBOW RICE PORRIDGE

The Chinese enjoy rice porridge or gruel on numerous occasions. For the Cantonese, it is a nourishing breakfast. For those recovering from an illness, it is soothing and easy to digest, and just about everyone enjoys it as a hearty, easy-to-prepare snack. I deviate from the traditional recipe by reducing the proportion of rice to broth, creating a lighter dish.

● Serves 6

1 pound boneless skinless chicken breasts

Marinade

2 tablespoons soy sauce

1½ tablespoons rice wine or sake

1 teaspoon sesame oil

1 teaspoon cornstarch

1 cup long-grain white rice

Cooking Liquid

10 cups Chinese Chicken Broth (page 367)

¼ cup rice wine or sake

1 teaspoon salt

2½ tablespoons corn or safflower oil

1 tablespoon minced garlic

½ tablespoon minced fresh ginger

1 tablespoon minced scallions (white part only)

6 dried Chinese black mushrooms, softened in hot water for 20
    minutes, stems removed, and caps cut into ¼-inch dice

3 carrots, trimmed, peeled, and cut into ¼-inch dice

1½ cups frozen peas, thawed

2 tablespoons soy sauce

Using a sharp knife or a cleaver, trim the chicken of any fat or sinew. Cut into ¼-inch dice and place in a bowl. Add the Marinade ingredients and toss lightly to coat. Cover with plastic wrap and refrigerate for 1 hour.

Using your fingers as a rake, rinse the rice in a colander under cold running water until the water runs clear. Drain. Combine the Cooking Liquid ingredients and set aside.

Heat a flameproof casserole or a wok, add 2 tablespoons of the oil, and heat until hot. Add the chicken and stir-fry over high heat until it loses its raw color and separates. Remove with a handled strainer or a slotted spoon and drain. Wipe out the pan.

Reheat the pan, add the remaining ½ tablespoon oil, and heat until hot. Add the garlic, ginger, scallions, and black mushrooms and stir-fry for about 10 seconds, until fragrant. Add the cooking liquid mixture and heat until boiling. Add the rice and carrots, and bring back to a boil. Cook over high heat, stirring occasionally, for about 2 minutes. Reduce the heat to low, cover, and simmer for about 1 hour, or until the porridge has the consistency of a thick soup. Skim the surface to remove any impurities. Add the peas, cook for about 30 seconds, and add the soy sauce. Transfer to a serving bowl and serve immediately.

SWEET-AND-SOUR
PORK STIR-FRY OVER RICE

he Chinese version of fast food is an all-purpose dish consisting of meat and vegetables spooned over rice. It is popular lunchtime fare in restaurants all over the Orient. Here is a pork rendition, liberally garnished with onions, red peppers, and mushrooms and bathed in a gutsy sweet-and-sour sauce—a superb topping for rice or noodles. ● Serves 6

1 pound boneless center-cut pork loin

Marinade

1½ tablespoons soy sauce

1 tablespoon rice wine or sake

1 teaspoon sesame oil

1 teaspoon cornstarch

Sauce

1 cup Chinese Chicken Broth (page 367) or water

3½ tablespoons soy sauce

2 tablespoons rice wine or sake

3 tablespoons ketchup

3 tablespoons sugar

2 tablespoons clear rice vinegar

1½ teaspoons cornstarch

3½ tablespoons corn or safflower oil

Seasonings

1½ tablespoons minced garlic

1 tablespoon minced fresh ginger

2 cups thinly sliced onions

1½ cups thinly sliced red bell peppers

1 cup mushrooms, trimmed and thinly sliced

⅓ pound snow peas, ends trimmed and veiny strings removed

6 cups hot cooked long-grain white rice

With a sharp knife or a cleaver, remove any fat or gristle from the pork loin. Cut into thin slices about ⅙ inch thick, then cut each slice crosswise into thirds. Place in a bowl, add the Marinade ingredients, and toss lightly to coat. Cover with plastic wrap and let stand for 30 minutes at room temperature.

Combine the Sauce ingredients and blend well.

Heat a wok or a skillet, add 2 tablespoons of the oil, and heat until very hot. Add the pork and stir-fry over high heat until the meat loses its raw color and separates. Remove with a handled strainer or a slotted spoon and drain. Wipe out the pan.

Reheat the pan, add the remaining 1½ tablespoons oil, and heat until very hot. Add the Seasonings and stir-fry over high heat for about 15 seconds, until fragrant. Add the onions and cook for about 1½ minutes, or until softened. Add the red peppers and mushrooms and stir-fry for about 2 minutes, until tender. Add the sauce mixture and heat until thickened, stirring constantly. Add the snow peas and pork and toss to coat. Transfer to a serving dish and serve spooned over the hot rice.

Variation: Substitute boneless chicken breasts, cut into 1-inch chunks, or meat, or medium shrimp for the pork.

BLACK BEAN–CHICKEN STIR-FRY OVER RICE

This fragrant stir-fry is redolent of garlic, ginger, and pungent black beans. The flavorful dish lends itself to variation: Try pork, beef, or seafood instead of the chicken and substitute broccoli or green beans for the snow peas. ● Serves 6

1 pound boneless skinless chicken breasts

Marinade

2½ tablespoons soy sauce

1½ tablespoons rice wine or sake

1 teaspoon sesame oil

1½ teaspoons cornstarch

Sauce

1 cup Chinese Chicken Broth (page 367)

2½ tablespoons soy sauce

2 tablespoons rice wine or sake

2 teaspoons sugar

1½ teaspoons cornstarch

3½ tablespoons corn or safflower oil

Minced Seasonings

2 tablespoons fermented black beans, rinsed, drained, and minced

1½ tablespoons minced garlic

1½ tablespoons minced fresh ginger

½ teaspoon crushed dried red chile peppers or chile pepper flakes

1 cup thinly sliced red onions

1½ yellow bell peppers, rinsed, cored, seeded, and thinly sliced

½ pound snow peas, ends trimmed and veiny strings removed

6 cups hot cooked long-grain white rice

With a sharp knife or a cleaver, remove any fat or sinew from the chicken. Holding the knife almost horizontal to the cutting board, cut into thin slices about ⅙ inch thick. If the breasts are very wide, cut each slice in half. Place in a bowl, add the Marinade ingredients, and toss lightly to coat. Cover with plastic wrap and refrigerate for 1 hour.

Combine the Sauce ingredients and blend well.

Heat a wok or a skillet, add 2 tablespoons of the oil, and heat until very hot. Add the chicken and stir-fry over high heat until it loses its pink color and separates. Remove with a handled strainer or a slotted spoon and drain. Wipe out the pan.

Reheat the pan, add the remaining 1½ tablespoons oil, and heat until very hot. Add the Minced Seasonings and stir-fry for about 15 seconds, until fragrant. Add the onions and peppers and toss lightly over medium heat for about 2½ minutes, or until the onions are softened. Add the sauce mixture and heat until thickened, stirring constantly to prevent lumps. Add the snow peas and cooked chicken, toss lightly to coat, and transfer to a serving dish. Serve spooned over the hot rice.

SOUPS

The repertoire of Chinese soups is extensive. There are light soups such as Egg Drop Soup and Summer Asparagus Soup with Crabmeat, clear broths garnished with meat, fish, seafood, and/or vegetables. These soups are often extraordinarily delicate, teasing the palate with a variety of tastes and textures.

Then there are thick soups such as Hot-and-Sour Soup and Vinegar and Pepper Seafood Chowder. Usually thickened with cornstarch, these are more substantial and heartier than their refined cousins. Full of meats or seafood, vegetables, and, occasionally, noodles, they are often served as a main course or a one-pot meal.

Chinese soups traditionally are served at the end of the meal, as the broth is believed to soothe the stomach and aid digestion. For family meals, where all the dishes are served simultaneously, soups are sipped like a beverage, with diners dipping their spoons in the broth between mouthfuls of other dishes. At formal dinners, soups punctuate a meal, signaling the progression of courses as the banquet moves from the beginning to the end.

I often defy Chinese convention and serve the light and delicate soups at the beginning of a meal, to tantalize diners and take the edge off their hunger.

For the busy cook, Chinese soups are especially attractive. The majority of soups in this chapter are not complicated affairs, but they can be prepared spontaneously with supplies at hand. In addition, most of the broths or bases can be prepared in advance and reheated before serving. Ingredients and garnishes may be cut or marinated in advance, then cooked just before serving.

CHINESE CHICKEN BROTH

Every good soup begins with a flavorful broth, and Chinese soups are no exception. Traditionally, Chinese broths are made with a combination of pork and chicken, but I prefer a simple chicken stock made with chicken bones, rice wine, smashed ginger, scallions, and water. Once the broth reaches a boil, simmer it slowly, uncovered, so that it does not become cloudy. Chicken broth will keep for up to a week in the refrigerator. It keeps almost indefinitely in the freezer. ● Makes 6 cups

2½ pounds chicken backs and necks, bones, and/or pieces with
      bones
9 cups water
¾ cup rice wine or sake
4 slices fresh ginger (about the size of a quarter), lightly smashed
      with the flat side of a knife or a cleaver
4 scallions, ends trimmed and lightly smashed with the flat side of a
      knife or a cleaver

Place the chicken parts in a pot with cold water to cover, and heat until boiling. Drain in a colander and rinse under cold running water.

Return the chicken parts to the pot and add the remaining ingredients. Heat until boiling, then reduce the heat to low and simmer uncovered for 1½ hours, skimming the surface periodically to remove any impurities. Strain the broth through a fine-meshed strainer and skim to remove any fat.

Note: Blanching the bones for broth in boiling water reduces the impurities, resulting in a clearer broth.

To make Chinese chicken broth from canned broth, combine 3 cups canned chicken broth, 3 cups water, ⅓ cup rice wine or sake, and 4 slices smashed ginger. Heat until boiling, reduce the heat to low, and simmer uncovered for 20 minutes. Strain and use as directed. This broth will keep refrigerated for up to a week.

EGG DROP SOUP

When lightly beaten eggs are drizzled into a hot thickened broth, they cook in seconds, forming thin, wispy streamers, or "egg drops"—hence the poetic name for this homey soup. It is a staple in our household, since I usually have the main ingredients, chicken broth, tomato, peas, and eggs, on hand. ● Serves 6

3½ tablespoons cornstarch

6 tablespoons water

1 teaspoon corn or safflower oil

1 medium tomato, cored and cut into ¼-inch dice

2 tablespoons minced scallions (white part only)

1 tablespoon soy sauce

Soup Base

6 cups Chinese Chicken Broth (page 367)

2 tablespoons rice wine or sake

1 teaspoon salt, or more to taste

1 cup frozen baby peas, defrosted

2 eggs, lightly beaten with 2 tablespoons water

1 teaspoon sesame oil

Combine the cornstarch and water and blend well.

Heat a large heavy pot, add the corn or safflower oil, and heat until hot. Add the tomato and scallions and stir-fry until fragrant, about 15 seconds. Add the soy sauce and then the Soup Base ingredients and heat until boiling. Reduce the heat to medium low and cook for 2 minutes, skimming the surface to remove any impurities. Slowly add the cornstarch thickener and cook, stirring constantly to prevent lumps, until slightly thickened. Add the peas, and remove from the heat. Slowly add the beaten eggs, pouring them in a thin stream around the edge of the pot and carefully stirring once or twice so that the eggs form thin streamers. Swirl in the sesame oil. Taste for seasoning and add salt if necessary. Transfer to a soup tureen or serving bowls and serve immediately.

CHINESE LEEK
AND POTATO SOUP

Leeks and potatoes are a natural pair, and in this humble soup their flavors contrast nicely with Chinese chicken broth and rice wine. The garnish of scallion greens and Chinese ham or prosciutto provides a flavorful counterpoint to the vegetables. ● Serves 6

4 potatoes (about 1½ pounds) peeled and cut into chunks about 1½ inches square

4 large leeks, split lengthwise in half, washed thoroughly, and cut into 3-inch lengths

4 cloves garlic, smashed with the flat side of a knife or a cleaver and peeled

6½ cups Chinese Chicken Broth (page 367)

½ cup rice wine or sake

1 teaspoon salt, or more to taste

¼ teaspoon freshly ground black pepper, or more to taste

3 tablespoons minced scallion greens

3 tablespoons minced Chinese ham or prosciutto

Combine the potatoes, leeks, garlic, chicken broth, and rice wine or sake in a large pot and heat until boiling. Reduce the heat to medium and simmer, partially covered, for about 35 to 45 minutes, or until the vegetables are tender. Remove from the heat and let cool slightly.

Strain the soup into a bowl, and return the broth to the pot. Place the leeks in a blender or a food processor fitted with a steel blade and purée until smooth. Add to the broth. Place the potatoes in the processor or blender and pulse until smooth; add a little of the broth if necessary. Do not overprocess or the potatoes will become gummy. Add to the broth. Season with the salt and pepper, and heat until piping hot. Taste for seasoning, and ladle into serving bowls. Sprinkle with the minced scallions and ham or prosciutto and serve.

Note: Puréeing the vegetable separately prevents the potatoes from becoming gluey.

TOMATO SOUP
WITH FRESH CILANTRO

Tomatoes are relatively new to China, but these days it is not unusual to see market tables spilling over with mountains of them. As a result, Chinese chefs have been inspired to create a host of new dishes featuring this "exotic" ingredient. This cold gazpacho-type soup celebrates late-summer vegetables. It is delightfully refreshing on a hot summer day. ● Serves 6

4 ripe tomatoes
2 cloves garlic, peeled
1 slice fresh ginger (about the size of a quarter), peeled
1 green bell pepper, rinsed, cored, seeded, and cut into chunks
1 large cucumber, peeled, halved, seeded, and cut into chunks
2 cups canned tomato juice or spicy tomato juice
2½ tablespoons clear rice vinegar
Juice of ½ lemon
¾ teaspoon ground cumin
1 teaspoon salt, or more to taste
¼ teaspoon freshly ground black pepper, or more to taste
½ cup minced scallion greens
3 tablespoons minced cilantro (fresh coriander)

Heat a medium pot of water until boiling. Core the tomatoes and, with a sharp knife, make an "X" in the skin of the rounded end of each one. Blanch in the boiling water for 15 seconds, then remove with a slotted spoon and immerse in cold water. Peel and cut into chunks.

With the machine running, drop the garlic and ginger into a blender or a food processor fitted with a steel blade and process until finely chopped. Add the green pepper, cucumber, and tomatoes and pulse until finely chopped. Transfer to a large bowl and stir in the tomato juice, rice vinegar, lemon juice, cumin, and salt and pepper. Taste for seasoning, and add more salt and pepper if necessary. If the mixture is too thick, add about ¼ cup of water. Cover with plastic wrap and chill for 2 hours.

Transfer the soup to a serving bowl or individual bowls, sprinkle the chopped scallions and cilantro on top, and serve.

Note: You can vary the texture of the soup from smooth to chunky, depending on how finely you chop the vegetables.

GINGER CLAM BROTH

Few tastes compare with that of clams steamed in a broth flavored with wine, smashed garlic, ginger, scallions, and their own juices. To prevent the clams from overcooking, it's vital to serve the soup as soon as the shells open. ● Serves 6

36 small littleneck or hard-shell clams

Soup Base

½ teaspoon corn or safflower oil

6 cloves garlic, smashed with the flat side of a knife or a cleaver and peeled

6 slices fresh ginger (about the size of a quarter), smashed with the flat side of a knife or a cleaver

4 scallions, trimmed and smashed with the flat side of a knife or a cleaver

3½ cups Chinese Chicken Broth (page 367)

¾ cup rice wine or sake

½ teaspoon salt, or to taste

Rinse the clams thoroughly. Place in cold water to cover and let sit for 1 hour. Drain.

To prepare the Soup Base, heat the oil in a large pot until very hot. Add the garlic, ginger, and scallions and stir-fry for about 10 to 15 seconds, until fragrant. Add the chicken broth, rice wine or sake, and salt and heat until boiling, reduce the heat to low and simmer for 10 minutes. Add the clams, cover, and cook for about 5 to 7 minutes over medium heat, just until the clams open. Discard any unopened clams, transfer to a serving bowl, and serve immediately.

Note: Littleneck clams toughen very quickly if overcooked, so cook them only until they are open.

SHRIMP
WONTON SOUP

There are not many dishes that are as satisfying as a rich chicken broth garnished with delicate shrimp wontons and fresh spinach. I often serve this as a complete meal in itself for a light lunch or dinner.

● Makes 48 wontons

¾ pound medium shrimp, peeled, deveined, rinsed, and drained

½ cup water chestnuts, blanched in boiling water for 10 seconds, refreshed in cold water, drained, and coarsely chopped

Seasonings

1½ tablespoons minced fresh ginger

1 tablespoon rice wine or sake

2 teaspoons minced scallions (white part only)

2 teaspoons soy sauce

1 teaspoon sesame oil

½ teaspoon salt

¼ teaspoon freshly ground black pepper

½ egg white, lightly beaten

1 tablespoon cornstarch

48 wonton skins

5 cups Chinese Chicken Broth (page 367)

1 teaspoon salt

½ teaspoon sesame oil

¼ pound fresh spinach, stems removed, rinsed thoroughly, and drained

Wrap the shrimp in a dish towel or paper towels and squeeze out as much moisture as possible. Place in a food processor fitted with a steel blade and process to a paste; or chop by hand, using a sharp knife. Transfer to a bowl.

Wrap the water chestnuts in a dish towel or paper towels and squeeze out as much moisture as possible. Add to the shrimp paste. Add all the Seasonings except the cornstarch and stir the mixture vigorously in one direction to combine the ingredients evenly. Add the cornstarch and stir to blend. The mixture should be quite stiff; if not, chill for about 1 hour, or until firm.

Wonton Soup

SERVES 4–6

THIS RECIPE is from SAVEUR producing editor Corinne Trang, whose family once lived in China.

4 cups chicken stock
1 piece ginger about ½" thick, crushed
2 scallions, white parts only, coarsely chopped
¼ lb. baby bok choy, trimmed (optional)
¼ tbsp. sesame oil
1 ½ tsp. Chinese light soy sauce
Pinch freshly ground white pepper
¼ tsp. cornstarch
¼ lb. medium shrimp, peeled and deveined
2 oz. lean ground pork
24 thin square wonton wrappers
2 tbsp. finely chopped scallions

1. For the broth, place stock, ginger, and coarsely chopped scallions in a medium pot. Add 2 cups water and bring just to a boil over medium-high heat. Skim, reduce heat to medium-low, cover, and simmer for 30 minutes. Strain and set aside.

2. If using bok choy, cook in a large pot of boiling water until tender, about 3 minutes. Drain, refresh in cold water, and set aside.

3. Combine sesame oil, soy sauce, and pepper in a medium bowl. Stir in cornstarch, making sure that it dissolves thoroughly. Pat shrimp dry, then finely chop. Add shrimp and pork to sesame oil mixture and stir to combine ingredients well.

4. Arrange a wonton wrapper, floured side down, on a dry surface, positioning it so that it looks like a diamond, with one corner facing you. Place 1 scant tsp. filling in center of wrapper, lightly dampen edges, then fold bottom corner up to top corner, pressing gently to remove any air pockets. Wonton should now look like a triangle. Dampen the right and left corners, then draw them together around the filling. Place wonton on a cookie sheet and cover with plastic wrap, then repeat with remaining wrappers.

5. To serve, reheat broth over medium-low heat. Cook wonton in small batches in a large pot of boiling water until they float, about 5 minutes. Drain, then divide between 4–6 large bowls. Add bok choy, if using, moisten wonton with broth, and garnish with chopped scallions.

PHOTOGRAPHS BY CHRISTOPHER HIRSHEIMER

First class

At this time we are boarding second-row passengers in th
and rich wood accents located throughout the cabin, inclu

 **LINCOLN**

Using a spoon or the tips of two chopsticks, place a scant teaspoonful of the shrimp filling in the center of each wonton skin, gather the edges of the skin around the filling, and pinch to completely enclose. (The shape will be like a little money bag.) Place the wontons on a tray lightly dusted with cornstarch.

Bring 3 quarts of water to a boil in a large pot. Add half the wontons, cover, and bring back to a boil. Reduce the heat, partially cover, and cook for 3½ to 4 minutes.

Meanwhile, combine the chicken broth, salt, and sesame oil in a large pot and heat until boiling, skimming any impurities from the surface.

Using a handled strainer, transfer the cooked wontons to soup bowls. Cook the remaining wontons in the boiling water, and transfer to the soup bowls. Meanwhile, remove the boiling chicken broth from the heat and add the spinach.

Ladle the hot broth and spinach over the wontons. Serve immediately.

Variation: Deep-Fried Shrimp Wontons: The shrimp wontons can be deep-fried in 350°F oil until golden brown, about 5 to 6 minutes. Serve with plum sauce and hot mustard.

SUMMER ASPARAGUS SOUP WITH CRABMEAT

Fresh asparagus and crabmeat are frequently paired in Chinese recipes, and one can understand why after tasting this exquisite dish. The sweet, pink crabmeat contrasts perfectly with the tender, emerald-green spears. Serve this soup at the beginning of a meal to whet the appetite or, as Chinese custom dictates, at the end, when the soothing broth will refresh the palate and aid digestion. ● Serves 6

1 pound asparagus

3 tablespoons cornstarch

6 tablespoons water

Soup Base

6 cups Chinese Chicken Broth (page 367)

2½ tablespoons rice wine or sake

1 teaspoon salt, or more to taste

1 teaspoon corn or safflower oil

2 tablespoons minced scallions (white part only)

1 tablespoon minced fresh ginger

½ pound lump crabmeat, picked through to remove any shells and cartilage

2 tablespoons rice wine or sake

½ teaspoon sesame oil

1½ tablespoons minced scallion greens

Snap off the tough ends of the asparagus and cut the stalks into 1-inch lengths. Combine the cornstarch and water and blend well.

Combine the Soup Base ingredients in a large pot, and bring to a simmer. Add the asparagus and cook until tender, about 4 minutes. Keep warm over low heat.

Heat a skillet until hot, and add the corn or safflower oil. Add the scallions and ginger and stir-fry until fragrant, about 10 seconds. Add the crabmeat and rice wine or sake and toss over high heat for 30 seconds. Transfer to the asparagus soup and bring to a simmer, skimming the surface to remove any impurities. Slowly add the cornstarch thickener to the soup, and cook until slightly thickened, stirring continuously to prevent lumps. Taste for seasoning, and add salt if necessary. Swirl in the sesame oil, and ladle into a serving bowl or individual bowls. Sprinkle the minced scallions on top, and serve immediately.

Variation: For an even more delicate flavor, substitute ½ pound snow peas (ends snapped and veiny strings removed) for the asparagus. Cook the snow peas just until tender, 1 to 2 minutes.

SWEET CORN SOUP

Fresh corn shaved from the cob gives this soup its satiny consistency and sweet flavor, and minced chicken imparts a delectable richness. I particularly love this soup at the height of corn season, when the butter-and-sugar varieties are at their peak. During the rest of the year, you can substitute frozen corn on the cob or creamed corn with excellent results.

● Serves 6

Soup Base

5 cups Chinese Chicken Broth (page 367)

3 tablespoons rice wine or sake

¼ cup long-grain white rice

¾ teaspoon salt, or more to taste

6 ears sweet corn, husked, or 2 cups thawed frozen corn,
    or 1½ 17-ounce cans creamed corn

¼ pound boneless skinless chicken

2 tablespoons rice wine or sake

2 tablespoons water

2½ teaspoons sesame oil

3 tablespoons minced scallion greens

Combine the Soup Base ingredients in a large heavy pot and heat until boiling. Reduce the heat to low, cover, and simmer for 15 minutes. Add the ears of corn (if using) and cook, covered, for 20 minutes longer. Remove the corn with a slotted spoon or a handled strainer and let cool slightly.

Strain the chicken broth and return to the pot. Purée the rice in a food processor fitted with a steel blade, adding a little broth, and return to the pot of broth. Cut the kernels from the corn and purée, adding a little broth. Add the puréed corn to the broth.

Chop the chicken meat to a paste in the food processor. Add the rice wine or sake, water, and 1 teaspoon of the sesame oil and pulse to blend. Add to the broth, stirring with a whisk to separate the chicken.

Heat the broth until boiling, reduce the heat to low, and cook for 1 minute to allow the flavors to mingle. Taste for seasoning, adding salt if necessary. Ladle the soup into serving bowls and sprinkle with the minced scallion greens. Drizzle the remaining 1½ teaspoons sesame oil over the soup, and serve.

SHRIMP AND SNOW PEA SOUP

For a striking marriage of color, flavors, and textures, try this soup full of plump shrimp, crisp snow peas, and smooth cellophane noodles. When cooked, the butterflied shrimp curl into flowerlike shapes.

● Serves 6

1 pound medium shrimp, peeled

Marinade

2 tablespoons rice wine or sake

1 teaspoon minced fresh ginger

1 teaspoon sesame oil

1½ teaspoons cornstarch

2 tablespoons water

Soup Base

½ teaspoon corn or safflower oil

2 teaspoons minced fresh ginger

2 teaspoons minced scallions (white part only)

6 cups Chinese Chicken Broth (page 367)

2 tablespoons rice wine or sake

1 teaspoon salt, or more to taste

½ 1.8-ounce-package bean threads or cellophane noodles, softened in hot water for 20 minutes and drained

¼ pound snow peas, ends trimmed and veiny strings removed

1½ tablespoons minced scallion greens

Using a sharp knife or a cleaver, slice the shrimp down the back so they will butterfly when cooked and remove the dark vein. Rinse and drain. Place in a bowl, add the Marinade ingredients, and toss lightly to coat. Cover with plastic wrap and refrigerate for 30 minutes.

Combine the cornstarch and water and blend well.

To prepare the Soup Base, heat the corn or safflower oil in a large pot until hot. Add the minced ginger and scallions and stir-fry over high heat for about 15 seconds, until fragrant. Add the broth, rice wine or sake, and salt and heat until boiling. Add the shrimp and the bean threads and bring back to a boil. Cook for about 1½ minutes over medium heat, skimming the surface for impurities, then add the snow peas and cook for about 1 minute. Taste for seasoning and add salt if necessary. Transfer to a soup tureen and sprinkle with the minced scallions.

SCALLOP SOUP

This simple, elegant soup combines thin scallop slices and spinach in a savory chicken broth. To finish, the soup is sprinkled with a garnish of minced peanuts and fresh cilantro, which accentuates the refined flavors. The freshest and sweetest scallops are essential to the success of this delicate soup.

● Serves 6

1 pound sea scallops, rinsed and drained

Marinade

3 tablespoons rice wine or sake

1 teaspoon minced fresh ginger

½ teaspoon sesame oil

½ teaspoon salt

Soup Base

5 cups Chinese Chicken Broth (page 367)

2 tablespoons rice wine or sake

1 teaspoon salt

½ pound fresh spinach, stems removed, rinsed thoroughly, drained, cut into thin julienne strips

Garnishes

1½ tablespoons chopped cilantro (fresh coriander)

1 tablespoon minced scallion greens

1 tablespoon finely chopped unsalted roasted peanuts

Cut the scallops horizontally into very thin slices. Place in a bowl, add the Marinade ingredients, and toss lightly to coat. Cover with plastic wrap and refrigerate for 30 minutes.

Remove the scallops from the refrigerator and let come to room temperature.

Combine the Soup Base ingredients in a large pot, and heat until boiling. Add the scallop slices, stirring to separate them, and heat just to a boil. Stir in the spinach. Pour into a soup tureen or individual soup bowls and sprinkle with the Garnishes. Serve immediately.

Variation: Substitute 1 pound firm-fleshed whitefish fillets, such as halibut or orange roughy, for the scallops. Cut the fillets into thin slices about ¼ inch wide and 2 inches long.

VINEGAR AND
PEPPER SEAFOOD CHOWDER

The Chinese mastery of seafood is exemplified by this sumptuous soup, studded with haddock, shrimp, and scallops. The seafood is poached lightly in a fragrant broth and its fresh, sweet flavor is accentuated by the pungent seasonings. ● Serves 6

1 pound scrod or haddock fillets, skin removed (see Note)
½ pound medium shrimp, peeled
½ pound sea scallops, rinsed and drained

Marinade

¼ cup rice wine or sake
1 teaspoon minced fresh ginger
½ teaspoon salt
1 teaspoon sesame oil

2 tablespoons cornstarch
¼ cup water

Soup Base

½ teaspoon corn or safflower oil
1 tablespoon minced fresh ginger
1 tablespoon minced scallions (white part only)
5 cups Chinese Chicken Broth (page 367)
2½ tablespoons rice wine or sake
1 teaspoon salt, or more to taste

3½ tablespoons clear rice vinegar, or more to taste
1 tablespoon Chinese black vinegar or Worcestershire sauce,
    or more to taste
1 teaspoon sesame oil
½ teaspoon freshly ground black pepper
3 tablespoons minced cilantro (fresh coriander)
2½ tablespoons minced scallion greens

Holding a sharp knife or a cleaver at a 45° angle, cut the scrod or haddock into paper-thin slices about 2 inches square. Place in a bowl. Slice the shrimp down the back to butterfly and remove the dark vein. Rinse, drain, and place

(continued)

in a bowl. Cut the scallops horizontally into thin slices and place in a bowl. Combine the Marinade ingredients and divide it equally among the bowls of seafood. Toss lightly to coat, cover with plastic wrap, and refrigerate for 30 minutes.

Combine the cornstarch and water and blend well.

To prepare the Soup Base, heat a large pot, add the oil, and heat until hot. Add the ginger and scallions and stir-fry for about 15 seconds, until fragrant. Add the broth, rice wine or sake, and salt and heat until boiling. Cook for 2 to 3 minutes to combine the flavors, then add the shrimp and fish, with the marinade, to the broth and bring back to a boil. Add the scallops and cook for about 1½ minutes, skimming the surface to remove any impurities. Slowly add the cornstarch thickener and cook, stirring to prevent lumps, until slightly thickened. Add both the vinegars, the sesame oil, and pepper. Taste for seasoning, and add more salt or vinegar if necessary. Ladle into a soup tureen or individual serving bowls and sprinkle with the minced cilantro and scallions. Serve immediately.

Note: If scrod and haddock are unavailable, substitute any firm-fleshed white-fish fillets.

HOT-AND-SOUR SOUP

With its intricate blend of tastes and textures, spicy hot-and-sour soup is one of the most popular of Chinese soups by far. Unfortunately, many Chinese-American restaurants prepare an inferior version, using hot chili oil to achieve a fiery flavor. My rendition, which is true to the authentic recipe, gets its piquant punch from generous amounts of black vinegar, black pepper, and ginger. The result is a subtle and more intriguing soup.

- Serves 6

1 pound firm tofu, cut lengthwise into slabs about 1 inch thick

2 tablespoons cornstarch

¼ cup water

1 recipe Chinese Chicken Broth (page 367) made without scallions

10 dried Chinese black mushrooms, softened in hot water to cover for 20 minutes, stems removed, and caps shredded

1½ cups finely shredded leeks, rinsed and thoroughly drained

Seasonings

3½ tablespoons Chinese black vinegar or Worcestershire sauce, or more to taste

2 tablespoons soy sauce

2 tablespoons minced fresh ginger, or more to taste

¾ teaspoon freshly ground black pepper

1 teaspoon sesame oil

½ teaspoon salt, or more to taste

1 large egg, lightly beaten

Wrap the tofu in paper towels or in a cotton towel and place a heavy weight, such as a skillet, on top. Let stand for 30 minutes to press out the excess water, then cut into thin julienne strips about 3 inches long and ⅙ inch thick.

Combine the cornstarch and water and blend well.

Place the chicken broth in a large heavy pot and heat until boiling. Add the black mushroom caps, leeks, and tofu to the chicken broth and heat until boiling. Boil for about 3 minutes, skimming the surface to remove any impurities. Add the Seasonings and heat until boiling. Taste for seasoning, and add vinegar, ginger, or salt if desired. Slowly add the cornstarch thickener, stirring constantly to prevent lumps, and cook until the broth has thickened.

(continued)

Remove from the heat and slowly add the beaten egg, pouring it in a thin stream around the edge of the pot and carefully stirring once or twice so the egg forms thin streamers and cooks completely. Transfer to a soup tureen and serve immediately.

Note: The soup can be reheated, but the broth may become thin during refrigeration, requiring additional cornstarch and water thickener. (If necessary, add 1 to 2 tablespoons cornstarch blended with 3 tablespoons water to the reheated soup and boil until thickened again.)

CHICKEN SOUP WITH RICE

The Chinese share the Western view that chicken soup is a soothing remedy for all ills, and there are hundreds of variations. During the cooler months, I often make this hearty rendition, which is embellished with thin slices of chicken, carrots, and celery and thickened with cooked rice. Accompanied with slices of crusty bread, this makes a filling lunch or dinner. Savor any leftover soup—the flavor increases upon reheating. ● Serves 6

¾ pound boneless skinless chicken breasts

Marinade

2 tablespoons rice wine or sake

1 tablespoon soy sauce

1 teaspoon sesame oil

1 teaspoon minced fresh ginger

1½ teaspoons cornstarch

2 tablespoons water

Soup Base

6 cups Chinese Chicken Broth (page 367)

2 tablespoons rice wine or sake

1 teaspoon salt, or more to taste

⅓ cup long-grain white rice, rinsed thoroughly and drained

¾ cup finely sliced carrots

¾ cup finely sliced celery

With a sharp knife or a cleaver, trim away any fat or sinew from the chicken meat. Holding the knife at an angle, cut the chicken into paper-thin slices about 2 inches square. Place in a bowl, add the Marinade ingredients, and toss lightly to coat. Cover with plastic wrap and refrigerate for 30 minutes.

Combine the cornstarch and water and blend well.

Combine the Soup Base ingredients in a large pot and heat until boiling. Add the rice and carrots and bring back to a boil. Reduce the heat to medium low and simmer for 10 minutes. Add the celery and cook for about 5 minutes, or until the rice is cooked and the vegetables are tender. Skim the surface to remove any impurities. Add the cornstarch thickener and cook, stirring constantly to prevent lumps, until slightly thickened. Taste for seasoning and add salt if necessary. Ladle into serving bowls and serve.

CHINESE
SWEETS

uite frankly, Chinese cooks are not renowned for their pastries and cakes. Too often, as a trip to a Chinese bakery will confirm, the offerings tend to be cloying and tasteless. In China, sweets are rarely served as dessert; instead they enjoy a broader role—with tea, as a snack, or in between courses at a banquet.

Nevertheless, I often crave a sweet at the end of a meal, as most Westerners do. For this reason, I've adapted a number of traditional Chinese sweets, and the results should delight even the toughest audience. For example, there's a light steamed lemon cake seasoned with fresh lemon zest and brown sugar, and a fruit salad brimming with juicy litchis and ripe cantaloupe and laced with plum wine. Or sample pears stuffed with honey and cinnamon and steamed until tender.

A significant number of Chinese are acquiring a craving for sweets too. As a result, Cantonese and Hong Kong chefs are now using a blend of Chinese and Western ingredients and techniques to create a host of new delicacies. In the same spirit of invention, I have developed a selection of cross-cultural desserts that reflect the Western penchant for sweetness, with an accent on convenience and, in many cases, lightness. There's a fresh strawberry sorbet spiked with plum wine, and orange slices with cinnamon, brown sugar, and candied ginger. And for those who desire more sumptuous offerings, try ginger-cinnamon ice cream, chewy gingersnaps, or buttery date-and-walnut nuggets.

POACHED PEACHES
IN CINNAMON-GINGER SYRUP

I remember with pleasure the luscious white peaches, dripping with sweet juice, that I devoured in the Far East. To my mind, these peaches are meant to be eaten plain, straight from the tree. Other varieties, however, benefit from embellishment. In this recipe, slightly underripe peaches are poached until tender in a sweet syrup infused with a cinnamon-ginger flavor. Serve hot or cold, garnished with scoops of vanilla or ginger ice cream if you like. ● Serves 6

6 slightly underripe peaches
2 lemons, halved
6 cups water
1½ cups sugar
2 cinnamon sticks
8 slices fresh ginger (about the size of a quarter), smashed with the
      flat side of a knife or a cleaver
1 tablespoon minced candied ginger

With a sharp paring knife, peel the peaches and cut in half, removing the pits. Rub the peaches all over with the cut lemons to prevent them from browning.

Combine the water, sugar, cinnamon sticks, and fresh ginger in a large non-aluminum pot and heat until boiling. Reduce the heat and simmer, uncovered, for 30 minutes.

Add the peaches and bring just to a simmer. Reduce the heat slightly and simmer gently for about 5 to 7 minutes, until just tender. A knife should pierce the center of a peach half easily. Remove with a slotted spoon and let cool slightly.

Remove the ginger from the poaching liquid and bring to a boil. Cook for 25 minutes, or until reduced to a thick syrup. Remove the cinnamon sticks and let cool slightly.

Arrange the peaches on a serving dish or in individual bowls. Pour the warm syrup over the peaches. Sprinkle with the candied ginger and serve.

Note: When choosing peaches for poaching, select firm, slightly underripe fruit, so they will not disintegrate or become mushy during cooking.

ALMOND JELLY AND MELON WITH FRESH STRAWBERRY SAUCE

Fresh fruit is often served for dessert at a Chinese meal. I like to combine fresh Chinese fruits and diamond-shaped pieces of almond jelly and bathe the whole lot in a fresh strawberry sauce. ● Serves 6

> 2½ tablespoons unflavored gelatin
>
> 3 cups warm water
>
> 2 tablespoons sugar
>
> ½ cup sweetened condensed milk
>
> 1½ tablespoons almond extract
>
> **Strawberry Sauce**
>
> 1 pint strawberries, rinsed and hulled
>
> ¼ cup freshly squeezed orange juice
>
> 2 tablespoons sugar, or to taste
>
> 1 tablespoon orange liqueur, such as Grand Marnier (optional)
>
> 2 cups ripe Crenshaw melon or cantaloupe cut into balls or
>   1-inch diamonds

Place an 8- or 9-inch square or round metal cake pan in the freezer to chill.

Sprinkle the gelatin over ½ cup of the water in a small saucepan and let sit until softened, about 5 minutes. Then heat the mixture over low heat until boiling, stirring constantly to dissolve the gelatin. Remove from the heat.

Combine the sugar, the remaining 2½ cups water, the condensed milk, and almond extract in a bowl and stir to dissolve the sugar. Stir in the dissolved gelatin. Pour into the chilled pan and refrigerate for about 4 hours, or until set.

Meanwhile, prepare the Strawberry Sauce: Purée the strawberries in a food processor fitted with a steel blade. Add the orange juice, sugar, and orange liqueur (if using) and pulse to blend. Transfer to a sauceboat or a pitcher, and refrigerate for 1 hour.

Place the melon balls or diamonds in a large serving bowl or in individual bowls. Cut the chilled almond jelly into 1-inch diamond-shaped pieces and place next to the melon. Pour the sauce over and serve.

STEAMED
LEMON CAKE

This moist, lemony confection has an ethereal texture similar to a sponge cake. Hot or cold, served plain or with ripe fruit and whipped cream, this dessert will delight even the most discriminating palate.

● Serves 10

2¼ cups all-purpose flour

2 teaspoons baking powder

½ teaspoon baking soda

1 teaspoon salt

6 large eggs, at room temperature

1½ cups tightly packed light brown sugar

1 cup milk

2 teaspoons vanilla extract

2 tablespoons finely minced lemon zest, blanched in boiling water
for 10 seconds

Juice of 1½ lemons

2 tablespoons unsalted butter, melted

Generously grease a 10-inch tube pan with softened butter, making certain that it is thoroughly coated.

Sift together the flour, baking powder, baking soda, and salt.

Break the eggs into a large bowl. Beat vigorously with an electric mixer at high speed until the eggs are light and lemon-colored and have tripled in volume, about 5 minutes. Add the brown sugar and beat for 3 minutes. Add the milk, vanilla extract, lemon zest, and lemon juice, beating well after each addition. Alternately fold in the dry ingredients and the melted butter. Pour the batter into the greased pan.

Fill a wok or a large pot with water for steaming and heat until boiling. Place the cake pan in a steamer tray over the boiling water or balance it on a trivet or an empty tuna can in the center of the pot (see page 7). Cover and steam over high heat for 1 hour, or until the cake is springy to the touch; check the water level after 30 minutes and add more boiling water if necessary. Remove from the steamer and let cool. Unmold the cake onto a platter, cut into slices, and serve.

Note: It's important to beat the eggs until they have tripled in volume so that the cake will be light and fluffy.

Variation: Substitute blanched minced orange zest for the lemon zest.

STEAMED APPLES WITH HONEY AND CINNAMON

In this luscious and simple dessert, cored apples are drizzled with honey and cinnamon and steamed, until tender. The natural juices make a superb sauce that is like nectar when served over vanilla ice cream. Pears are equally good prepared in this manner. ● Serves 6

6 firm Red Delicious apples
2 lemons, halved
3 tablespoons honey
1½ teaspoons ground cinnamon
Vanilla or ginger ice cream for serving (optional)

Peel the apples and rub all over with 1 lemon half. Cut a slice about ½ inch thick off the top of each apple and set aside. (These will serve as lids.) Trim the bottom of each apple so it will sit upright. Using a melon baller or a spoon, core and seed the apples. Squeeze the juice of the lemons inside.

Arrange the apples upright in a 9-inch pie pan or on a heatproof plate. Spoon ½ tablespoon of the honey into each apple and sprinkle ¼ teaspoon of the cinnamon on top. Cover the apples with their "lids."

Fill a wok or a large pot with water for steaming and heat until boiling. Place the pan of apples in a steamer tray set over the boiling water or balance the pan on a trivet or an empty tuna can in the center of the pot (see page 7). Cover and steam for 25 minutes, or until the apples are tender when pierced with a knife. Transfer to serving plates and, if desired, fill each apple with a scoop of vanilla or ginger ice cream.

Variation: You can bake the apples in a preheated 375°F oven for 35 minutes, or until tender; do not peel.

STEAMED PEARS WITH HONEY AND CANDIED GINGER

For a simple yet elegant fall or winter dessert, stuff pears with honey and candied ginger and steam until tender. During the warmer months, the cooked fruit may be served chilled for a light and refreshing sweet. ● Serves 6

6 slightly underripe Anjou or Bosc pears
2 lemons, halved
6 tablespoons honey
6 thin slices candied ginger (about the size of a silver dollar),
    cut into fine julienne shreds
Vanilla ice cream for serving (optional)

Cut a thin slice off the bottom of each pear so that it will stand upright. Peel the pears and rub all over with 1 lemon half to prevent them from turning brown. Slice about 2 inches off the top of each pear and set aside. With a melon baller or a spoon, carefully remove the cores and seeds. Do not cut through the bottom of the pears.

Arrange the pears on a pie plate or a heatproof plate. Combine the honey and candied ginger and spoon the mixture into the pears. Place the tops on the pears and, if necessary, secure with toothpicks.

Fill a wok or a large pot with water for steaming and heat until boiling. Place the plate of pears in a steamer tray over the boiling water or balance the plate on a trivet or an empty tuna can in the center of the pot (see page 7). Cover and steam for 30 minutes, or until the pears are tender when pierced with a knife. Serve hot or chilled, with scoops of ice cream if desired.

ORANGE SLICES WITH CINNAMON, BROWN SUGAR, AND CANDIED GINGER

This recipe was inspired by my friend Ruth Bauer, who often serves juicy, sliced oranges sprinkled with brown sugar and cinnamon at brunch. One day, on impulse, I added a bit of minced candied ginger—so simple yet unbelievably good. As the oranges sit in the sugar mixture, they produce a succulent natural sauce. ● Serves 6

6 navel oranges, peeled and cut into ½-inch-thick slices

¼ cup tightly packed light brown sugar

1 teaspoon ground cinnamon

1 tablespoon minced candied ginger

Arrange the orange slices side by side on a serving platter. Combine the brown sugar, cinnamon, and candied ginger and sprinkle over the oranges. Let sit for 15 minutes at room temperature, and serve.

Variation: Substitute grapefruit slices for the oranges.

CHINESE FRUIT SALAD

Few desserts are as refreshing as a fruit salad. For a unique approach, I mix and match fresh and canned Chinese and Western fruits, starting with ripe melon and adding litchis and loquats, with a bit of their syrups. Plum wine and a sprinkling of candied ginger are the finishing touch.

● Serves 6

> 1 pint ripe strawberries, rinsed and hulled
>
> 2 tablespoons sugar, or to taste
>
> 2 cups ripe cantaloupe or honeydew cut into balls or 1-inch diamonds
>
> 1 20-ounce can litchis in syrup
>
> 1 15-ounce can loquats in syrup
>
> 1 cup plum wine
>
> 3 tablespoons finely minced candied ginger

If the strawberries are large, cut in half lengthwise. If they are not very sweet, add the sugar, toss lightly to coat, and let sit for 1 hour at room temperature.

Place the strawberries in a serving bowl and add the melon. Drain the litchis and loquats, reserving about ¼ cup of the syrup from each, and add to the strawberries. Pour the reserved syrup over the fruit, add the plum wine and candied ginger, and stir gently to mix. Cover with plastic wrap and refrigerate for at least 1 hour. Spoon the fruit and sauce into bowls and serve.

Note: If you prepare the fruit salad early in the day, let the strawberries sit in the sugar (if using) separately and add them to the salad just before serving.

GINGERSNAPS

Cookies are not a traditional Chinese delicacy, but these chewy rounds, flavored with vanilla, brown sugar, and candied ginger, are perfect as a snack with tea or at the end of a Chinese meal. ● Makes 40 cookies

1¾ cups all-purpose flour

⅓ teaspoon salt

½ teaspoon baking soda

8 tablespoons (1 stick) unsalted butter, softened to room temperature

1¼ cups tightly packed light brown sugar

1 large egg

1¼ teaspoons ground ginger

1 tablespoon finely minced candied ginger

1 teaspoon vanilla extract

Sift together the flour, salt, and baking soda.

With an electric mixer, beat the butter and sugar in a large bowl until light and fluffy, about 4 to 5 minutes. Beat in the egg until well blended. Stir in the ground ginger, candied ginger, and vanilla extract and combine well. Slowly add the dry ingredients in two additions, beating until just incorporated. Turn the dough out onto a sheet of aluminum foil and roll into a long roll about 1½ inches thick. Wrap in the foil and chill in the freezer for about 1 hour, or until firm.

Preheat the oven to 375°F.

Using a sharp knife, cut the dough into slices about ¼ inch thick. Arrange 1½ inches apart on ungreased cookie sheets, and bake for 10 to 12 minutes, or until golden brown. Transfer to wire racks and let cool.

WALNUT-DATE NUGGETS

These buttery cookies are studded with bits of dates and walnuts, two ingredients that are especially dear to the Chinese. These keep well, so make a double batch and store in airtight containers or freeze to have on hand. ● Makes 48 cookies

    2 cups all-purpose flour
    ¼ teaspoon baking soda
    ½ teaspoon salt
    ½ pound (2 sticks) unsalted butter, softened to room temperature
    ¾ cup sugar
    2 teaspoons vanilla extract
    ¾ cup pitted dates, coarsely chopped
    ½ cup coarsely chopped walnuts
    Confectioners' sugar for dusting

Sift together the flour, baking soda, and salt.

With an electric mixer, cream the butter and sugar in a large bowl until light and fluffy, about 5 minutes. Beat in the vanilla extract. On low speed, beat in the dry ingredients in two additions, beating until just incorporated. Stir in the dates and walnuts. Turn the dough out onto a large sheet of plastic wrap, wrap tightly, and chill in the refrigerator for at least 2 hours, or overnight.

Preheat the oven to 350°F.

Roll teaspoonfuls of the dough into balls and arrange them about 1½ inches apart on ungreased baking sheets. Bake for 12 to 15 minutes, until set and lightly golden around the edges. Using a spatula, transfer the cookies to wire racks and let cool. Just before serving, sprinkle lightly with confectioners' sugar.

ORANGE-ALMOND CRISPS

These rich cookies, similar to shortbread, are studded with chopped almonds and grated orange zest. For two memorable variations, try substituting either grated lemon zest or vanilla extract and ground cinnamon for the orange zest. ● Makes about 28 cookies

  1 cup all-purpose flour
  ½ cup cornstarch
  12 tablespoons (1½ sticks) unsalted butter, softened to room
        temperature
  ½ cup confectioners' sugar
  2 tablespoons finely grated orange zest
  1 teaspoon almond extract
  ½ cup finely chopped blanched almonds

Sift together the flour and cornstarch.

Process the butter and sugar in a food processor fitted with a steel blade for 2 to 3 minutes, until light and fluffy. Add the orange zest and almond extract and process to blend. Alternately add the flour mixture and the chopped almonds in several additions, pulsing just until blended. Turn the dough out onto a large sheet of plastic wrap, wrap well, and chill in the refrigerator for about 1 hour, until firm enough to shape.

Place the dough on a large sheet of aluminum foil and roll into a long snake-like piece about 1½ inches in diameter. Wrap in the foil, and chill in the freezer for 1 hour.

Preheat the oven to 375°F.

Using a sharp knife, cut the dough into ¼-inch-thick slices. Arrange 1½ inches apart on ungreased cookie sheets, and bake for about 10 minutes, or until the edges are golden. Using a spatula, transfer to wire racks to cool.

GINGER-CINNAMON
ICE CREAM

The Chinese are credited with inventing ice cream, but in the Far East, it is generally savored as a between-meals snack rather than a dessert. Nevertheless, to my mind, there are few confections that end a Chinese meal with such finesse as homemade ice cream, and I love to create different flavors. This creamy mixture combines the pleasing tastes of fresh and candied ginger with the spicy tang of cinnamon. ● Makes 1 quart

2 cups milk

2 cups heavy cream

10 slices fresh ginger (about the size of a quarter), lightly smashed with the flat side of a knife or a cleaver

2 cinnamon sticks

¾ cup sugar

5 egg yolks

½ teaspoon ground cinnamon (optional)

2 tablespoons chopped candied ginger

Combine the milk, cream, smashed ginger, cinnamon sticks, and sugar in a large nonaluminum saucepan and heat just to a simmer, stirring to dissolve the sugar. Cover and let sit at room temperature for 2 to 3 hours to infuse the mixture. Then strain through a colander, discarding the ginger and cinnamon sticks, and return to the saucepan.

With an electric mixer, beat the egg yolks until light and lemon-colored, about 5 minutes. Add to the cream mixture and whisk lightly to blend. Heat over low heat, stirring with a wooden spoon, until the mixture thickens and coats the back of the spoon, about 5 to 7 minutes. Stir in the ground cinnamon (if using). Transfer to a bowl and let cool to room temperature, then chill for 2 hours.

Freeze in an ice cream maker according to the manufacturer's instructions, folding in the candied ginger just before completely frozen. Serve immediately, or transfer to airtight containers and freeze for up to 2 days.

Note: The ice cream base should be well chilled before placing it in the ice cream maker. If the mixture is warm or at room temperature, it will take much longer to freeze.

STRAWBERRY-PLUM WINE SORBET

Good fruit sorbets fill the mouth with the vibrant taste of sweet, fresh fruit. Ripe strawberries, complemented by sweet plum wine, give this ice its superb flavor. Serve as an *entremets* between courses to cleanse and refresh the palate, or at the end of the meal as a refreshing dessert.

● Makes 1 quart

> 1 pint fresh strawberries (about ¾ pound), rinsed, hulled, and patted dry
> ¾ cup sugar
> ¾ cup water
> 1 cup plum wine
> Juice of ½ lemon

Purée the strawberries in a food processor fitted with a steel blade.

Combine the sugar and water in a saucepan and heat until boiling. Reduce the heat to low and simmer for 5 minutes. Transfer to a bowl and stir in the strawberry purée, plum wine, and lemon juice. Let cool, then chill for 2 hours.

Freeze the chilled mixture in an ice cream maker according to the manufacturer's instructions until fairly firm and stiff. Then transfer to an airtight container and place in the freezer to firm up completely. For the best texture, remove from the freezer about 10 minutes before serving to soften slightly.

Note: To prepare the sorbet without an ice cream maker, pour the cooled mixture into an ice cube tray and freeze, stirring with a fork every 30 minutes, until completely frozen. Serve, or pack into an airtight container and freeze.

INDEX